Labor Market Issues
along the U.S.-Mexico Border

Labor Market Issues
along the U.S.-Mexico Border

Edited by
Marie T. Mora and Alberto Dávila

The University of Arizona Press   Tucson

The University of Arizona Press
© 2009 The Arizona Board of Regents
All rights reserved

www.uapress.arizona.edu

Library of Congress Cataloging-in-Publication Data

Labor market issues along the U.S.–Mexico border /
edited by Marie T. Mora and Alberto Davila.
        p.   cm.
    Includes bibliographical references and index.
    ISBN 978-0-8165-2700-7 (cloth : alk. paper)
    1. Labor market—Mexican-American Border Region.
2. Mexican-American Border Region—Economic conditions.
3. Mexican-American Border Region—Commerce.
4. Mexican-American Border Region—Emigration and
immigration. I. Mora, Marie T., 1969– II. Davila,
Alberto E.
    HD5725.M48L33 2009
    331.120972'1–dc22   2009025775

Contents

Acknowledgments

Marie T. Mora and Alberto Dávila would first like to thank and acknowledge our colleagues who contributed to this volume for their hard work, patience, and commitment to this project. They also express their appreciation to the anonymous referees of this manuscript as well as to Patti Hartmann at the University of Arizona Press for their insightful suggestions and comments. They further thank Alma D. Hales for her excellent research assistance. Finally, Alberto Dávila acknowledges financial support from the V.F. "Doc" and Gertrude M. Neuhaus Endowment at the University of Texas-Pan American.

Labor Market Issues
along the U.S.-Mexico Border

Introduction

Marie T. Mora and Alberto Dávila

FIVE MILLION WORKERS ARE EMPLOYED in a variety of settings along the U.S.-Mexico border. From blue-collar employment to the service sector to professional vocations, the majority of these labor market activities occur in border "twin" cities—pairs of cities sprinkled along the two-thousand-mile frontier separated only by the international boundary. Figure I.1 shows a map of Mexico and the United States that identifies the six northern border states of Mexico and the four southern border states of the United States, along with the major twin-city pairs. The five largest city pairs (Tijuana and San Diego; Ciudad Juárez and El Paso; Reynosa and McAllen; Matamoros and Brownsville; and Nuevo Laredo and Laredo) alone account for three-quarters of the employment in U.S. counties and Mexican *municipios* (similar to counties) located along the international boundary.[1]

Many residents along the U.S.-Mexico border view the twin city across the border as part of the same community, and they frequently cross to the other side for the purposes of shopping, going to restaurants, entertainment, visiting family and friends, receiving medical services, and in many cases, working.[2] Despite the geographic, economic, and cultural dependencies of these twin cities, however, their labor market outcomes often differ considerably from each other, as well as from those of their respective country's interior regions in certain regards. Indeed, as will be discussed throughout this volume, areas along the U.S. side of the border tend to have relatively low earnings and high unemployment rates compared to the rest of the United States, despite experiencing rapid population and economic growth. In contrast, workers on the Mexican side of the international border tend to be more prosperous than those in other parts of Mexico, although their earnings are considerably lower than workers on the U.S. side of the border.[3]

These socioeconomic differentials—in conjunction with renewed attention to U.S. immigration and border-security issues—have captured

FIGURE I.1 The U.S.-Mexico border region and the largest border twin city pairs.

the interest of social scientists and policymakers, particularly in recent times. Interest in such border-related topics was exemplified by the large turnout at the Lineae Terrarum international borders conference held in late March 2006 in the border cities of El Paso, Ciudad Juárez, and Las Cruces. We were each independently invited to present papers at this conference and decided to collaborate on both of our presentations by focusing on issues related to labor market outcomes along the U.S.-Mexico border before and after the implementation of the North American Free Trade Agreement (NAFTA). Both of us already had been involved in other border-related studies, but this conference reinforced our view that many other related interesting and important issues had yet to be investigated under an umbrella of common themes.

Moreover, the recent media coverage on immigration, as well as on border security issues (e.g., the so-called Minutemen Project), has raised awareness—sometimes with a negative tone—in the rest of the United States about this unique geographic region. Questions are being asked about the determinants of immigration as well as the potential effects on employment, wages, and the use of public goods in areas located near the Mexican border. Despite such attention, few studies exist that offer a set of in-depth analyses of how recent socioeconomic, demographic, and policy changes influence a variety of labor market outcomes on both sides of the U.S.-Mexico border.

To fill this research void, we invited a group of scholars interested in border-related socioeconomic issues to contribute chapters to this book. Many of the contributing authors have at some point during their careers been employed at universities located near the U.S.-Mexico border, including the University of Texas–Pan American, the University of Texas at El Paso, Tecnológico de Monterrey, New Mexico State University, and San Diego State University. Other contributors have worked in the interior regions of border states (namely, the Federal Reserve Bank of Dallas and Texas A&M University). While the majority of the chapters incorporate data analysis into the discussion, they have been written so as to be accessible to a wide range of readers, not just academics.

We should note at the outset that there is no general consensus on how to define the U.S.-Mexico border region. We did not attempt to standardize the definition here, instead leaving the decision on identifying the border region to the different authors. This said, the appendix to this manuscript provides the variety of definitions used throughout this volume, along with a description of the different datasets employed.

Clearly, there are many policy-related themes of importance to U.S.-Mexico border labor market issues, but there are some that dominate the current discourse: migration, trade, gender, education, earnings, and employment. While each on its own could warrant an entire manuscript,[4] their intersections are also of interest. For example, standard migration theory predicts that earnings differentials across regions, such as between Mexico and the United States, give rise to labor migration. But what implications does such migration have on the educational outcomes, employment rates, gender-related employment outcomes, and so forth across regions? Of course, we do not claim to address *all* of the possible permutations and combinations across these themes, as such an undertaking would result in an entire series of volumes. This manuscript does, however, provide new insight into these issues, as the different contributors worked under the same general umbrella of themes.

To provide historical context into these themes, particularly those regarding migration, trade, gender, and employment, Anthony P. Mora outlines the history of the borderlands from 1821 to the present in the following chapter. This chapter discusses the struggles to limit and define national identities in an area with tremendous fluidity and diversity, as well as the differing historical events that helped shape local circumstances and the socioeconomic outcomes of individuals in both nations. Mora also outlines some key labor agreements between the United States and Mexico that have affected employment opportunities on both sides of the border during the past several decades.

In chapter 2, Thomas M. Fullerton Jr., James H. Holcomb, and Angel L. Molina Jr. contribute to the education and employment themes as they provide an overview of socioeconomic and demographic changes, including those related to education and employment, that have occurred on the U.S. side of the border during the past few decades. They note that border populations exhibit relative youth, rapid population growth, low educational attainment, and low per-capita income. In addition, Fullerton, Holcomb, and Molina suggest that U.S.-border labor markets are becoming more service and information oriented, so that education has become increasingly important for employment in U.S. border counties.

The chapter by James T. Peach and Richard V. Adkisson (chapter 3) continues with a similar approach by focusing on the importance of trade to the U.S. side of the international border with Mexico. In particular, it examines the evolution of economic activity in the border region to consider whether the implementation of NAFTA in January 1994 affected the socioeconomic outcomes, including employment, in the region. Peach and Adkisson first outline the economic changes anticipated during the NAFTA debate and then compare pre-NAFTA trends to post-NAFTA trends to observe whether these expected changes actually came to pass.

The next chapter (chapter 4), by John Sargent, Melissa Najera, and Linda Matthews, provides an interesting discussion of the importance of trade to the Mexican side of the U.S.-Mexico border, giving insights into the intersections of trade, gender, and migration. Part of this chapter examines the evolution of maquiladoras (manufacturing facilities, often owned by the world's largest multinational corporations) since the implementation of NAFTA, paying particular attention to changes in employment and aspects of the employer-employee relationship in this industry. This chapter discusses the role of NAFTA in the rapid growth of the maquiladora industry during the 1990s, as well as the maquiladora contraction (partly related to low-cost competition from China) that began in late 2000. In addition, basing their analysis on ethnographic evidence, Sargent, Najera, and Matthews evaluate various aspects (including gender) of the maquiladora work experience in 1992 and 2002, such as workers' turnover intentions and their perceptions regarding health and safety.

Still focusing on the Mexican side of the border, in chapter 5, Hector J. Villarreal analyzes how salary differentials between the northern Mexican border and the rest of Mexico have changed since 1994. This chapter contributes to our understanding of migration and education on the Mexican side of the border. Much of Villarreal's discussion focuses on the role of education in determining labor-market income. This chapter also relates salary trends to Mexican domestic and international migration.

We, along with Alma D. Hales, explore in chapter 6 the earnings of salaried and self-employed individuals who work in the Mexican and U.S. border regions versus the earnings of their counterparts in the rest of these countries. Thus, with respect to the themes of migration and earnings, we confirm that workers on the U.S. side of the border earn less than those in the U.S. interior, even when controlling for differences in observable characteristics, such as education. However, the relatively low earnings on the U.S. side of the border are considerably larger than the earnings of Mexican workers directly across the border. Mexican border workers, in turn, earn more on average than their counterparts in the rest of Mexico. Given these differences, we discuss the possibility of wage conversion across the regions following the predictions of migration theory. We further consider whether individuals in the border and interior regions of Mexico are "pushed" into self-employment because of poor labor-market conditions or "pulled" into this sector because it offers relatively attractive returns.

Inserting the theme of gender into the intersection of migration and earnings, in chapter 7, Rogelio Sáenz, Lorena Murga, and Maria Cristina Morales examine the determinants of wages among Mexican immigrant women on the U.S. side of the border, with particular attention paid to whether they worked in jobs typically held by Mexican immigrants. They find that Mexican immigrant women pay a penalty for living in the U.S. border region (versus migrating further northward), as well as for working in jobs where Mexican immigrants are clustered. However, the cost of working in a Mexican immigrant job is less severe along the border than in the U.S. interior for these women.

The chapter by Pia M. Orrenius, Madeline Zavodny, and Leslie Lukens (chapter 8) continues to explore migration, gender, and earnings themes, focusing on factors affecting Mexican migration to the border region, including U.S. border enforcement and economic conditions. The authors find that migrants to the U.S. border region are more likely to be female, to have first migrated within Mexico, and to lack migrant networks than are migrants to the U.S. interior. Border migration has also remained highly sensitive to Mexican and U.S. business cycles, much more so than migration to the U.S. interior. Moreover, reinforcing the Sáenz, Murga, and Morales chapter, Orrenius, Zavodny, and Lukens find that female Mexican immigrants on the U.S. side of the border earn significantly less than those in the U.S. interior.

Catalina Amuedo-Dorantes and Cynthia Bansak in chapter 9 examine an important (and widely discussed) aspect of the migration theme: the net effect of Mexican migration on public coffers in U.S. border states. They find that many Mexican migrants who reside in U.S. states near Mexico have both Social Security and federal taxes withheld from their paychecks, regardless of legal status. In addition, Amuedo-Dorantes and Bansak show that Mexican migrants as a group have become less likely to make use of public services (e.g., schools, unemployment insurance, food stamps, and medical services) over time. Contrary to public perception, provided evidence shows, undocumented Mexican immigrants in border states are less likely to use public services than their legal counterparts.

Under the intersection of the migration and trade themes, in chapter 10 we note that nearly all of the debate on immigration and border security ignores the fact that thousands of U.S. residents cross the international border on a daily basis to work in Mexico. These cross-border workers tend to be more educated and earn higher wages than their otherwise similar counterparts who live and work on the U.S. side of the border. In addition, we find that despite the recent growth in border security-related measures and rising violence in Mexican border cities, the cross-border earnings premium remained steady between 2000 and 2005.

André Varella Mollick in chapter 11 contributes to the list of themes presented here by analyzing employment trends on the U.S. side of the border. He begins his discussion by noting the relatively high unemployment rates in U.S. border cities. Mollick also finds that there is more variation in the employment composition in U.S. border cities than in other large cities in the interior of border states.

Finally, a series of policy implications is provided in chapter 12, drawn from the issues put forth in the other chapters of this book. Using the context of the lagging socioeconomic conditions characterizing the U.S. border region versus those of the U.S. interior, this chapter includes a discussion of policy prescriptions that could be useful for improving these conditions on the U.S. side of the border without dampening the relative success of workers employed on the other side. We conclude by outlining other related topics worthy of future research.

A Fixed Border's Shifting Meanings

The United States and Mexico, 1821 to 2007

Anthony P. Mora

Introduction

Even at the moment when Mexico won independence from Spain in 1821, its relationship with the United States was already strained by land disputes, migration, and even violence. Creating, maintaining, and explaining the meaning of a definitive borderline has vexed the two nations ever since. To understand how some of our modern concerns about the U.S.-Mexico border developed, we need to consider how the two nations' complicated histories intertwined at the frontier. This chapter provides a historical narrative that highlights the various turns and twists that Mexican and Euro-American residents have faced since the nineteenth century.[1] At times, these border settlers shaped the direction of the two nations. In other circumstances, they were left to the whims of power brokers in the far-away capitols of Mexico City and Washington, DC.

While the cartographical boundary line between the United States and Mexico has been imagined as a constant since 1854, the meaning of that line and who can cross it has changed significantly over time. Indeed, even creating an exact survey of that line did not occur until relatively recently. Struggles over the border shifted from a nineteenth-century battle to control land to a twentieth-century battle to control groups of people and capital. Throughout these two centuries, the critical questions were always about how much the two nations should blur their borders.

Nations on the Edge: Border Negotiations in the Nineteenth Century

Before Mexican independence, Spain jealously guarded its imperial economy and territories from entry by the United States (Weber 1994; Kessell 2002). Northern territories like New Mexico and Texas could not trade with the United States, nor could U.S. citizens legally reside in those areas. Indeed, Spain had reason to be suspicious of the rapidly expanding republic on its northern frontier. When Thomas Jefferson acquired the Louisiana Territory in 1803, he made an audacious claim that his agreement with France extended to the Rio Grande, which included most of modern-day Texas and half of New Mexico (Weber 2003). Spain kept vigilant watch over its northern neighbor to ensure that it did not pursue such claims.

Spain's concerns, however, would ultimately be moot as pressures from within collapsed its empire. Wars for independence swept through Latin America in the first decades of the nineteenth century. Mexico itself emerged from ten years of bloody fighting as a new nation in 1821. More than 600,000 people died in that conflict, reducing the total population by 10 percent (González 2000). The economic cost of the independence war, moreover, hampered the fledgling nation, leaving it with a substantial national debt.

As a new nation, Mexico was hardly comparable with the neighboring United States. The northern republic was booming with industrial development and had enjoyed several generations of relative political stability. The Mexican population, in contrast, was predominantly rural for the first half of the nineteenth century (Meyer and Sherman 1995). Mexico's gold and silver mines, rather than industrial development, had been the driving force of the colonial economy. The actual coinage produced in Mexico, however, dropped from more than $26 million in 1809 to less than $6 million in 1821 (Meyer and Sherman 1995:304). At the same time, the price of agricultural goods soared and unemployment became rampant.

Matters only deteriorated as Mexico experienced constant political instability in the central government in the first decades of the country's independence. Between 1822 and 1848, fifty regimes traded control of the nation. The style of government shifted uncomfortably from a federalist republic to an autocratic centralist government and back again (Krauze 1997). The infamous Antonio López de Santa Anna figured prominently in these struggles as he drifted in and out of power after independence (Weber 2003). This political chaos kept the nation's economy stagnant and Mexico defaulted on its international loans in 1827 (Roeckell 1999).

An uncertain government coupled with economic woes necessarily resulted in discontent within the nation, especially in outlying areas. Northern provinces responded by turning to the more robust U.S. economy (Reséndez 2005). Mexican citizens, particularly along the northern frontier, eagerly welcomed Mexico City's immediate reversal of the trade ban with the United States and an end to Spain's inflated prices (Reséndez 2005).

William Becknell was the first Euro-American trader to take advantage of the policy change, making a round-trip journey between Franklin, Missouri, and Santa Fe, New Mexico, within months of Spain's ousting. News that Becknell turned a 1,000 percent profit created a sensation, prompting hundreds of Euro-American traders to create the highly profitable trade route known as the Santa Fe Trail. Countless caravans of goods trekked nine hundred miles from Independence, Missouri, through Santa Fe, and south to Chihuahua (Reséndez 2002).

Similar enthusiasm for trade appeared throughout Mexico's northern territories. Within a year of independence, Alta California experienced a complete change in its economy when trading vessels from Boston and Britain appeared. In exchange for much-needed manufactured goods from these ships, *californios* created an extensive local industry that produced hides and tallow. During the 1820s and 1830s, trappers and traders in both New Mexico and California integrated themselves into the existing Mexican society and established permanent residences, including such famed figures as Jedediah Smith, Kit Carson, Charles Bent, and James Magoffin (Weber 2003). For the most part, these Euro Americans rarely advocated revolution against the Mexican government or U.S. annexation. In the first decades after independence, they seemed content taking advantage of the new economic situation along the border.

All the same, Mexican officials increasingly disapproved of the growing number of Euro Americans who failed to leave with the trade caravans. The governor of New Mexico warned in 1827 that "every day the foreigners are becoming more influential over the miserable inhabitants of this Territory" (Weber 2003:56). A year later, Mexico and the United States agreed that establishing a clearly defined border between the nations was a priority (Reséndez 2005). When the Mexican border commission arrived in Texas, however, they found an alarming situation. The few Euro-American settlers in New Mexico and Alta California appeared inconsequential compared to the swarms of U.S. immigrants who had established themselves in Texas.

That influx into Texas had started when Mexico upheld an agreement originally drafted between the Spanish government and Moses Austin to settle a limited number of foreigners in Texas. Spain (and later Mexico) had hoped that they could create a buffer colony that would defend Texas if the United States decided to invade. Stephen Austin, Moses' son, implemented this contract after his father's death. In exchange for a sizable land grant, Euro-American settlers pledged to become Mexican citizens, integrate with the existing communities, and obey Mexican civil authorities and laws. The contract also implicitly required these settlers' conversion to Catholicism, as Mexico permitted only one religion in the nation (Weber 1982).

Few people, if anybody, predicted the ultimate cost that Mexico would pay for opening its border to U.S. immigrants. While the initial agreements had stipulated just a few hundred people would be permitted to settle in Mexico, Euro Americans surged into Texas. Their population increased by one thousand people annually between 1823 and 1830. That number tripled during the 1830s. By 1835, Euro Americans outnumbered Mexicans ten to one in eastern Texas (Reséndez 2005).

On April 6, 1830, the Mexican Congress passed a controversial law that addressed the perceived crisis in Texas. Mexico City explicitly forbade any further immigration from the United States and established military garrisons with explicit orders to defend the region from further U.S. encroachment. To pay for all of this, Congress authorized the construction of customhouses at several strategic locations to ensure that the government collected revenues from the lucrative trading occurring at the northern border (Reséndez 2005). Officials clumsily enforced these new laws, which escalated the tensions between remote Texas and Mexico City. Both Euro Americans and Mexicans in Texas (tejanos) had long been frustrated over their limited representation in either the state or federal government. Texas, after all, was merely a subdistrict of the state of Coahuila. The 1830 law only enforced the presumption in Texas that the people making decisions about trade and immigration were too far removed from the border to understand the stakes involved. For their own economic prosperity, tejanos often advocated for an open border with the United States as much as Euro Americans did (Reséndez 2005).

Slavery put Euro-American Texans even further at odds with Mexico City. President Vicente Guerrero emancipated all slaves in Mexico on September 15, 1829.[2] Extreme outrage in Texas, however, resulted in a temporary exemption for that region (Weber 1982). Euro Americans, 75 percent of whom migrated to Texas from slave states in the U.S. South, resented the federal government interfering with their "private property" (Weber 2003:89). When the Mexican government explicitly banned slavery again in 1835, wild rumors circulated that the federal Mexican army planned to invade Texas, free the black slaves, and imprison all Euro Americans (Weber 1982). In a short time, most Euro-American settlers in the territory became united in favor of independence or, preferably, annexation by the United States (Weber 2003). Though they were not explicitly supported by the United States as they had hoped, delegates meeting at Washington-on-the-Brazos declared Texas a nation distinct from Mexico on March 2, 1836.

Santa Anna seized on the Texas crisis as a means to shore up his own deteriorating authority as Mexico's central leader. He had already arrived in Texas with an army of six thousand soldiers even before the rebels officially declared independence (Krauze 1997). His military force quickly crushed resistance at San Antonio, including those barricaded in the now-famed Alamo mission, as well as the rebel forces in Goliad. The Mexican general raised the ire of the local settlers when he executed four hundred prisoners of war after his victories (Weber 2003).

Perhaps buoyed by his initial military successes, Santa Anna decided to divide his military force into smaller units. He led a truncated contingent further east, seemingly believing that he would not face any further challenges by military forces. This miscalculation ultimately cost him. Texan rebels surprised Santa Anna near the present-day site of Houston on April 21. These Texans fought fiercely under the remembrance of the Alamo and Goliad. When the battle ended, hundreds of Mexicans soldiers were dead and Santa Anna was a prisoner of the revolutionaries (Weber 2003).

The executive made several public and secret arrangements with his captors, including Texan independence and the withdrawal of Mexican troops, in exchange for his personal safety and return to his home in Veracruz. The revolutionaries also resurrected ideas about the Texas boundary that had been circulating since the Louisiana Purchase. Under Spain and Mexico, Texas's administrative boundary ended at the Nueces River. The Texan rebels, however, drew on previous U.S. claims that Texas encompassed a much larger geography. Despite the fact that Mexico had never recognized these claims, Santa Anna signed the Treaty of Velasco and declared that the Texas boundary extended along the Rio Grande (which effectively meant that half of New Mexico would have been annexed as well). When the treaties arrived in Mexico City, the Mexican Congress explicitly rejected their legality due to the fact that they had been signed while Santa Anna was a prisoner. Mexico never recognized Texas as an independent nation (Weber 2003).

Other rebellions soon erupted across Mexico, following Texas's lead. Alta California revolted against the centralist government in 1836. The next year, New Mexico and Sonora also took up arms against the reigning regime. Yucatán, the southernmost state, seceded in 1838 and remained in revolt for almost a decade. Tamaulipas, Nuevo León, and Coahuila declared independence in 1840 (Weber 2003). With these scattered revolts shaking the country, Mexico had little opportunity to secure Texas.

Texans hoped to break their own stalemate with Mexico City when they circulated a proposal to key leaders in 1845. If Mexico agreed to their independence, Texans would pledge not to join the United States. Moreover, Texas suggested that the British government could serve as an arbitrator for the border dispute. Though many officials in Mexico City appeared amenable to these terms, Texas withdrew its offer when it learned that Britain would not support its fabricated claim to the Rio Grande (Griswold del Castillo 1990). Texans also became alarmed when certain British officials suggested that the abolition of slavery in Texas be a requirement of the negotiations (mostly to make Texas less desirable for U.S. annexation) (Roeckell 1999).

Meanwhile, circumstances had changed in the United States. Some U.S. officials anxiously imagined that the British interest in Texas was part of a larger plan to dominate North American trade (Chávez 2006). Popular sentiment in the United States, expressed through a notion of "manifest destiny," convinced many Euro Americans that the United States was preordained for westward expansion. James Polk won his election to the presidency in 1844 largely based on a campaign that advocated annexing Texas and expanding the U.S. share of the Pacific coast. Congress acted on this mandate even before Polk's inauguration by admitting Texas as a state on February 28, 1845. This move created a predictable international crisis. Since Mexico never acknowledged Texan independence, that government argued that Texans did not have the authority to negotiate its admission into the United States.

Polk had little regard for Mexico's protests. He initially sent John Slidell with a proposal to purchase all of Mexico's northern territories in exchange for recognizing the Rio Grande as the Texas boundary. Mexican officials responded coldly to these offers, and understandably, they did not view selling *more* territory to the United States as a fair bargain for losing Texas (Griswold del Castillo 1990). Unable to persuade Mexico to accept his offers, Polk decided to use military force to secure the contested section of Texas. General Zachary Taylor led a group of U.S. troops south of the Nueces River (Texas's historical border under Spain and Mexico). A Mexican cavalry unit engaged U.S. troops at their makeshift fort near the city of Matamoros on April 24, 1846, ultimately causing the death of eleven U.S. soldiers.

The U.S. president used the incident to push a declaration of war through Congress. Polk claimed that "American blood has been shed on American soil" and that war was the only possible response. The proposed declaration required a congressional vote within two hours, giving almost no time for debate. Many, especially members of the rival Whig party, doubted Democrat Polk's version of the conflict. All the same, it passed the House of Representatives 174 to 14 and the Senate 40 to 2 on May 13, 1846 (Chávez 2006:140–42).

Despite a number of stunning U.S. victories early in the war, including the occupation of Alta California and New Mexico, Mexico refused to negotiate an immediate settlement (Weber 1982). Through 1847, the U.S. and Mexican armies fought extraordinarily bloody battles. Polk and his military advisors had underestimated the depth of Mexicans' commitment to defending their nation. Only after U.S. General Winfield Scott occupied Mexico City in September did Mexican negotiators finally agree to end the war (Weber 2003).

An Imperfect Treaty

Officials from both the United States and Mexico crafted an agreement known as the Treaty of Guadalupe Hidalgo on the outskirts of Mexico City in the last months of 1847. The document retroactively legitimated most of the U.S. land claims, such as declaring the contested area between the Nueces and the Rio Grande rivers part of Texas. The United States also acquired New Mexico, most of Arizona (which was part of New Mexico at the time), and Alta California, meaning that Mexico lost half of its total territory. The treaty established a new international boundary that ran along the Rio Grande for Texas; made the Gila River the southern boundary for New Mexico; and terminated one marine league south of San Diego, California. In exchange for these concessions, the U.S. government paid Mexico $15 million (Griswold del Castillo 1990:39–41).

Articles VIII, IX, and X of the treaty outlined specific protections for Mexicans who lived in the ceded territories. Settlers could retain their Mexican citizenship and still reside in the newly made U.S. territories if they asserted their inclination within one year of the treaty's adoption. If they did nothing in that year, Mexicans automatically became U.S. citizens. Negotiators also gave specific guarantees for Mexicans' religious practices, ownership of property, and civil protection within these articles.

Once the treaty reached the U.S. Senate, however, these measures were either altered or deleted entirely. President Polk expressed his personal animosity to Article X, which had protected Mexican land grants in Texas. The Senate followed his recommendations and expunged the article entirely (Griswold del Castillo 1990). The Senate also redrafted Article IX. The original article, among other things, had specified that Mexicans' political rights "shall be on an equality with that of the inhabitants of the other territories of the United States" (Griswold del Castillo 1990:46). The Senate substituted more ambiguous language from previous treaties that ceded Florida and Louisiana from Spain and France. U.S. officials assured the Mexican government that the changes would not result in their former citizens being disenfranchised or dispossessed, conveniently ignoring that numerous people in both Florida and Louisiana had filed lawsuits and complaints against the U.S. government based on that same diplomatic language in those previous treaties (Griswold del Castillo 1990). Indeed, state and national courts would frequently rule that local laws superseded the treaties' provisions (Griswold del Castillo 1990).

Mexicans in the ceded territories faced difficult choices immediately after the war. Most decided to take their chances with the new regime. Hundreds, though, took advantage of offers by the Mexican government for cash and land grants to relocate south of the new borderline. The settlers created a number of new towns and considered themselves patriotic Mexicans. The most famous of these communities was La Mesilla, which was located just south of the new boundary between New Mexico and Chihuahua (see Baldwin 1938).

Much to the dismay of the Mesilla residents, the colony became embroiled in yet another diplomatic crisis between Mexico and the United States in 1853 (Garber 1923). Leaders in the southern United States wanted to build a transcontinental railroad connection to Alta California and believed that lands in present-day southern New Mexico and Arizona would be the best option for a level, all-weather route to the Pacific. The United States claimed additional lands in Sonora and Chihuahua, including La Mesilla, arguing that the Treaty of Guadalupe Hidalgo had imprecisely defined the boundary between the nations.

James Gadsden, the U.S. minister to Mexico in 1853, ultimately negotiated the purchase of the territory south of the Gila River with Antonio López de Santa Anna, who had once again claimed the presidency of Mexico (Weber 1982:274–275). When the Senate confirmed the purchase in 1854, it established the boundary line between the two nations that exists today (though the exact surveying of that line would occur much later). Unfortunately for the people of La Mesilla who hoped to remain in Mexico, it also meant that they became part of the United States after all. (For more discussion about Mesilla, see Mora [2009].)

Land and Violence along the Nineteenth-Century Border

Mexicans living in the ceded territories faced economic difficulties and the increasing hostility of their newly arriving neighbors. Through the first decades after the war, for instance, Mexicans' incomes in New Mexico remained constant. Yet the surging Euro-American migration strained the territory's resources and drove the price of food and supplies to new highs. In the first five years after the Treaty of Guadalupe Hidalgo, the price of corn rose from \$3.50 to more than \$4.50 per bushel. Eggs, similarly, doubled in price. Mules cost four times more by 1858 than they had in 1848 (González 1999:87). This rapid inflation coupled with stagnant earnings meant that most Mexicans became mired in poverty in their first decade as U.S. citizens.

Mexican women were the hardest hit by the rapidly changing economy. Most Mexican women reported that their total estate was worth less than fifty dollars in the nineteenth century (González 1999). More and more women had to become wage-earning workers so that their family could afford basic necessities. Seventy-five percent of all Mexican women in New Mexico worked as laundresses, domestics, or seamstresses in 1860. By 1870, the number of Mexican women employed in these low-wage jobs increased by 5 percent. By 1880, almost 90 percent of Mexican women worked for wages (González 1999).

These women not only faced the same economic crisis that Mexican men faced, but also the loss of civil rights they had enjoyed under Mexican law. Prior to the war, women in Mexico frequently conducted business in public, retained their property after marriage, and filed suits in local courts.[3] Mexicans did not see widows who managed their property or poor married women selling items or earning wages in public places as particularly unusual or threatening (Lecompte 1981). This is not to say, of course, that Mexicans had an egalitarian view of gender. Most expected a woman's main duties to involve her home and family. Although women had some access to public venues, Mexico's laws and common practices defined women's roles in relation to men and assumed that they "belonged" to a family headed by a man (González 1999).

U.S. law, however, even more severely limited women's abilities to act as independent agents. Married women, under the Euro-American legal system, lost their property and were expected to stay out of public places to preserve their "purity." Mexican women in the United States found that they no longer had access to local courts to settle disputes.

Even if Mexican men had more access than women to legal venues, they faced an uphill battle to secure their land titles, despite the Treaty of Guadalupe Hidalgo's guarantees. At the end of the war, New Mexico had the largest Mexican population of the ceded territories. It also had the oldest historical settlements in the northern frontier of Spain's empire. Initially, Congress assumed direct responsibility for assessing the claims in New Mexico (which included Colorado and Arizona as well). By 1880, Congress had only acted on seventy-one titles out of one thousand claims filed with the surveyor general in New Mexico (Weber 2003). The slowness of the bureaucracy and the complexity of the legal process left many in New Mexico vulnerable. A powerful group of Euro-American lawyers and a few Mexican Americans took advantage of this situation. Sometimes they acquired land as legitimate payment for their legal services. Other times, they forged grants or tricked Mexicans out of their land titles. More than 80 percent of grant holders lost their lands in New Mexico after the U.S. invasion, despite explicit guarantees in the Treaty of Guadalupe Hidalgo. (For more a through discussion of the land grant issue, see Montoya [2002].)

Similar patterns played out across the border. California experienced the most dramatic population changes in the last half of the nineteenth century. The discovery of gold and the profitability of Pacific trading resulted in a rapid surge of Euro-American migration. Mexicans and Native Americans quickly found that their existing land claims were disregarded more often than not by Euro Americans who set themselves up as squatters. Numerous cases of Euro Americans burning crops, stealing cattle, or physically intimidating Mexican vaqueros have been documented (Weber 2003).

Congress also passed the California Land Act in 1851, which established a complicated set of procedures for Mexicans to prove the validity of their land claims to a local board. Unsuccessful petitions, the law dictated, converted the property in question to public domain. Many had to pursue the matter beyond the local board and into the court system. Californios waited an average of seventeen years before their cases found resolution (Weber 2003). Any success, moreover, was often a pyrrhic victory, as the length of the legal battle frequently bankrupted the plaintiff.[4]

Many Mexicans expressed their dissatisfaction with their treatment under the U.S. flag, including some who resorted to violence. Joaquin Murrieta, a bandit in Alta California during the gold rush, became a legend after the California Rangers executed him in 1853. The following year, John Rollin Ridge, a sympathetic Cherokee author, published

Murrieta's biography. Ridge claimed that Murrieta had been driven to crime by the injustices that accompanied Euro Americans' arrival in California. Though an outlaw, Murrieta had a Robin Hood mystique dramatized in numerous *corridos* (folk songs) that configured him as avenging Mexicans against greedy "foreigners" (Weber 2003:206).

Like the feelings of californios and New Mexico's settlers, tejanos' unhappiness often centered on land disputes and the state's disregard for their civil rights. Anti-Mexican sentiment had been escalating in Texas since the revolt against the Mexican government. The 1836 Texan Constitution provided a quasi-legal means to dispossess Mexicans by stipulating that any people who refused to fight the Mexican government, or who otherwise aided the enemy, forfeited their lands. Euro Americans in Texas manipulated this law or resorted to violence to force out Mexican title holders.

The shift in land ownership occurred rapidly in central and eastern Texas. Mexicans in Nueces County, for example, owned the majority of land through fifteen individual grants in 1835. By the time the United States ended the war with Mexico in 1848, only seven Mexicans still retained their grants in Nueces. Another decade later, only one Mexican still had a land claim in that county (Weber 2003). These same circumstances were repeated throughout the state, but they were a bit slowed in the border counties of Webb, Zapata, and Starr (Weber 2003).

Some tejanos, frustrated by a lack of legal protection, fought back through more militant means. Mention of Juan Nepomuceno Cortina's name created a feeling of dread for many Euro-American Texans after he invaded Brownsville in 1859. Cortina, who was born to a landholding Mexican family, became incensed at the treatment Mexicans received from their Euro-American neighbors. Euro Americans, especially the Texas Rangers, often beat, arrested, or even lynched innocent Mexicans with impunity. After a conflict with a local marshal escalated to gun violence, Cortina retaliated as a self-proclaimed agent of justice for all Mexicans in Texas. He led an armed party into Brownsville and freed Mexicans imprisoned in the local jail.

Cortina issued two proclamations that explained his actions and demanded the protection of Mexicans' civil rights along the border. His sense of justice, however, also included violent retribution. The Mexican leader murdered three Euro Americans whom he considered "criminal, wicked men, notorious among the people for their misdeeds" (as quoted in Weber 2003:233).

Despite this violence, many living on both sides of the border embraced Cortina. He became a legend when his band of sixty men defeated the Brownsville Militia and the dreaded Texas Rangers, who had been dispatched to apprehend him. Only the arrival of the U.S. Cavalry forced Cortina's retreat into Mexico. Even after this defeat, many Mexicans still regarded Cortina as a daring transnational hero.

Violence continued to flare up periodically on the U.S. side of the border through the last decades of the nineteenth and early twentieth century. An international crisis, in one instance, developed around the salt trade near El Paso in 1877. Mexican settlers in El Paso built a road to the Guadalupe Salt Lakes in 1868. For a decade, Mexicans from both sides of the border believed that the lakes were a natural resource that was available to anyone who mined it. Charles H. Howard therefore created a furor when he claimed an exclusive domain over the lakes as his personal property and sought to charge a fee for the salt in 1877. Tensions quickly escalated out of control. Mexicans united in a common cause across the international boundary line and threatened Howard. The enterprising Euro American called upon the Texas Rangers to protect his claim, which only prompted a bitter reprisal from a Mexican mob. In a difficult battle, the Rangers ultimately surrendered and the Mexican group executed Howard (Weber 2003).

News of this border violence quickly traveled across Texas. When a stronger contingent of Rangers arrived on the scene, they executed several Mexicans and committed a number of atrocities, including raping a Mexican woman, as revenge (Weber 2003). Mexicans ultimately lost the dispute and were required to start paying for the salt.

Angry settlers in northern New Mexico also stepped outside the legal system in the 1890s through their participation in the secret organization known as the Gorras Blancas (White Caps). This vigilante group targeted Euro Americans who acquired land titles under dubious circumstances. Many of these contested grants were originally issued by Spain and Mexico for communal pasture lands. The United States, however, created legal mechanisms that eroded the community's ability to use these ranges, concentrating land ownership among a few individuals. As a protest to the "land grabbers," the Gorras Blancas destroyed miles of their fences, upended railroad ties, cut telegraph lines, and burned houses to the ground (Weber 2003).[5] While the Gorras Blancas had some support among the Mexican community, this group eventually collapsed with the arrest of its leaders. By the early twentieth century, many New Mexicans were persuaded to find political solutions and placed their faith in the Progressive party.

Just at the time that the Gorras Blancas fell apart in New Mexico, Texas's Rio Grande Valley would again be riddled with violence at the start of the twentieth century. The railroad's arrival in Brownsville brought a wave of Euro-American settlers into the valley in 1904. In a familiar chain of events, these new settlers quickly obtained many Mexican-owned lands, often through squatting and brutal intimidation. A number of lynchings of Mexicans occurred, but nobody faced prosecution for the crimes. Indeed, the Texas Rangers themselves, ostensibly guardians of the law, executed sixteen Mexicans between 1907 and 1911 under questionable circumstances (Dunn 1996).

In 1911, a group of four hundred Texas-Mexican leaders assembled in Laredo and publicly decried the lynching and dispossession of their fellow countrymen. That gathering, in turn, inspired groups of Mexicans from both sides of the border to conduct raids on property owned by Euro Americans whom they considered responsible for border oppression. As the violence escalated, a militant proclamation appeared under the title "El Plan de San Diego" in November 1915. It called for the creation of a new republic that would be carved out of Texas, New Mexico, Colorado, Arizona, and California. This nation, the authors promised, could be won if African Americans, Japanese, Native Americans, and Mexicans united against their common Euro-American foe. The Plan de San Diego, in other words, advocated a race war that would result in the death of all Euro-American men older than sixteen (Dunn 1996; see also Johnson 2005).

Hysteria gripped both Mexicans and Euro Americans. The United States responded promptly by sending 1,900 Army troops into the Rio Grande Valley, along with the Texas Rangers. Most Mexicans obviously did not support the extremist violence in the Plan de San Diego. During the tense months in 1916, however, the Rangers indiscriminately attacked Mexican families.[6] Even mid-century historian Walter Prescott Webb, who generally celebrated the Texas Rangers, characterized their actions in 1915 and 1916 as "a reign of terror" (Dunn 1996:10). By the end of 1916, many hundreds of innocent Mexicans had lost their lives.

While these violent conflicts attracted the most attention, they obviously involved only a small minority of the Mexican population. Even if they privately supported and celebrated figures like Murrieta or Cortina, most nineteenth-century settlers focused on eking out a living while coming to terms with the newly imposed U.S. legal system.

The Mexican population in the nineteenth-century United States remained relatively static and was mostly composed of Mexican families whose ancestors had lived in the ceded territories at the time of the Treaty of Guadalupe Hidalgo. Some migration to mining communities in Arizona and California occurred, but it was relatively modest. Only 8,086 California residents, for instance, reported their birthplace as Mexico in the 1900 census (Sánchez 1993:19).[7] Starting in the early twentieth century, though, dramatic changes in both Mexico and the United States resulted in a rapid Mexican migration that dramatically altered the landscape of the border states.

Twentieth-Century Migration and the New Border Population

Estimates suggest that between six hundred thousand and one million Mexicans migrated to the United States between 1900 and 1929 (Reisler 1976:265–73). On the U.S. side, changes in agricultural technology created a massive demand for unskilled labor. Irrigation projects transformed California and Texas from arid lands in 1900 to the largest producers of fruits of vegetables by 1929 (Sánchez 1993). California put two million acres under cultivation between 1909 and 1929. Irrigation in Texas likewise increased the amount of land being farmed by 317 percent between 1909 and 1917 (Sandos and Cross 1983:48). Both states desperately needed workers for these expanding agricultural enterprises. At the same time, Congress severely limited immigration into the United States from the eastern hemisphere. The Chinese Exclusion Act of 1882 had already cut off immigration from most of mainland Asia. The "Gentleman's Agreements" of 1907 and 1908 with Japan eliminated California's main source for agricultural labor just as the new boom started. Congress then passed a series of immigration acts in 1917, 1921, and

1924 that excluded almost all nonskilled or semiskilled workers from Eastern and Southern Europe.

Mexico, however, was not included in most of those immigration measures. Indeed, agricultural growers directly lobbied Congress and the president to exempt Mexicans from any restrictions (Stern 2004). In instances in which the laws did apply to Mexican immigrants, officials often looked the other way. The Immigration Act of 1917's requirements for a head tax and a literacy test, for instance, exempted Mexican immigrants until 1921. Even after that time until 1930, the high demand for Mexican laborers usually meant that border officials rarely enforced those requirements (Sánchez 1993). Mexicans therefore found an attractive set of jobs that had been left empty when the flow of immigration essentially ended from Asia and Europe (Sánchez 1993). To illustrate, the number of Mexicans employed in California's citrus orchids or packing houses grew exponentially in the first decades of the twentieth century. In 1914, 2,317 Mexicans worked for the industry; that number increased to 7,004 just five years later. By 1926, more than 10,000 Mexicans worked in the citrus industry (Garcia 2001:60).

The massive influx of Mexican workers exposed contradictory sentiments about immigration in the United States. Business and agricultural leaders in the United States imagined Mexican labor as critical to the success of the developing border region. However, other Euro Americans, as will be discussed later, responded to this sudden wave of immigration as a threat to the safety and health of the United States.

On the other side of the border, the massive construction of railroads that had occurred between 1875 and 1910 had made migration to the United States easier than ever (Sánchez 1993). Workers also had many reasons to leave their native land. Mexico's economy and political stability had collapsed by the turn of the century. The dictator Porfirio Díaz, who ruled the nation almost uninterrupted for thirty-five years, instituted economic policies that blatantly favored wealthy land owners and foreign investors. Most Mexican laborers earned less than subsistence wages or suffered total unemployment (Sánchez 1993). Tensions within the nation eventually escalated into a full revolution against Díaz in 1910. For more than a decade, Mexico became embroiled in a series of bloody civil wars that prompted many people to seek refuge north of the border.

At times, the Mexican Revolution crossed the border in the form of violent attacks on U.S. citizens and property. These incidents inevitably prompted an anti-Mexican response among those who wished for tighter control of immigration. Pancho Villa's forces participated in the most famous of these incidents in March 1916. Early in the morning, Villistas raided Columbus, New Mexico, and killed eighteen U.S. citizens. The United States responded by sending General "Blackjack" Pershing and twenty thousand troops into northern Mexico to apprehend Villa. Pershing ultimately returned to the United States empty handed; however, the raid itself created a massive surge of attacks on Mexicans in the United States.

Between 1916 and 1919, several other incidents were brought about in west Texas by a number of factions. The Texas Rangers cemented their negative reputation in the Mexican American community through indiscriminately violent reprisals (Dunn 1996). On November 15, 1922, the Mexican federal government filed an official protest to the United States accusing the government of ignoring the lynching of Mexican citizens on U.S. soil, particularly in Texas (*Los Angeles Times* 1922).

Although violent episodes fueled nativist fears and even violent reprisals, immigration authorities in the United States were still somewhat unconcerned about the overall Mexican migration in the early twentieth century. Despite most male migrants' obvious poverty upon arrival, official and unofficial policies permitted almost unlimited access to the United States. "We know that any able-bodied [Mexican] man who may be admitted," one immigration official explained to his superiors in Washington, DC, "can immediately secure transportation to a point on the railroad where employment will be furnished him" (as quoted in Sánchez 1993:52). By the end of the decade, more than 150,000 Mexicans were migrating to the United States each year, so that the total Mexican population in the country reached 1,422,533 by 1930 (Stern 2004:304). This rapid immigration mostly impacted border states like Texas and California, but it also created Mexican enclaves in areas far from the border, including the Midwest.[8] Henry Ford's rapidly expanding Wayne-County automobile plants, for instance, filled three thousand vacancies with the newly arriving Mexicans (Valdés 1988).

Cities boomed on the U.S side of the border during the first couple of decades in the twentieth century. Mexicans most likely earned more on the U.S. side of the border than in Mexico, but a border-interior earnings gap appeared to develop among workers in the United States in the early 1900s (Mora 2005). Workers on the U.S. side of the border had an average occupational income equivalent to their counterparts in other parts of the United States in 1900. By 1920, however, workers in the U.S. border region earned more than 10 percent less than their counterparts in other parts of the nation (Mora 2005). The U.S. economy benefited from the extra labor arriving from Mexico even as the wages paid for work decreased because of the abundance of that same labor. (More discussion on border-interior wage differentials will be provided in later chapters.)

Not surprisingly, a worker's gender also impacted the wages earned in the United States. Both men and women migrated across the border during the early decades of the twentieth century. Their experiences differed, however, in the types of jobs available to them. In 1930, 45 percent of Mexican men worked in agriculture, 24 percent in manufacturing, and 13 percent in transportation. Mexican women more often worked in the service sector (38 percent), blue-collar employment (25 percent), and agriculture (21 percent) (Ruiz 1998:9; see also Deutsch 1987, Ruiz 1987, and Devra Weber 1994). These occupational differences, and their earnings implications, still exist today, as will be discussed by Rogelio Sáenz, Lorena Murga, and Maria Cristina Morales later in this volume.

As mentioned, immigration officials considered Mexican men immediately employable and therefore approved their entrance into the nation. In contrast, Mexican women, especially women traveling alone, faced much scrutiny, as border inspectors considered them "likely to become a public charge" (Ruiz 1998:11). As a result, women's applications to enter the United States received special hearings. Numerous Mexican women found that the United States denied their request to enter the nation even if they could demonstrate that they had cash in hand (Ruiz 1998). Despite these extra challenges, Mexican women still made their journey and built a life for themselves in the booming southwestern economy.

When that boom cooled at the end of the 1920s, however, Mexican men soon started to experience the same scrutiny that Mexican women had faced all along. Border raids, as mentioned, had already exacerbated nativist fears in the United States. Widespread hysteria and anti-immigrant sentiments only increased in the 1920s. Leading Euro-American medical authorities made accusations that Mexicans spread disease, violence, and disorder wherever they lived. Scientific racism contributed to more intensive efforts to control migration across the border as a matter of public health during the 1920s.[9] On May 28, 1924, Congress officially created the Border Patrol to apprehend individuals migrating into the United States at nondesignated entry points (Stern 2004). Mounted patrols of the border had already existed since 1904, but those first incarnations of a border patrol had mostly been charged with preventing Asians and Europeans from entering the United States through Mexico. In March 1915, for instance, Congress authorized "mounted inspectors" to apprehend Asians who might try to cross the U.S.-Mexico border in an effort to evade the Chinese Exclusion Act. That version of a border police almost entirely ignored Mexican migrants. The newly empowered 1924 Border Patrol, however, had a specific goal of regulating Mexican immigration. The number of Mexicans deported from the United States had rapidly surpassed the number of Europeans being deported by the end of the 1920s (Stern 2004).

Repatriation and the Closed Border

Anti-Mexican sentiment in the United States reached a fevered pitch with the onset of the Great Depression. Local, state, and federal government officials explicitly blamed rising unemployment on immigrants (Gutiérrez 1995; see also Balderrama and Rodríguez 1995). Mexican communities consequently faced overt pressure from the Border Patrol, civic agencies, and other government institutions to leave the United States. This campaign of repatriation resulted in almost eighty thousand individuals being sent to Mexico per year between 1927 and 1937. Estimates suggest that as many as six hundred thousand Mexicans, including many U.S. citizens, migrated to Mexico during the Depression decade (Gutiérrez 1995:72). The Mexican federal government tacitly supported these campaigns as consulates encouraged citizens to relocate across the border rather than alienating the U.S. government (Gutiérrez 1995; Valdés 1988).

As Mexican immigrants became scapegoats for the nation's economic woes, many became disenchanted with the United States. Lyrics from a popular corrido entitled "Los deportados" appealed to the sentiments of many immigrants:

Los güeros son muy malores [sic]	*The Anglos are very bad fellows*
Se valen de la occasion	*They take advantage*
Y a todos los mexicanos	*And to all the Mexicans*
Nos tratan sin compassion.	*They treat us without pity.*
Hoy traen la gran polvareda	*Today they bring great disturbance*
y sin consideración	*And without consideration*
Mujeres, niños, y ancianos	*Women, children, and old ones*
Nos llevan a la frontera,	*They take us to the border,*
Nos echan de esta nación.	*They eject us from this country.*
Adiós paisanos queridos	*Goodbye dear countrymen*
Ya nos van a deportar	*They are going to deport us*
Pero no somos bandidos	*But we are not bandits*
Venimos a camellar.	*We came to toil.*[10]

Though repatriation campaigns occurred almost everywhere Mexican immigrants lived, Southern California and the Midwest were the hardest-hit areas. These also happened to be the areas where unemployment skyrocketed in the United States. While cities like San Antonio only paid an average of $0.24 per capita (worth approximately $3.00 in mid-2007) for welfare expenses, Los Angeles welfare expenses per capita reached $3.40 (about $42 in mid-2007) in the first six months of the Depression, Chicago expenses climbed to $2.41 ($30 in mid-2007), and Detroit expenses reached an astounding $6.59 ($82 in mid-2007) (Valdés 1988:4).[11] In Detroit, automobile employment fell 54 percent between 1929 and 1932 (Valdés 1988:3), and the weekly wage for those in the industry plummeted from $33.05 to $10.62 (the equivalence of falling from $413 to $133 in mid-2007).

Los Angeles returned tens of thousands of Mexicans, including many of their U.S.-born children, to Mexico in the first year of the Depression (Gutiérrez 1995). Midwestern states and cities passed laws that explicitly limited job opportunities for Mexican immigrants (Valdés 1988). Under these conditions, it is not surprising that many Mexicans opted to return to Mexico of their own accord.

In the first decades of the twentieth century, Mexican immigration transformed the United States. Mexican immigrants' labor made agricultural expansion possible and kept the industrial machines running in many of the nation's major cities. Yet a re-invention of the meaning of the border accompanied their migration. By 1930, rather than construing the boundary line as marking the divide between two distinct government structures, the United States envisioned the border as a barrier that should prevent the flow of people.

The Bracero Program

World War II would modify this view of the border only slightly. The war rekindled the call for Mexican labor just as rapidly as the Depression had created the disdain for their presence. Demand for food and manufactured goods in Europe increased the need for agricultural produce even before the United States officially committed to the battle. Franklin Roosevelt signed the Selective Service Act in 1940, moreover, taking a significant number of young workers for military service. Agricultural businesses thereafter advocated for the legal recruitment of Mexican labor (Gutiérrez 1995).

Congress obliged by passing a binational agreement, known as the Bracero Program, to recruit Mexican laborers in August 1942. The exact terms of the agreement changed several times in its two decades of existence, but both nations consistently demanded several key components in each incarnation. The United States stipulated that Mexican workers could only be employed in areas with a documented labor shortage so as to prevent accusations that the program deprived U.S. citizens of jobs. Moreover, the U.S. Secretary of Labor had to certify that the newly arriving workers would not adversely affect local wages or working conditions (Gutiérrez 1995). For its part, the Mexican government demanded that its citizens be guaranteed a certain wage; be exempt from U.S. military service; be free from racial discrimination; and be provided housing, food, and return transportation to Mexico (Gutiérrez 1995). For the first four years of the program, Mexico also refused to allow Mexicans to work in Texas because of the racist atmosphere in that state (Miller 1981). Eventually, though, the government relented on this last point.

The Mexican federal government had total discretion in how it allocated the Bracero permits to its citizens. As a result, almost 50 percent of Braceros came from Mexico's least-developed areas in northern and western states like Durango, Guanajuato, Jalisco, Michoacán, San Luis Potosí, and Zacatecas (Sandos and Cross 1983). All the workers were men between the ages of eighteen and forty-five, with most being between eighteen and thirty (Gutiérrez 1995). The Bracero Program grew rapidly during the war years. In the first year, 4,189 Mexicans signed on as Braceros. Only two years later, 62,091 Braceros worked in U.S. agricultural fields (Gutiérrez 1995). As had been the case with unregulated immigration in the early twentieth century, Braceros found work throughout the United States, not just in the Southwest. More than forty-seven thousand Braceros, for instance, worked in Idaho, Washington, and Oregon between 1943 and 1947 (Gamboa 1987).

Both the Mexican and U.S. governments declared the Bracero Program a major success. Corruption and abuse, however, plagued the system. Workers in Mexico almost always had to pay a bribe to a local official to obtain a Bracero contract (Sandos and Cross 1983). Once in the United States, workers found that employers interpreted the mandate to provide adequate food and shelter fairly loosely. Camps often served spoiled food to workers in unsanitary conditions (Gamboa 1987; Martinez 1948). In the Pacific Northwest, growers expected six workers to live together in a sixteen-by-sixteen-foot cloth tent year round (Gamboa 1987:381). The Braceros regularly complained of freezing conditions in the winter and unbearable heat in the summer. Similar complaints appeared in New York, where Mexican workers lived in poorly ventilated barracks that lacked basic necessities, like clean sheets. Meanwhile, Euro-American workers doing the same job reportedly lived in separate and superior barracks nearby (Martinez 1948).

Despite these types of violations, the two countries continued to renew the program for twenty years, until it ended in 1965. Though lauded by many, the Bracero Program eventually became a political liability in the United States (Craig 1971). Labor unions attacked the program as threatening industrial jobs because Braceros might illegally remain in the United States once their agricultural contract expired (Gonzáles 1999). Likewise, small farmers saw that the Bracero Program gave unfair advantage to agribusiness, which could afford the labor contracts. Finally, even major Latino civil rights organizations opposed the program by arguing that it undermined their economic and social positions within the United States. Congress ultimately decided not to renew the agreement in 1964 and it expired the following year. By that time, more than 4.6 million Mexicans had found temporary employment thanks to the Bracero Program (Sandos and Cross 1983).

Racism also continued as a major problem on the U.S. side of the border in the middle of the twentieth century. Even as the Bracero Program attracted tens of thousands of Mexicans to fill jobs in the United States, the nation witnessed another round of scapegoating of Mexican labor in the middle of the twentieth century. Between 1942 and 1965, nearly five million Mexicans were apprehended and deported by the United States (Durand and Massey 1992). When the United States faced an economic slump in 1952, renewed calls for stricter control of the border appeared. One histrionic essay in the *Stanford Law Review* from 1954 authoritatively claimed that "to law enforcement agencies, public health authorities, labor groups, and the community at large, the Wetback invasion presents critical problems" (*Stanford Law Review* 1954:287). The Immigration and Naturalization Service (INS) initiated a number of raids and militaristic maneuvers against undocumented workers in 1954. Known collectively as "Operation Wetback," these maneuvers allowed the U.S. government to ultimately deport more than a million Mexicans (Gutiérrez 1995).

Not all the criticism of Mexican migrants came exclusively from Euro Americans. Indeed, most of the best-known U.S. Latino civil rights groups had a complicated relationship with Mexican nationals. While U.S. citizens of Mexican descent expressed sympathy for recent immigrants, most of the civil rights organizations had explicit citizenship requirements for membership. The League of United Latin American Citizens (LULAC, formed in 1921), the American G.I. Forum (formed in 1948), and César Chávez's United Farm Workers (UFW, formed in 1962) usually supported stiffer restrictions on immigration from Mexico (Gutiérrez 1995; see also García 1989). As mentioned, almost all these groups were likewise involved in campaigning for the demise of the Bracero Program in 1964. The Mexican American leaders of the American G.I. Forum even went as far as to publish a broadside entitled *What Price Wetbacks?* in 1952. This publication named immigration "the fundamental problem facing the Spanish-speaking population of the United States." It called for remarkably stringent immigration laws and increasing the power of the Border Patrol (Gutiérrez 1995:154).

The positions of two organizations in the 1930s, however, sharply contrasted those of most other Latino organizations in the United States. The United Cannery, Agricultural, Packing, and Allied Workers of American (UCAPAWA, founded in 1937) and El Congreso de Pueblos de Habla Española (founded in 1938) both contended that immigrant workers had a right to work in the United States and a right to organize (Gutiérrez 1995). Leaders of these groups suggested that divisions along citizenship lines prevented workers from recognizing their shared oppression. Despite some initial successes, neither the UCAPAWA nor El Congreso maintained their momentum through World War II. UCAPAWA scaled back its scope to focus mainly on cannery workers and El Congreso more or less dissolved under accusations of being a Communist tool. It would not be until the late 1980s that any union would try to organize both Mexican Americans and Mexican nationals living in the United States.

Late Twentieth-Century Reforms

After the demise of the Bracero Program, migration across the border continued to be the most consistent and least resolvable diplomatic issue between the United States and Mexico. The U.S. Congress passed the Hart-Cellars Immigration and Naturalization Act in 1965, which eliminated the national-origin quotas established in 1924. Instead of using the 1924 quotas, the United States restricted the total number of visas from anywhere in the eastern hemisphere to 170,000, and it likewise established the first-ever immigration quotas (120,000) for the western hemisphere (Simon and Deley 1984).

Meanwhile, Mexico faced almost unending economic crises in the last three decades of the twentieth century. Starting around 1965, Mexico witnessed a shift in industrialization that centered on its border with the United States. A sudden proliferation of maquiladoras (to be discussed in more detail by John Sargent, Melissa Najera, and Linda Matthews in chapter 4) changed the economy of northern Mexico from Tijuana to Matamoros. As will be noted by James T. Peach and Richard V. Adkisson in chapter 3, this process would escalate exponentially after Mexico joined the General Agreement of Tariffs and Trade (GATT) in 1986, and even further with the implementation of the North American Free

Trade Agreement (NAFTA) in 1994. The first agreements in the mid-1960s that spawned maquiladoras called for "twin plants" to be constructed on each side of the U.S.-Mexico border. The factories on the U.S. side, under this plan, would produce individual components that would then be assembled in their partner plants on the Mexican side. The final product would then be sent back into the U.S. market with tariffs only applying to the low cost of Mexican labor used for assembly (González 2000).

In practice, however, U.S. corporations used this program as a means to avoid stiffer labor and environmental regulations north of the border. Rather than the series of linked transnational plants envisioned in 1965, U.S. corporations usually constructed only a warehouse on the U.S. side of the border. General Motors Corporation, which would become the largest private employer in Mexico by 1990, built eleven new maquiladoras in Mexico. At the same time, it closed eleven factories in the United States and dismissed twenty-nine thousand workers (González 2000:234). Such decisions created resentment in the United States and a notion that Mexico was "stealing U.S. jobs."

Maquiladoras' rapid development accompanied major population shifts in the border region. Migration both within and between the United States and Mexico resulted in a radical demographic change between 1950 and 1990. Only sixteen million people lived in the four southwestern U.S. states and six northern Mexican states in 1940. By 1990, the number of people residing in these border states had swelled to sixty million (Meyer and Sherman 1995:689–90). (Recall that the border states are highlighted in figure I.1 in the introductory chapter.) Contrary to popular assumptions, these border states' populations were highly urban.

In the midst of these shifts in demographics, Mexican immigration re-emerged as a dominant political issue in the United States during the late 1970s and early 1980s. Despite the growth of the maquiladoras, unemployment remained high in Mexico and surplus labor depressed wages in the last decades of the twentieth century. Between 1980 and 1996, an estimated 17 million new workers entered the Mexican labor market. During that same period, however, Mexico only created two million new jobs (Gutiérrez 1999:505, n. 46). The collapse of the oil industry in the 1980s only exacerbated Mexico's social and economic problems (Chávez

2006). Many Mexicans continued to seek a better chance for employment by crossing the border (Samora 1971).

Both President Gerald Ford and President Jimmy Carter proposed comprehensive immigration legislation to Congress, but neither effort resulted in significant changes (e.g., Pear 1982). Ronald Reagan made immigration reform a central component of his agenda when he assumed the presidency in 1981. Just months after taking office, Reagan's attorney general, William French Smith, declared that the nation had "lost control of our borders" and that a major overhaul was required (*New York Times* 1981). By July 1981, the Reagan administration had reversed the INS policy on detention that had been in place since 1954. Previously, immigrants had been released from custody while their case was pending. The new policy, however, considered detention as a means to deter unwanted immigration (Dunn 1996).

Under Reagan, the border between the United States and Mexico became increasingly militarized. Congressional appropriations for the INS rose 130 percent between 1980 and 1988 (Dunn 1996:42). Funding for Border Patrol staff positions, in particular, jumped 90 percent, and the budget for the Detention and Deportation program, a centerpiece of the new changes, jumped 191 percent (Dunn 1996:45, 49).

The amount of military equipment increased at a similar rate during the 1980s. The Border Patrol operated two helicopters in 1980; it had five by 1982, and twenty-two by 1988 (Dunn 1996:43). The INS increased the number of night-vision scopes from 59 to 344, while 22 new Border Patrol stations and four traffic-inspection checkpoints were also approved for construction (Dunn 1996:45).

Officials in the Reagan administration partially explained this military increase by directly linking illegal immigration with drug trafficking during the administration's second term. They downplayed the fact that less than 1 percent of individuals apprehended by the Border Patrol were found carrying drugs. Instead, they created an idea that migration could be blamed for the nation's drug addictions. Attorney General Edwin Meese confidently declared, "The uncontrolled flow of illegal aliens gives the drug traffickers the ideal opportunity to get lost in the crowd" (Brinkley 1986).

These types of unsubstantiated proclamations have led some to suggest that the Border Patrol's efforts at apprehension were linked more to the Reagan administration's domestic agenda than to a sudden increase in migration. The number of apprehensions of undocumented immigrants by the Border Patrol, they note, doubled between 1981 and 1986, the period during which the Reagan administration pressured Congress for new immigration legislation. Indeed, Alan C. Nelson, commissioner of the Immigration and Naturalization Service, released statistics about apprehensions that he contended showed a "startling surge" of illegal migration from Mexico to the United States while Reagan and Congress negotiated the final details of immigration reform in 1986 (Senon 1986).

Passage of the Immigration Reform and Control Act (IRCA) reflected the U.S. preoccupation with undocumented workers. The bill instituted the first-ever penalties for U.S. employers who hired undocumented immigrants, ranging from $250 to $10,000 (Pear 1986; Baker 1997). It also created a one-time-only program for undocumented workers to become permanent U.S. residents and citizens. To qualify for the program, the bill stipulated that migrants needed to file an application within twelve months of the law being enacted; prove continuous residency in the United States since before January 1, 1982; show a "minimal understanding of ordinary English"; and demonstrate knowledge of U.S. government institutions and history (Reinhold 1986; *New York Times* 1986). About 1.7 million people received legal status through the program (Baker 1997). The IRCA also contained a Special Agricultural Worker (SAW) program that provided different criteria for obtaining legal status. SAW permitted undocumented individuals to apply for legal status in the United States if they had worked for ninety days in U.S. agriculture between May 1985 and May 1986 (Gonzáles 1999).

Many Mexicans and Mexican Americans expressed concern, however, that the bill was accompanied by even more funding for weapons and officers in the Border Patrol. The emphasis on policing, they argued, resulted in abuse by agents during the 1980s and 1990s. One case that gained a great deal of attention involved a Border Patrol agent, Edward Cole, shooting a twelve-year-old Mexican citizen named Humberto Carrillo Estrada across the international border line. Reportedly, Estrada and some of his friends pelted Cole and two other agents with stones while standing on the Tijuana side of the border. Cole retaliated by firing at and wounding Estrada. The agent never faced charges in the case, as the U.S. district attorney claimed that he lacked jurisdiction (Cummings 1985). Such events suggested to community activists that the Border Patrol operated without much oversight or concern for human rights.

In human rights debates, Mexican women often became critical to organizations seeking social justice on the border. During the 1970s and 1980s, women composed between 35 and 50 percent of undocumented workers entering the United States from Mexico (Simon and Delay 1984). Their unique experiences, however, have often been understudied by scholars on both sides of the border. Sáenz, Murga, and Morales offer a starting corrective to this problem in chapter 7 by focusing their analysis on the earnings of female Mexican immigrants in U.S. border states. Pia M. Orrenius, Madeline Zavodny, and Leslie Lukens also discuss gender-related outcomes among Mexican migrants in chapter 8.

While academics have been slow to notice, women figured prominently in grassroots activism that created movements such as the Justice for Janitors campaign in 1985. Sponsored by the Service Employees International Union (SEIU), this campaign addressed the shared needs of immigrant workers and U.S. citizens working in the service industry. When Mexican American María Elena Durazo became president of the Local 11 chapter of the Hotel Restaurant Employees Union in March 1989, she declared immigrants the "future of L.A." (Ruiz 1998:137).

Justice for Janitors launched several successful campaigns in Pittsburgh, Denver, San Diego, Los Angeles, and Washington, DC, through the 1980s and 1990s (Kelley 1997). These successes hinged on the creation of powerful alliances between African American, Mexican American, and immigrant workers. In Los Angeles, the number of janitors belonging to a union rose from 10 percent in 1987 to 90 percent in 1995 (Kelley 1997). In April 1995, Justice for Janitors won a major pay increase from seven of the leading Los Angeles janitorial contractors.

African American and Latina women composed the majority of the SEIU membership and several key leadership positions in Washington, DC. These women organized grassroots demonstrations against a private janitorial company that had a history of intimidation and labor busting in March 1995. They eventually won a victory when the National Labor Relations Board ruled in their favor at the end of the year (Kelley 1997).

NAFTA and the Nineties

Revising immigration laws accompanied changing ideas about the meaning of trade and capital investment along the border. Mexico announced in August 1982 that it would not be able to meet the interest payments on its foreign debt (Rosen and McFadyen 1995). The debt crisis and concurrent economic recession prompted the Mexican federal government to start a long process of major economic and trade reforms. Miguel de la Madrid, who assumed the Mexican presidency in 1982, reversed Mexico's long-standing opposition to joining the General Agreement on Tariffs and Trade (GATT) in 1986.

The GATT, the forerunner to the current World Trade Organization, involved an ongoing series of agreements that lowered trade restrictions between nations. Joining the GATT was critical, de la Madrid argued, because Mexico's economic future depended on its participation in the world economy (Rosen and McFadyen 1995). Government policies, as a result, changed to promote Mexico's imagined advantage of low wages and flexible labor in that world market. Among other things, de la Madrid believed one key to economic growth centered on creating more exports and attracting foreign industry, especially maquiladora development, along the U.S.-Mexico border. Despite the continued creation of jobs in maquiladoras, however, the rest of the national economy failed to rebound. During the 1980s, almost half of Mexico's labor force lived below the nation's poverty line. Moreover, real wages declined by 50 percent during de la Madrid's tenure (Grinspun and Cameron 1995:42).

Changes in trade restrictions started by de la Madrid would advance dramatically in the following decade. On November 17, 1993, the U.S. Congress approved the North American Free Trade Agreement (NAFTA). (The effects of NAFTA on employment and other economic outcomes in the border region will be discussed in more detail in chapters 3 and 4.) NAFTA's successful passage is often credited to George H. W. Bush and Carlos Salinas de Gortari. In July 1988, Salinas was declared president of Mexico after a questionable election (Salinas would later order records of the actual vote burned) (Krauze 1997:770). The newly installed president surrounded himself with young economists who mostly had degrees from prestigious U.S. universities. Based on their training, they configured a plan that accelerated the privatization of state industries, renegotiated Mexico's foreign debt, and further eased restrictions on trade with its northern neighbors (Krauze 1997).

Salinas found a receptive audience to the last part of his plan in his conservative U.S. and Canadian counterparts, President George Bush and Prime Minister Brian Mulroney. The first hints of the new agreement appeared when Bush and Salinas met in Houston, Texas, in 1988. The Mexican president successfully argued that creating NAFTA would reduce Mexican migration to the United States by creating new jobs in Mexico. Moreover, he suggested that the combined resources of the United States, Mexico, and Canada would make a trading bloc that could rival Europe and Asia (Krauze 1997).

For NAFTA to take effect, though, Salinas had to dismantle hard-won constitutional protections that came about after the Mexican Revolution. In particular, he oversaw the removal of Article 27, Section VII, in the Mexican Constitution, which had guaranteed land reparations to indigenous groups throughout Mexico, a major component of the revolution's reforms. He further dismantled restrictions on foreign investment and sold 261 public-sector enterprises (Chávez 2006:329).

Easing trade restrictions along Mexico's northern border and changing the Constitution had tremendous social and economic consequences.[12] On January 1, 1994, a clandestine guerrilla organization known as the Zapatista Army of National Liberation (EZLN) took control of six cities in the southern state of Chiapas. Led by the mysterious and masked subcommander Marcos (probably Rafael Sebastián Guillén Vicente, a Tampico intellectual), the EZLN made full use of the Internet and media to articulate their position (Chávez 2006). NAFTA and other "neo-liberal" policies, they argued, opened the Mexican border to cheap, mass-produced U.S. agricultural products and ended crop subsidies. Mexican farmers, as a result, could not compete with the mechanically fertilized and harvested U.S. crops, especially corn. The Chiapas uprising brought about a great deal of debate about whether Mexico's new economic policies benefited the wealthy at the expense of the poor (Gilbreth and Otero 2001).

By the time Ernesto Zedillo Ponce de León assumed the Mexican presidency in 1994, it was already known that much of the Salinas-era economic growth was built on questionable principles or simple manipulation of economic figures. During Zedillo's first month in office, the government devalued the Mexican peso, sending the country into an economic crisis. The United States under Bill Clinton intervened to prevent a free-fall of the peso's value, but the Mexican economy would still be fairly crippled (Krauze 1997).

Free trade, meanwhile, resulted in the growth of maquiladoras on the Mexican side of the border, which is the focus of discussion by Sargent, Najera, and Matthews later in this volume. The 1990s witnessed a massive boom in the maquiladora industry, leading to the creation of seven hundred thousand jobs in Mexico's northern cities. As Sargent, Najera, and Matthews note, about 75 percent of those jobs were in just three industries: electronics, automobile parts, and apparel. Maquiladoras produced $78 billion in exports in 2002 alone (*New York Times* 2003b).

Yet the maquiladoras have been connected with controversies and even violence. There have been accusations of various types of abuse and sexual harassment within maquiladoras (Ortíz-González 2004). Moreover, when the U.S. economy started to decline in 2000, almost three hundred thousand of those new jobs were eliminated (see the Sargent, Najera, and Matthews chapter; and *New York Times* 2003b). More than 340 maquiladoras closed between 2000 and 2003, many of them relocating to China, where labor was even cheaper than in Mexico (*New York Times* 2003a). China's elevation to a full partner in the World Trade Organization (and the accompanying changes in tariff restrictions) allowed that nation to compete with the same labor advantages as Mexico. Between 1997 and 2006, for example, the number of jobs in China's versions of maquiladoras increased from eighteen million to forty million (see chapter 4). Mexico's labor pool no longer appeared as attractive to transnational corporations as it had in the late 1990s. To compensate, as noted by Sargent, Najera, and Matthews in chapter 4, Mexican federal, state, and local governments have attempted to cater to more knowledge-intensive industries, such as software development or aerospace engineering, manufacturing, and repair. Those efforts, though, have failed to regenerate all the jobs lost in maquiladoras after 2000.

On the U.S. side of the border, several states began passing anti-immigrant laws shortly after NAFTA's passage. California's Proposition 187 was one of the most visible and punitive of these measures. Though it was later struck down by federal court, voters approved the proposition, which denied undocumented workers access to virtually all public services (health care, public education, and welfare) (Gutiérrez 1999). (Ironically, as will be discussed by Catalina Amuedo-Dorantes and Cynthia Bansak in chapter 9, illegal immigrants in U.S. border states are less likely to use these services than their legal counterparts.) California voters followed this measure with Proposition 209, which banned affirmative action programs in the state, and Proposition 227, which banned bilingual education in public schools (Gutiérrez 1999). Even as NAFTA opened the border to the free flow of capital, the United States continued to insist that the border be closed to the free migration of workers.

The Millennium Border

Debates about the meaning of the U.S.-Mexico border would continue to inform U.S. politics after the turn of the millennium. During the 2000 U.S. presidential election, both the major candidates made the border a key component of their campaigns. Each assured voters that they would rethink the U.S. relationship with its southern neighbor if elected. Republican George W. Bush promised to form a "special relationship" with Mexico, in which differences would be "differences among family, not rivals" (Streeby 2002:288). Similarly, Democrat Al Gore hailed NAFTA as the first step toward deepening a sense of unity between Mexico and the United States. Both candidates also tacitly acknowledged that border migration had significantly changed U.S. demographics as they each produced Spanish-language advertisements (Streeby 2002).

Despite this bipartisan acknowledgment that the United States and Mexico were intimately intertwined because of their shared border, the U.S. media and policymakers have continued to fret about the meaning of the transnational boundary. President George W. Bush unsuccessfully sought to make immigration reform a signature issue in his second term as president. Twelve senators, both Democrats and Republicans, worked with Bush for three months in early 2007 to craft a bill that would have made the most comprehensive changes to U.S. immigration law in two decades (Hernandez 2007; Pear and Huilse 2007). In many ways, it mirrored key components of Reagan's IRCA of 1986. The new bill proposed increasing funding for military equipment and staff in the Border Patrol by $4.4 billion; stiffer penalties for employers who knowingly hired undocumented workers; and a pathway for citizenship for undocumented workers who already resided in the United States. One portion of the bill that was significantly different from the 1986 law, though, involved the creation of a new guest-worker program like the previous Bracero Program (Pear and Zeleny 2007).

Despite Bush's endorsement and its bipartisan authorship, Congress rejected the proposal. Initially, the bill failed to advance beyond debate in the Senate by a vote of fifty to forty-five (supporters needed sixty votes to move it forward) on June 7, 2007. It received a surprise resurrection a week later, but failed again with a vote of fifty-three to forty-six on June 28. Both Republicans and Democrats voted against the bill. Conservative Republicans argued that it wrongly provided "amnesty" to those who had broken the law. Senator John Cornyn, a Republican from Texas, explained that he opposed the reform partly because "criminals might slip through" the process (Pear 2007). Meanwhile, those on the political left took issue with the guest-worker program. Tom Harkin, a Democratic senator from Iowa, declared that the immigration bill would have driven down wages for Americans "on the lower rungs of the economic ladder" (Pear and Huilse 2007).

Debate around and the failure of the 2007 immigration bill suggests how uncertain the United States remains about its border with Mexico. The imagined constancy of the actual 1854 boundary line belies the ongoing controversies over the meaning of that line for the past century and a half. When settlers from Mexico and the U.S. encountered each other in the nineteenth century, the border signified a challenge to managing and controlling land. By the twentieth century, the conflict between the two nations centered on the flow of workers and capital investment. Far from being an arbitrary line on maps, the border has greatly impacted the daily lives of those living at the edge of two nations.

Labor Market Evolution[1]

Thomas M. Fullerton Jr., James H. Holcomb, and Angel L. Molina Jr.

Introduction

Border areas of the United States currently face a variety of economic challenges. In particular, border-region labor markets are becoming more service and information oriented. Similar to in the rest of the United States and other high-income economies, job creation in border counties has moved away from goods-producing sectors. Such changes mean that income performance depends increasingly on worker productivity that is primarily a function of formal education.

This chapter provides an overview of the demographic and socio-economic trends and changes that have characterized labor markets on the U.S. side of the border in recent years. The U.S. southern border region is defined here as the twenty-three counties physically adjacent to Mexico; see the appendix to this volume for more information. Despite some heterogeneity across these counties, as will be discussed here, their underlying demographic and socioeconomic characteristics—such as age distributions, educational attainment, and per-capita income—often distinguish this region from the United States as a whole.[2]

Basic Demographics

One of the striking demographic changes affecting the U.S. border region in the past few decades has been its rapid population growth. The aggregate population of the twenty-three U.S. border counties more than doubled between 1970 and 2005, with San Diego County, California, comprising nearly half the border population throughout those years. During the same period, the population of the United States as a whole increased by only 46 percent. In 1970, the border counties collectively accounted for 1.4 percent of the national population, but by 2005, this figure grew to 2.3 percent. The above average growth rate stems from a combination of immigration and fertility patterns causing the border-region population to expand fairly rapidly (Fullerton 2003; Johnson and Rendell 2004; Hanson 2006).

While the border-region residential population growth rate is impressive, the total figure masks substantial heterogeneity. Among these twenty-three counties, several are highly urbanized, such as San Diego County in California; Pima County (which includes the metropolitan statistical area [MSA] of Tucson) in Arizona; El Paso County in Texas; and Hidalgo County, Texas (which includes the McAllen MSA). In fact, the population of Hidalgo County, Texas, increased by 274 percent (growing from 181,540 to 678,650 residents) between 1970 and 2005—the fastest-growing county of the 23 border counties during the thirty-five-year period, and one of the fastest-growing counties in the United States overall.

In contrast, seven counties within this group individually have fewer than ten thousand residents, one of which (Terrell County, Texas) actually lost half its population between 1970 and 2005 (dropping from 1,940 to 990 residents). With this in mind, it is often difficult to define a prototypical "border county." However, as noted above, several common characteristics distinguish this region from the rest of the United States.

For one, the populations of border counties tend to be relatively young. In 1970, 34.3 percent of the national population was age seventeen or younger; by 2005, that figure declined to 24.8 percent, reflecting the aging of the U.S. population. The corresponding border county figures were noticeably higher than the national figures for these years. Only five border counties in 2005 (Pima County, Arizona; and Jeff Davis, Brewster, Terrell, and Kinney counties in Texas) had smaller under-eighteen populations than the national average.

This age pattern has important implications for border-county public finances: the demand for educational services in younger counties will tend to be higher than in older counties, causing higher pressures to finance those services via property taxation or other mechanisms (Poterba 1997; Aleman 2006). A relatively young region also tends to generate less output than do regions with more experienced labor forces (Kogel 2005).[3]

Consider also that while about half of the U.S. border counties have a relatively low share of people age sixty-five and older, these counties have a comparatively high percentage of individuals younger than the age of eighteen. The border counties, therefore, have relatively high *population dependency ratios* (defined as the percentage of people who are either too young or too old to work and thus depend on others for their care). For example, in 2005, the average population dependency ratio was 40 percent in border counties, compared to 37.2 percent in the United States overall.[4]

Another demographic feature of interest pertains to the number of persons per household in border counties compared to the number observed for the United States as a whole. As discussed by James T. Peach and Richard V. Adkisson in the following chapter, the number of persons per household in border counties tends to exceed the number that is observed for the United States as a whole. Moreover, while the national average household size trended down from 2.8 to 2.6 persons between 1980 and 2005, this average rose from 2.8 to 3.0 persons between 1980 and 2005 in the border counties. Such divergences have potentially important regional economic implications, particularly when considering that household demographics influence the demand for a wide array of goods and services, affecting regional housing stocks, automobile fleet sizes, fiscal performance, and retail store investment among other things (Montgomery 1996; Clark 2007; Mullins and Wallace 1996; Singh, Hansen, and Blattberg 2006).

While the household size and age distribution patterns mentioned above might be useful demographic phenomena, income and ethnicity also play a role. Income is negatively correlated with household size and, as will be discussed below and in other chapters in this book, income levels are lower along the border than in the U.S. interior. Also, Hispanics tend to reside in larger-family households than non-Hispanics in the United States, and the border region has experienced an increase in the presence of Hispanics.

Indeed, perhaps the most noticeable change in border county demographics relates to ethnicity (Sutton and Day 2004). Between 1980 and 2005, this region's population share of Hispanics rose from 36 percent to just more than 50 percent. Excluding San Diego County, the latter figure rose to 68.3 percent. Also, there were nine border counties (almost all in Texas) in 2005 in which the percentages exceeded 80 percent. On the surface, these data might appear trivial. Related policy issues arise, however, as these counties frequently exhibit education, language, and income characteristics that differ from those observed in other parts of the nation (Dávila and Mora 2000; Almada et al. 2006). For example, lower rates of English-language proficiency and educational attainment often correlate with Hispanic-population enclaves (e.g., Vélez and Sáenz 2001).

General Economic Trends

One of the most difficult problems that has hampered border economic development subsequent to 1970 has been below-average educational attainment (Fullerton 2001). Most of the U.S. border counties have had lower average educational levels than the nation as a whole during the past couple of decades, as observed in table 2.1. For example, in 1980, two-thirds of the adult U.S. population earned a high school education, compared to just more than half of those in the border counties. By 2005, 84 percent of this U.S. population had completed high school, but only 71 percent of the border population had this level of schooling.

This said, as reported in the second half of table 2.1, encouraging gains developed between 1980 and 2005 in many border counties with respect to the presence of college graduates. Even with those fairly modest increases in enrollment, however, the lack of educational attainment represents a major, if not *the* major, impediment to development in the border counties. In fact, the increase in the representation of college graduates between 1980 and 2000 in border counties did not keep pace with the United States as a whole, particularly when excluding San Diego. In 1980, 14.4 percent of the border population (minus San Diego) had finished college, compared to 16.2 percent of the U.S. population. Two decades later, one-fifth of the border county population had a college degree, compared to more than one-quarter of the United States overall.

Numerous studies point to continually increasing returns to education and the rising importance of education in the determination of labor market incomes (Welch 2000; Juhn, Murphy, and Pierce 1993; Ashenfelter and Rouse 1999). Under such circumstances, even if educational distributions remain unchanged, border counties will probably continue to lose ground relative to the rest of the United States with respect to labor market outcomes.

Given these educational gaps, it is not surprising that per-capita incomes tend to be relatively low throughout the U.S. border region (table 2.2). Although border incomes have grown in real terms, they have generally not kept pace with the rest of the country. In 1985, U.S. border county per-capita income averaged $9,809—approximately 66.5 percent of the national average. By 2005, border per-capita incomes had risen to $20,809, averaging only 60.4 percent of the national estimate. In fact, table 2.2 shows that, exclusive of San Diego County, border per-capita incomes lagged behind the national average by an even larger margin during the same period. In the Texas border counties alone, recent estimates suggest that below-average educational attainment contributed to an aggregate income loss of more than $9.4 billion in 2000 (Almada et al. 2006). This translates into a $4,800 per-capita income loss, nearly two-fifths of the gap shown for that year in table 2.2.[5]

Because border per-capita incomes lag behind those of the rest of the country, retail sales should also be expected to lag behind what is observed in other regions. However, this is not always the case, because consumers from Mexico cause retail sales to exceed the expected domestic levels in several border counties (Patrick and Renforth 1996; Hadjimarcou and Barnes 1998; Adkisson and Zimmerman 2004). In 2002, the retail sales-to-income ratio for the United States was 0.34 (see table 2.3). This ratio is very close to the 0.36 average for the twenty-three border counties during the same year.

Once again, however, the aggregate figure masks substantial variability among the different border markets. As table 2.3 shows, in 2002, nine counties whose sales-to-income ratios were 0.45 or greater contained well-known shopping destinations for Mexican customers, including Laredo (Webb County), McAllen (Hidalgo County), and Brownsville (Cameron County) in Texas, as well as Calexico (Imperial County) in California and Nogales (Santa Cruz County) in Arizona. It follows that the retail sales generated by Mexican nationals shopping in certain U.S. border communities are considerable, suggesting the vulnerability of these areas to changes in Mexican economic conditions.

Table 2.3 also shows there were five border counties in Texas that had sales-to-income ratios of 0.21 or less in 2002. Without exception, these

TABLE 2.1 Educational Attainment Percentages for the Population Ages 25 and Over

County	High School or More				4-Year College or More			
	1980	1990	2000	2005	1980	1990	2000	2005
San Diego County, CA	78	81.9	82.6	84.7	20.9	25.3	29.5	33.9
Imperial County, CA	50.9	53.2	59	62.4	9.6	9.7	10.3	11.6
Yuma County, AZ	61.6	64.9	65.8	69.5	10.9	12.7	11.8	13.5
Pima County, AZ	74.6	80.5	83.4	86.7	20.7	23.3	26.7	30.1
Santa Cruz, AZ	54	57.2	60.7	NA	13.2	10.8	15.2	NA
Cochise County, AZ	68.8	75.7	79.5	85	13.8	16.1	18.8	22.2
Hidalgo County, NM	NA	71.6	68.8	NA	9.1	11.7	9.9	NA
Luna County, NM	NA	58.8	59.8	NA	10.7	11.1	10.4	NA
Doña Ana County, NM	NA	70.4	70	72.6	19.3	21.9	22.3	23.7
El Paso County, TX	59.5	63.7	65.8	67.5	14	15.2	16.6	17.1
Hudspeth County, TX	46.3	48.1	46.1	NA	9.3	8	9.7	NA
Jeff Davis County, TX	55	69.5	74.7	NA	22.4	25.1	35.1	NA
Presidio County, TX	41.1	43.9	44.7	NA	12.2	11.8	11.7	NA

Brewster County, TX	67.5	73.2	78.6	NA	23.5	28	27.7	NA
Terrell County, TX	59.9	66.3	70.9	NA	11.4	12	19	NA
Val Verde County, TX	51.1	56.1	58.7	NA	12.2	13	14.1	NA
Kinney County, TX	40.1	56.2	66.9	NA	7.4	11	17.7	NA
Maverick County, TX	32.2	37.5	42.1	NA	8.4	7.3	9.1	NA
Webb County, TX	41.5	47.8	53	58.5	9.8	11.1	13.9	17.9
Zapata County, TX	41.3	50.1	53.1	NA	7.2	6.9	8.7	NA
Starr County, TX	26.6	31.6	34.7	NA	6	6.7	6.9	NA
Hidalgo County, TX	41.1	46.6	50.5	58.2	10.8	11.5	12.9	15.3
Cameron County, TX	43.8	50	55.2	61.3	10.5	12	13.4	13.7
Border Counties	51.8	58.9	61.9	70.6	17.4	20.4	22.9	26.2
Border without San Diego	50.4	57.9	61	69.1	14.4	15.9	17.5	19.9
United States	66.5	75.2	80.4	84.2	16.2	20.3	24.4	27.2

Sources: U.S. Census Bureau Decennial Census; U.S. Census Bureau Quick Facts; and U.S. Census Bureau American Community Survey.

TABLE 2.2 Per-Capita Incomes

County	1985	1990	1995	2000	2005
San Diego, CA	16,548	20,852	23,533	32,799	40,569
Imperial, CA	11,213	16,018	16,313	17,751	21,899
Yuma, AZ	12,037	13,764	17,029	16,507	21,005
Pima, AZ	13,089	16,002	19,275	24,173	28,869
Santa Cruz, AZ	9,919	12,000	13,597	16,868	19,967
Cochise, AZ	11,200	13,829	15,582	19,733	26,866
Hidalgo, NM	9,243	12,893	16,883	15,865	20,589
Luna, NM	8,695	11,131	12,702	14,591	19,165
Doña Ana, NM	10,244	12,611	15,119	17,827	23,070
El Paso, TX	9,803	12,284	14,793	18,560	23,256
Hudspeth, TX	10,136	9,458	10,264	14,133	14,804
Jeff Davis, TX	13,075	13,344	13,858	17,081	19,499
Presidio, TX	9,133	9,050	10,800	13,446	14,583
Brewster, TX	9,535	13,023	14,760	21,674	27,422
Terrell, TX	14,204	15,684	17,761	24,892	20,039
Val Verde, TX	9,205	11,151	13,164	16,794	22,133
Kinney, TX	8,851	9,367	12,029	16,614	20,813
Maverick, TX	5,478	7,023	8,960	11,509	14,690
Webb, TX	6,986	9,406	12,122	15,067	18,809
Zapata, TX	7,169	8,032	9,939	12,204	14,592
Starr, TX	4,691	5,479	7,845	9,556	12,197
Hidalgo, TX	7,465	9,282	11,073	13,574	16,359
Cameron, TX	7,681	9,853	12,143	14,912	17,410
Border Counties	9,809	11,806	13,893	17,223	20,809
Border without San Diego	9,502	11,395	13,455	16,515	19,911
United States	14,758	19,477	23,076	29,843	34,471

Source: U.S. Bureau of Economic Analysis.

are rural counties that do not have major ports of entry linking them to Mexico. Consumers within these rural markets frequently shop at retail locations located in neighboring counties within driving distance.[6]

The U.S. border-region population growth discussed above has also been accompanied by increased labor supplies. From 1985 to 2005, total employment grew by 50 percent (from 2.2 million to 3.6 million) in the U.S. border area (table 2.4). At the same time, the growth in jobs was not in the traditionally high-wage manufacturing industry. As table 2.4

TABLE 2.3 Sales-to-Income Ratios

County	1992	1997	2002
San Diego, CA	0.34	0.31	0.31
Imperial, CA	0.44	0.42	0.45
Yuma, AZ	0.46	0.45	0.34
Pima, AZ	0.44	0.41	0.4
Santa Cruz, AZ	0.84	0.59	0.65
Cochise, AZ	0.34	0.36	0.35
Hidalgo, NM	0.4	0.47	0.7
Luna, NM	0.48	0.55	0.4
Doña Ana, NM	0.39	0.39	0.35
El Paso, TX	0.52	0.44	0.41
Hudspeth, TX	0.23	0.17	0.13
Jeff Davis, TX	0.26	0.12	0.1
Presidio, TX	N/A	0.27	0.28
Brewster, TX	0.39	0.38	0.4
Terrell, TX	0.12	0.14	0.11
Val Verde, TX	0.45	0.46	0.48
Kinney, TX	N/A	0.1	0.1
Maverick, TX	N/A	0.52	0.59
Webb, TX	0.96	0.64	0.59
Zapata, TX	0.23	0.21	0.21
Starr, TX	0.47	0.47	0.51
Hidalgo, TX	0.64	0.53	0.56
Cameron, TX	0.56	0.46	0.49
Border Counties	0.41	0.37	0.36
Border without San Diego	0.5	0.45	0.44
United States	0.34	0.36	0.34

Source: U.S. Bureau of Economic Analysis.

shows, in each of the U.S. border labor markets with total employment greater than 150,000 in 2005, similar to the United States as a whole, the percentage employed in manufacturing declined relative to 1985. These job losses in the U.S. border region were offset by gains in public utility and broadly defined service-sector payrolls (the details of which can be provided by the authors). Although much of the public utility and service employment growth was concentrated in the larger counties (e.g., San Diego and El Paso), several small and medium-sized counties also had a rapid expansion in this general payroll category.

TABLE 2.4 Employment Data

County	Total Employment (in Thousands)					Percent in Manufacturing				
	1985	1990	1995	2000	2005	1985	1990	1995	2000	2005
San Diego, CA	1166.8	1437.4	1451.3	1733.5	1822.6	10.9	9.8	8.7	8.1	6.3
Imperial, CA	41.2	52.7	58.8	61.8	67.2	3.4	3.0	3.3	3.2	3.7
Yuma, AZ	41.2	51.1	60.2	68.3	82.9	4.0	4.4	2.9	3.6	3.6
Pima, AZ	293.0	321.7	384.6	444.4	486.2	11.1	8.8	7.8	7.9	6.3
Santa Cruz, AZ	10.0	13.5	14.5	15.8	17.4	9.2	8.5	7.3	6.7	3.6
Cochise, AZ	37.1	40.6	45.3	50.8	58.1	5.5	4.0	3.1	2.7	1.9
Hidalgo, NM	2.6	2.8	3.2	2.4	2.5	21.3	22.2	18.4	N/A	N/A
Luna, NM	5.4	6.5	8.1	8.9	10.9	5.5	6.6	7.1	10.9	11.3
Doña Ana, NM	48.8	58.2	66.1	75.6	87.5	7.0	6.9	4.4	4.6	4.1
El Paso, TX	232.7	269.7	300.0	326.3	349.2	15.9	15.6	15.8	12.1	7.1
Hudspeth, TX	1.2	1.2	1.3	1.4	1.5	3.9	3.6	1.1	N/A	N/A
Jeff Davis, TX	0.8	1.0	1.1	1.2	1.4	N/A	N/A	N/A	N/A	N/A
Presidio, TX	1.9	2.1	2.1	2.5	2.7	N/A	N/A	1.4	1.2	N/A

Brewster, TX	4.0	4.2	4.6	5.6	6.0	2.2	1.2	1.2	2.6	1.6
Terrell, TX	0.8	0.8	0.7	0.9	0.7	N/A	N/A	N/A	N/A	N/A
Val Verde, TX	15.0	15.2	17.5	20.3	23.4	4.0	2.8	3.6	3.1	9.4
Kinney, TX	1.0	1.0	1.0	1.1	1.3	N/A	1.7	N/A	N/A	N/A
Maverick, TX	8.4	10.2	12.3	15.6	18.4	11.5	11.6	11.0	6.6	N/A
Webb, TX	42.5	54.3	69.1	86.2	103.4	4.5	3.4	2.6	2.5	1.7
Zapata, TX	2.4	2.6	3.5	4.2	5.0	0.9	0.9	0.7	0.8	0.9
Starr, TX	8.5	10.8	14.2	16.8	20.4	0.5	0.5	0.9	0.9	1.0
Hidalgo, TX	113.7	135.9	164.8	214.4	267.4	9.8	10.2	8.5	6.0	3.5
Cameron, TX	85.5	99.4	118.7	140.7	156.2	11.4	12.3	11.8	9.4	5.0
Border Counties	2164.6	2592.9	2803.0	3298.6	3592.2	10.7	9.7	8.8	7.8	5.7
Border without San Diego	997.8	1155.5	1351.7	1565.1	1769.6	10.5	9.7	8.9	7.4	5.0
United States	124509.7	139380.9	148982.8	166758.8	174249.6	15.9	14.1	12.9	11.5	8.5

Source: United States Bureau of Economic Analysis.

As also pointed out by André Varella Mollick in chapter 11, the information here illustrates that the border economy is not immune to the structural changes affecting the United States as a whole. The service sector jobs that frequently pay well usually require a formal education that goes beyond the level typically associated with a high school diploma. The lower average schooling levels along the U.S.-Mexico border therefore place many border counties at a competitive disadvantage.

Demographic change in the United States and Mexico will continue to play influential roles in the employment growth patterns observed in border regions. Although the populations of both the United States and Mexico are aging, those in the United States are aging more rapidly. As estimated by the United Nations, in 2025, the aging index—defined as the number of persons age sixty or older per one hundred persons younger than fifteen—will be 133.8 for the United States but only 58.2 for Mexico (Department of Economic and Social Affairs 2001). The more ample labor supplies in Mexico and the border regions may cause manufacturers interested in serving North American markets to move even more production to these areas. (This issue will be discussed in more detail by John Sargent, Melissa Najera, and Linda Matthews in chapter 4.)

In fact, geographic proximity to the maquiladoras in Mexico has promoted entrepreneurial opportunities in the service sector in northern Mexico (Ladman 1979). Many of these jobs have developed in transportation and warehousing activities that help distribute the manufactured goods from the factories in Mexico. Despite concerns that the maquiladora expansion has come at the expense of jobs in the U.S. border region (recall Mora's discussion in the previous chapter; also see Gruben 1990), substantial evidence exists that growth on the two sides of the border is complementary in nature (e.g., Hanson 2001). André V. Mollick, Abigail Cortez-Rayas, and Rosa A. Olivas-Moncisvais (2006), for example, estimate that a 10 percent increase in Mexican maquiladora industry output generates an approximate 1.1 percent growth in jobs in El Paso and Brownsville (located on the north side of the international boundary). Moreover, the foregoing demographic changes within the United States and Mexico, in combination with a strengthening Chinese currency, may offer significant growth opportunities to border areas. As will be discussed by Peach and Adkisson and by Sargent, Najera, and Matthews in the next two chapters, the maquiladora industry will continue to evolve as global economic conditions change, which can affect employment on both sides of the border.

Concluding Remarks

As job creation in U.S. border counties moves away from goods-producing sectors and toward the service and information sectors, regional income performance depends increasingly on worker productivity that is primarily a function of formal education. With the relatively low levels of U.S. border county educational attainment outlined here, per-capita income performance across this region tends to be much lower than in the rest of the United States, which is likely to continue. Improving high school and post-secondary graduation rates will be difficult and likely require many years to achieve.

Moreover, proximity to the border relates to an additional set of labor market concerns. Beyond the fact that immigration from Mexico has been associated with lower levels of educational attainment, geographic location causes labor markets on the U.S. side of the border to face *dual business-cycle risks,* emanating from changing economic conditions in both the United States and Mexico. For example, peso devaluations have frequently caused retail disruptions on the U.S. side of the border. Given the reliance of many U.S. border communities on Mexican shoppers, these devaluations can affect their employment and income levels. Even in the absence of currency instabilities, labor market weakness can also occur on the U.S. side of the border when recessions occur in Mexico (e.g., Fullerton 2003). More insight into these issues is provided in the following chapter by Peach and Adkisson, who specifically consider labor market and other macroeconomic outcomes related to the North American Free Trade Agreement.

The material in this chapter deals primarily with demographic changes on the north side of the international boundary between the United States and Mexico. That does not mean, however, that structural changes are not affecting labor markets on the Mexican side of the border. As detailed by Sargent, Najera, and Matthews in chapter 4, the industrial composition of the maquiladora sector has evolved substantially during the last decade and a half in all of the metropolitan areas stretching from

Matamoros to Tijuana. Given this trend, the scales of industrial activity in these labor markets are likely to increase in future years. Accordingly, many of the internal migration patterns discussed by Hector J. Villarreal in chapter 5, as well as by Pia M. Orrenius, Madeline Zavodny, and Leslie Lukens in chapter 8, should continue in future years as workers from other regions in Mexico respond to formal-sector job openings in northern border areas.

3

NAFTA and Economic Activity along the U.S.-Mexico Border[1]

James T. Peach and Richard V. Adkisson

Introduction

Trade agreements among nations, such as the North American Free Trade Agreement (NAFTA), have far-reaching domestic and international consequences. The NAFTA negotiations during 1992 and 1993 generated an intense debate over the potential macroeconomic consequences of a "free-trade" agreement for the United States. The fervency of the debate has continued over the years since the first provisions of NAFTA took effect on January 1, 1994, and to date, there is no widespread agreement on the impacts of NAFTA.

The purpose of this chapter is to examine the evolution of economic activity in the U.S.-Mexico border region in the years before and after NAFTA's implementation. We restrict the analysis to the U.S. side of the border and consider changes over two periods: a twelve-year pre-NAFTA period and a twelve-year post-NAFTA-implementation period. (Employment issues on the Mexican side of the border will be considered in the next two chapters.) The U.S. border region deserves special consideration for at least two reasons. First, because of its proximity to Mexico and its pre-NAFTA industrial structure, the impacts of NAFTA in the border region are likely to be more intense than in non-border regions of the nation. Second, the region attracted considerable attention during the NAFTA debate, particularly with regard to employment and environmental issues.

NAFTA is only one policy tool at work in the border economy and in U.S.-Mexico relations. Independent of NAFTA, other policies, events, and trends exist. In particular, trade liberalization has been evident at least since Mexico joined the General Agreement on Tariffs and Trade (GATT) in 1986. The World Trade Organization, an extension of the

GATT, concluded its Uruguay round of multilateral negotiations in 1994, the same year NAFTA was first implemented. As mentioned by John Sargent, Melissa Najera, and Linda Matthews in the next chapter, the longstanding Multifiber Arrangement that closely controlled international production of textiles and apparel was also phased out during this period. Likewise, migration has continued to be a substantive border issue and, especially since the terrorist attacks of September 11, 2001, border security has become increasingly policy-relevant (Bailey 2004).

Potential and Realized NAFTA Effects

In general, the purpose of NAFTA was to reduce trade barriers between the United States, Mexico, and Canada. Like most other trade agreements, NAFTA is an extraordinarily complex document that is more than two thousand pages long. The NAFTA document is long and complex because of numerous exceptions to the concept of free trade. These exceptions include, among others, temporary or permanent exceptions for military goods, timber and lumber products, and petroleum products. NAFTA even prohibited (a) the United States and Canada from producing and selling tequila, (b) the United States and Mexico from producing and selling Canadian whiskey, and (c) Mexico and Canada from producing and selling Kentucky bourbon. Further, numerous behind-the-scenes working groups have produced an unknown number of modifications to the original NAFTA agreement. Many of these side agreements accelerated the removal of tariffs or clarified some of the more ambiguous parts of the original document. Evaluating the economic effects of such a complex, continually evolving document is itself a complex task.

Viewed from an historical perspective, NAFTA is neither the most significant nor the most controversial aspect of U.S. trade policy.[2] Nevertheless, NAFTA has been and continues to be controversial. To illustrate, Fred C. Bergsten (2005:xiv) has observed, "Today, NAFTA continues to be almost as controversial as it was during the ratification debate in the U.S. Congress in the summer and fall of 1993." During the Congressional debate on NAFTA, the controversy was focused on seven major themes at the national or macro level: employment, trade flows, migration, foreign direct investment (FDI), economic growth, the environment, and political stability in Mexico. The proponents and critics of NAFTA continue to disagree on most of these issues.

With the exception of increased trade flows and FDI, the evidence remains mixed concerning NAFTA's potential effects on these themes. And, in each case, there is no a priori reason to expect that the NAFTA impact on the border region would be the same as its effects nationally, with many reasons to suspect the contrary.

Employment

The most emotional issue in the NAFTA debate was its potential employment effect, and this issue remains at the top of the list of controversial NAFTA issues. During the early 1990s, NAFTA proponents and critics made starkly contrasting claims concerning employment. Ross Perot, an independent presidential candidate in 1992, stated that as many as 5.9 million U.S. jobs were at risk because of NAFTA (Perot and Choate 1993), and he proclaimed that NAFTA would cause a "giant sucking sound" as U.S. jobs relocated to Mexico. NAFTA proponents uniformly suggested and still maintain that U.S. employment would increase as a result of NAFTA.

The evidence regarding NAFTA's impact on U.S. labor markets is mixed. This is not a surprising result, given the relatively small impact of NAFTA on economic growth (to be discussed below). Yet controversy remains. Mary E. Burfisher, Sherman Robinson, and Karen Thierfelder (2001:129) concluded that NAFTA effects on U.S. labor markets "are indeed small and are overwhelmed by other U.S. macroeconomic trends such as a rapidly growing economy." However, Gary Clyde Hufbauer and Jeffrey Schott (2005) estimate that the United States has experienced a net gain of 171,000 jobs as a result of NAFTA—an estimate consistent with the 1993 forecast of the U.S. trade representative.

NAFTA critics remain unconvinced. Robert Scott and his colleagues at the Economic Policy Institute (EPI) presented alternative estimates suggesting that the net impact of NAFTA was a loss of slightly more than a million jobs, "including 560,000 due to growing trade deficits with Mexico and 456,000 with Canada" (Scott et al. 2006:9).

Trade Flows

While disagreement still exists regarding NAFTA's impact on total U.S. employment, nearly all analysts agree that the impacts are industry specific;

this issue will be discussed in more detail in subsequent chapters. We note here, however, that NAFTA supporters asserted that the increased trade flows resulting from the agreement would increase employment in both the United States and Mexico. NAFTA's effect on Canada was largely ignored in the U.S. debate because the United States and Canada had already signed a free trade agreement in 1988. U.S.-Mexico trade flows, which had been increasing before NAFTA, did increase substantially after 1994. U.S. exports of goods and services to Mexico increased from $68.1 billion in 1994 to $169.6 billion in 2006, while imports from Mexico increased from $64.8 billion to $229.2 billion during the same time period (U.S. Dept. of Commerce, International Economic Accounts 2007). This increase has been described by Willem Thorbecke and Christian Eigen-Zucchi (2002:647) as "an explosion of exports and imports between the U.S. and Mexico."

Whether such changes would have occurred without NAFTA remains a meaningful and unsettled question. For example, a Congressional Budget Office (CBO) report (May 2003) describes several non-NAFTA factors that have affected U.S.-Mexico trade flows, including macroeconomic conditions in both countries, security issues after September 11, Mexico's 1994–95 economic crisis, and exchange rate fluctuations. The results of a CBO model of U.S.-Mexico trade suggest that "without NAFTA, both U.S. exports to and imports from Mexico would have grown almost as much as they did with NAFTA, and they would have fluctuated almost identically to the manner in which they did with NAFTA" (CBO 2003:17). In any case, the increase in U.S.-Mexico trade has meant substantially larger shipments of goods through major border-region ports-of-entry.[3]

The increase in U.S.-Mexico trade flows is reflected in greater openness of the U.S. and Mexican economies. Figure 3.1 shows that Mexico has increased its merchandise trade (imports plus exports) as a share of gross domestic product (GDP) substantially, especially since the early 1990s. Over the quarter-century documented in this figure, Mexico's openness by this measure roughly tripled.[4] The increase in U.S. openness was somewhat smaller but still substantial. By this measure, the United States was twice as open at the end of the period as it was in the beginning. Meanwhile, the United States has also become more trade interdependent, with Mexican trade making up more than 10 percent of total U.S. merchandise trade since the mid-1990s. Mexico is more obviously

Percentage

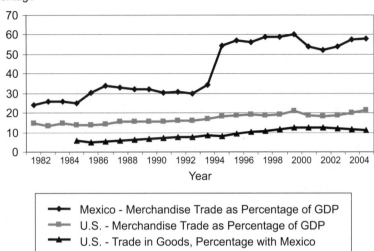

FIGURE 3.1 U.S.-Mexico trade and openness. *Sources:* World Bank, World Development Indicators, U.S. Bureau of the Census, Foreign Trade Statistics.

dependent on U.S. trade. Especially to the extent that increasing trade flows are transported by land, economic activity in the border region should be influenced by the increased trade.

Migration

Migration from Mexico to the United States was always an underlying concern during the NAFTA debates. NAFTA supporters typically argued that NAFTA would reduce migration from Mexico to the United States as expanding trade opportunities also expanded economic and employment growth in Mexico. In essence, it was suggested that NAFTA would offer at least a partial solution to the perceived Mexico-to-U.S. migration problem. Evaluating the NAFTA migration effect is a complex and possibly insoluble problem. Despite considerable effort by demographers (Passel 2006) and others to provide estimates of Mexican migration to the United States, no one really knows the size of these flows. A common figure used in the 2007 debate over immigration reform in Congress was 12.1 million "illegal" immigrants residing in the United States, with just more than half (6.2 million) from Mexico (Passel 2006). Indeed, this figure found its way into the draft legislation. Yet considerable uncertainty remains about both the stock and flow of migrants in the United States, and much less is known about the effect of NAFTA on Mexican-U.S. migration flows.

Patricia Fernández-Kelley and Douglas S. Massey (2007) argued that migration from Mexico to the United States probably increased during the NAFTA years. Their argument is that increased enforcement under the 1986 Immigration Reform and Control Act as well as increased capital mobility under NAFTA have reduced the number of Mexican migrants to the United States—and presumably to the border region—who eventually return to Mexico.[5]

Foreign Direct Investment

NAFTA was also expected to alter the pattern of foreign direct investment (FDI) in member nations. Total FDI in Mexico increased dramatically after the signing of NAFTA, going from $4.5 billion in 1993 to $11.0 billion in 1994. It reached a peak in 2001 at $27 billion but had fallen to $18.8 billion by 2005 (World Bank 2007). However, the 2001 peak was driven primarily by the purchase of BANAMEX by Citibank; a more normal post-NAFTA expectation would have been an annual FDI in the $12–16 billion range, with a slightly increasing trend (Scott, Salas, and Campbell 2006:41). U.S. FDI in Mexico accounted for a large portion of the total but followed a pattern similar to that of total FDI. U.S. FDI in Mexico in 1993 was $2.5 billion (55.6 percent of Mexico's total FDI), increasing to $4.5 billion in 1994 (40.6 percent of Mexico's total), and peaking in 2001 at $14.2 billion (52.4 percent of Mexico's total) (U.S. Department of Commerce 2007). While certain provisions of NAFTA facilitated FDI flows, some of the increase in these flows probably would have occurred even without NAFTA. The economic instability in Mexico during the 1980s and continuing through the 1995 economic crisis was without doubt a deterrent to FDI.

Investment data for the border region in particular are not available, but in a study on border trade using data from 1975–1989, Gordon H. Hanson (1996:2) gave two reasons why NAFTA would promote a re-allocation of resources toward the U.S.-Mexico border region. First, the change in transportation needs and patterns would increase the demand for transportation and distribution services; second, U.S. firms importing inputs from Mexican firms would relocate to the border region to minimize transportation costs. Similarly, Lonnie L. Jones, Teofilo Ozuna Jr., and Mickey Wright (1991) predicted favorable conditions for investments in businesses that facilitate international trade, and they saw an increased need for infrastructure development along the border. Hanson and Jones, Ozuna, and Wright all recognized that NAFTA would affect industries differently but anticipated it would have an overall positive economic impact on the border region.

Economic Growth

It is exceedingly difficult to evaluate the effects of NAFTA on economic growth (i.e., the growth of real gross domestic product [GDP]) in either the United States or Mexico. When NAFTA was implemented in 1994, the United States was in the midst of its longest expansion in history (March 1991 to March 2001), and it is not possible to attribute this expansion or the economic slowdown in the early 2000s to NAFTA. The U.S. economy (with its GDP in 2006 equal to $13.2 trillion) is considerably larger than the value of its exports to Mexico ($169.6 billion in 2006, or 1.28 percent of U.S. GDP) or its imports from Mexico ($229.1 billion, or 1.73 percent of U.S. GDP). Since a large but unknown portion of U.S.-Mexico trade would have occurred without NAFTA, the effect of NAFTA on U.S. GDP is almost certainly very small. For example, in 2003, the CBO concluded that, "NAFTA has increased annual U.S. GDP, but by a very small amount—probably no more than a few billion dollars, or a few hundredths of a percent" (CBO 2003:xiv).

Mexico began the NAFTA era with its deepest recession (the 1994–1995 economic crisis) since the Great Depression of the 1930s. While the Mexican economy began its recovery by late 1995, its economic growth rate has been variable and modest in the NAFTA years. From 1994 to 2005, Mexico's real GDP increased at an average annual rate of 2.74 percent, somewhat less than the comparable figure for the United States (3.25 percent). The CBO's (2003) study concluded that Mexico's real GDP probably increased due to NAFTA by the same order of magnitude (a few billion dollars) as U.S. GDP did.

The condition of the two national economies is extremely important in the borderlands. During the 1990s NAFTA debate, analysts generally agreed that the impacts would vary by region and industry (Jones, Ozuna, and Wright 1991; Betts and Slottje 1994; Weintraub 1993) and that the overall impact in the United States would be small (Lustig, Bosworth, and Lawrence 1992). Border analysts have long known that healthy economic growth rates at the national level in both nations are reflected in border-region economic activity. Recall that in the previous chapter of this book, Thomas M. Fullerton Jr., James H. Holcomb, and Angel L. Molina Jr. refer to this as a "dual business-cycle risk."

Environmental Issues

NAFTA-related environmental issues were (and remain) an important part of the NAFTA debate. While these concerns are binational, it was widely recognized that the intense (pre-NAFTA) environmental problems of the border region might be intensified with increases in cross-border trade and production sharing expected as a result of NAFTA's implementation. Such fears resulted in the NAFTA side agreement on the environment and the creation of the North American Development Bank (NADBANK), the Border Environmental Cooperation Commission (BECC), and the Commission for Environmental Cooperation (CEC). Gary Clyde Hufbauer and Jeffrey Schott (2005:181) assessed the environmental effects of NAFTA in mixed terms: "As a result, collaboration has improved between local, national and international agencies. Nevertheless, border conditions are bad and in some respects may be getting worse." It should be noted that both Hufbauer and Schott were strong advocates of NAFTA from the earliest days of the debate and remain convinced of its generally beneficial effects.

Political and Economic Stability

Many proponents of NAFTA argued that the increased prosperity in Mexico that could be expected as a result of reducing trade barriers would mean greater political and economic stability for Mexico. On the same day of the start of the NAFTA implementation (January 1, 1994), the Mexican political establishment was stunned by the Zapatista rebellion in Chiapas. In March 1994, the Institutional Revolutionary Party (PRI) presidential candidate Luis Donaldo Colosio was assassinated in Tijuana. The year did not improve. In September, the attorney general was assassinated, and by late December, Mexico had entered its worst economic crisis since the Great Depression. Both political and economic conditions improved in Mexico from late 1995 to the early 2000s, at which time the United States entered its economic slowdown and the export-oriented Mexican economy suffered as well. In 2006, a closely contested presidential election and allegations of voter fraud threatened Mexico's political stability again.

Political and/or economic instability in Mexico impact border-region economic activity as well. An early indication that the U.S. border region was expected to experience economic gains from NAFTA was the pattern of U.S. senatorial and Congressional voting for the agreement. Leo Kahane (1996:406) examined the NAFTA vote and concluded that "expected job losses were empirically important in describing both the House and Senate voting patterns on NAFTA." Expected job gains were an important predictor of House votes but were less influential on the Senate vote. Except in California, U.S. border-region senators and members of Congress voted heavily in favor of NAFTA, suggesting a general expectation of positive border-region impacts (Congressional Quarterly, Inc. 1994).

Other factors suggested that NAFTA might lead to a decrease in employment and income on the U.S. side of the border. The principal motivation for "free trade agreements" is to make borders, and hence border regions, less important by removing tariffs and other barriers to the cross-border movement of goods and services. Reduced tariff rates, for example, might have a substantial negative impact on cross-border retail trade. Why would Mexican shoppers travel to the U.S. side of the border to purchase U.S.-made goods that they could buy in post-NAFTA Mexico at the same or almost the same prices? While other intervening factors might have influenced the outcome, Richard V. Adkisson and Linda Zimmerman (2004) provide fairly strong evidence that retail trade on the U.S. side decreased as a result of NAFTA.

In many respects, assessing the impact of NAFTA on the border region is a more difficult task than assessing its impact at the national level. In addition to the national-level effects, the border region's history of high population growth rates, high unemployment rates, low levels of per-capita income, and an industrial structure very different from the national economies of both the United States and Mexico presents serious analytical problems. The border region's heterogeneity adds more complexity to the task. No attempt will be made in this chapter to sort out the various NAFTA-related effects on the border region. Rather, this chapter will now complement the previous chapter by Fullerton, Holcomb, and Molina by examining changes in key economic and demographic variables specifically in the years before and after NAFTA.

Economic and Demographic Trends

Population

Population growth (or decline) is a basic economic indicator at the regional level. Standard migration theory, as well as numerous empirical studies, suggests that people move away from areas of low income and high unemployment to areas of high income and low unemployment. This issue will be discussed in more detail by Hector J. Villarreal in chapter 5 and by Alberto Dávila, Marie T. Mora, and Alma D. Hales in chapter 6. Recall from the previous chapter that the border region as a whole has experienced higher population growth rates than the national average during the past few decades. However, nearly 90 percent of the growth occurred in the eight border metropolitan statistical areas (MSAs—see this volume's appendix), and this growth has been particularly rapid since the 1940s, long before NAFTA.

Table 3.1 displays border-region population growth rates for the pre-NAFTA-implementation period (1982–1993) and post-NAFTA-implementation period (1994–2005). The historical pattern of rapid population growth in the border region continued through both periods. In the earlier period, from 1982 to 1993, the overall border population increased by 32 percent, nearly 2.5 times the national increase of 12.9 percent. In the post-NAFTA years, overall border population growth has slowed down, growing by only 20.4 percent (still about 1.5 times the national growth rate of 13.4 percent). Thus, while the long-term trend continues, border population growth rates have moderated somewhat in comparison to the national rate.

TABLE 3.1 The U.S.-Mexico Border Region: Selected Growth Indicators

Area	Average Annual Percent Change in Population		Average Annual Percent Change in Per-Capita Income		Unemployment Rate		MSA Per Capita Income as a percent of U.S. Per-Capita Income	
	1982 to 1993	1994 to 2005	1982 to 1993	1994 to 2005	Average 1991–93	Average 2003–05	1993	2005
San Diego, CA	2.5	1.0	5.0	5.2	7.2	4.7	103.8	117.7
Yuma, AZ	2.7	3.2	4.6	2.9	25.1	16.0	71.2	60.9
Tucson, AZ	2.2	2.1	4.7	4.1	4.5	4.8	84.0	83.7
Las Cruces, NM	3.6	1.8	5.0	4.3	8.2	6.3	65.7	66.9
El Paso, TX	2.0	1.1	5.0	4.5	11.5	7.8	64.4	67.5
Laredo, TX	3.3	3.2	5.3	4.2	10.9	7.5	54.0	54.6
McAllen, TX	3.4	3.5	5.0	3.5	21.6	9.1	49.1	47.5
Brownsville, TX	2.3	2.3	5.0	3.5	14.4	8.6	54.3	50.5
Non-MSA Border*	2.1	1.5	4.6	3.8	26.4	11.0	—	—
Border Counties*	2.5	1.6	4.9	4.5	10.6	5.8	—	—
(w/o San Diego)	(2.5)	(2.2)	(4.7)	(3.9)	(13.9)	(6.4)	—	—
California	2.1	1.2	4.6	4.2	6.6	5.1	—	—
Arizona	3.1	3.2	4.6	4.2	8.8	6.1	—	—
New Mexico	1.7	1.4	5.1	4.3	7.3	5.7	—	—
Texas	1.8	2.0	5.1	4.4	7.2	6.0	—	—
United States	1.0	1.1	5.5	4.1	7.1	5.5	—	—

* Per-capita income rate weighted by population. Unemployment weighted by labor force.

Sources: (1) Population estimates are from the U.S. Department of Commerce, Bureau of Economic Analysis. Annual estimates are for July. Changes calculated by authors. (2) Per-capita income from U.S. Department of Commerce, Bureau of Economic Analysis, Regional Accounts, weights and averages calculated by authors. (3) Unemployment rates from the Bureau of Labor Statistics, Local Area Estimates, various tables. Averages and weights calculated by authors.

Changes in growth rates were not constant across the border region. In the largest border MSA, San Diego, population grew more slowly than the national rate during the post-NAFTA years. Two MSA populations (Yuma and McAllen) expanded even faster than they had in the earlier period. Of the 363 MSAs in the United States, three border MSAs (Yuma, Laredo, and McAllen) were among the 25 fastest-growing MSAs in the nation for the 1994–2005 period. Of interest, two border-state populations, Arizona and Texas, grew faster than the nation in the latter period.

Demographic momentum—the tendency of a population to grow due to its age-sex distribution even in the face of stable or declining fertility rates—virtually assures high population growth rates in the region for decades to come. Despite historically high in-migration rates, Census Bureau estimates suggest that three-fourths of the border region's population change between 2000 and 2006 can be attributed to a "natural" increase. This compares to two-thirds that could be attributed to a natural increase in the mid-to-late 1990s.

Income

Recall from the previous chapter that relatively low levels of per-capita income have been another persistent feature of the border region (see also Hansen 1981; Peach 1997; Fullerton 2001). Many things could help explain the low level of income along the border, but as discussed by Fullerton, Holcomb, and Molina in chapter 2, a particularly strong candidate is the low educational levels of the border population. In 2005, the simple correlation between per-capita income and the percentage of high school graduates twenty-five years old and older was 0.872, a very high correlation. Generally speaking, income levels decrease from the west to the east along the border. Later in this book, other studies investigate these earnings gaps by "adjusting" for educational-level differences between workers along the U.S.-Mexico border and those in interior regions (e.g., see chapters 5–7).

As seen in table 3.1, the average annual rate of growth of per-capita income for the United States, each of the four border states, and seven of the eight border MSAs (with San Diego as the exception) was lower in the post-NAFTA period than in the pre-NAFTA period. However, changes in per-capita income levels in the nation, border states, or MSAs should not be attributed only to NAFTA-related economic activity. As described earlier, NAFTA effects at the national level probably amounted to only a few billion dollars in a very large and dynamic economy.

With the exception of San Diego, the border region MSAs remain a long way from convergence with national averages. Indeed, as with the overall border counties discussed by Fullerton, Holcomb, and Molina in chapter 2, excluding San Diego, per-capita income in the border MSAs fell slightly from 65.3 percent of the national average in 1993 to 64.0 percent in 2005. A dozen years after NAFTA implementation, three border MSAs (Laredo, McAllen, and Brownsville) had per-capita income levels either below or barely exceeding half the national average, while per-capita income in three of the other MSAs (Yuma, Las Cruces, and El Paso) was less than 70 percent of the national average (table 3.1). Per-capita income in the non-MSA border counties fell from 62.0 percent of the national average in 1993 to 60.1 percent of the national average in 2005. In brief, the evidence so far does not suggest that NAFTA resulted in substantial improvements in per-capita income levels along the border relative to the U.S. interior.

Unemployment and Employment

Border unemployment rates are substantially higher than national unemployment rates, as will be addressed later in more detail by André Varella Mollick (chapter 11). Still, table 3.1 shows that the unemployment rate in the eight border MSAs fell from an average of 11.1 percent (56 percent higher than the national rate) in 1991–93 to 7.1 percent (29 percent higher than the national rate) in 2003–2005. Similarly, as shown in table 3.2, total employment in the border region increased faster than in the nation in both the pre- and post-NAFTA periods. On average, 1.8 percent of the nation's wage and salary employment was in the border region in the earlier period compared to 1.96 percent in the later period. In short, some evidence exists that the border region has improved its relative unemployment position in the post-NAFTA era, even if per-capita income levels have remained relatively low.

The middle columns of table 3.2 report the average wage per job in 1993 (the year before NAFTA implementation) and 2005 (twelve years

TABLE 3.2 The U.S.-Mexico Border Region: Selected Growth Indicators

Geographic Area	Total Wage and Salary Employment		Percentage Change in Employment		Average Wage per Job (1982–84 Dollars)		Percentage Change in Real Wage 1993–2005
	1993	2005	1982 to 1993	1994 to 2005	1993	2005	
San Diego, CA	1,149,933	1,495,758	35.3	30.0	18,002	22,232	23.5
Yuma, AZ	49,922	72,746	42.9	41.7	12,731	14,544	14.2
Tucson, AZ	289,284	385,535	39.5	25.0	15,140	18,054	19.2
Las Cruces, NM	51,523	72,465	44.0	38.8	13,169	14,317	8.7
El Paso, TX	254,150	288,321	29.6	11.2	13,940	15,060	8.0
Laredo, TX	57,797	87,969	55.4	43.9	12,292	13,977	13.7
McAllen, TX	125,886	215,817	35.6	64.3	11,900	12,871	8.2
Brownsville, TX	94,932	127,700	31.4	28.4	12,051	12,614	4.7
Non-MSA Border*	149,337	192,049	24.8	25.0	13,227	15,302	15.7
Border Counties*	2,222,764	2,938,360	35.0	29.6	15,866	18,789	18.4
(w/o San Diego)	(1,072,831)	(1,442,602)	(24.8)	(29.2)	(13,576)	(15,219)	(12.1)
California	13,310,401	16,082,910	21.5	19.9	19,954	23,490	17.7
Arizona	1,710,146	2,637,335	52.1	45.6	16,183	19,375	19.7
New Mexico	683,120	856,406	29.6	20.3	14,988	16,834	12.3
Texas	7,986,963	10,269,066	17.7	24.6	17,318	20,295	17.2
United States	118,722,000	140,967,000	22.1	15.9	17,932	20,556	14.6

* Average wage per job weighted by wage and salary jobs.

Notes: Wages per job adjusted to 1982–84 dollars using CPI for all urban U.S. consumers. All items, 1982–84=100, Department of Labor, Bureau of Labor Statistics.

Source: Data from U.S. Department of Commerce, Bureau of Economic Analysis, Regional Economic Information System. Percentage changes, averages, and population weights calculated by authors.

after NAFTA implementation). The table also reports the percentage changes in average real wages. Several things are apparent. First, not surprisingly given the low per-capita income levels discussed earlier, wages are lower along the border than they are elsewhere in the nation. This issue will be further discussed in later chapters, particularly chapters 6, 7, and 8. In the meantime, border wages were about 88 percent of national wages in 1993 and about 91 percent in the post-NAFTA period. However, the difference is more extreme if the high-income MSA, San Diego, is omitted from the calculations. Excluding San Diego, border wages were 76 percent of the national figure in 1993 and 74 percent of the national average in 2005. As with per-capita income, it is likely that education has an important role in this, as might industrial structure.[6]

Concluding Remarks

The basic regional economic indicators examined above complement those reported in the previous chapter by specifically focusing on the pre-NAFTA-implementation and post-NAFTA-implementation periods. It appears that NAFTA has done neither great harm nor good to the U.S. border region relative to the United States as a whole. Population growth in the border region in the post-NAFTA period was not as rapid as in the pre-NAFTA period. Yet border-region population and employment growth rates remain higher than in the nation as a whole. While border region per-capita income in both metropolitan and nonmetropolitan counties grew at a slower rate in the post-NAFTA period than in the pre-NAFTA period, lower per-capita income growth rates in the post-NAFTA period can also be observed at the state and national levels. Border region unemployment rates (metropolitan and nonmetropolitan) were consistently lower in the post-NAFTA years than in the pre-NAFTA period, but again, this pattern was apparent in the nation and the border states as well. Wage and salary employment in the border region increased in the post-NAFTA period as was the case in the nation. Outside of San Diego, real wages in the border region increased in the post-NAFTA period, but not as fast as they did in the rest of the nation.

Regional variation in economic activity is a permanent feature of large nations. Although far from homogeneous, the U.S. side of the border region has been an economically less prosperous area throughout most of its recent history compared to the United States overall. NAFTA has not clearly, at least yet, produced substantial, measurable improvements in economic conditions along the U.S. side of the border. It is possible that there could be long lags between NAFTA implementation and its regional consequences. More likely, there are other factors at work. A strong correlation between border-county income levels and educational attainment levels suggests that many border residents are unlikely to find high-wage employment opportunities regardless of the effects of NAFTA. Trade policies benefit those who have the education and skills to adjust to rapidly changing labor and product markets. In the border region, the need for adequately funded and aggressive education and workforce training programs is reinforced by the NAFTA experience.

4

Labor Market Dynamics and a Look Inside Border Maquiladoras

John Sargent, Melissa Najera, and Linda Matthews

Introduction

Beginning in the 1960s, many of the world's largest multinational companies (MNCs) have located manufacturing facilities in Mexican border cities (Sklair 1993). The reasons for these investments are clear. Maquiladoras historically have been allowed to import raw and intermediate materials duty free into Mexico, process those items, and then export their output to the United States under a highly favorable tariff regime. Border facilities allow MNCs supplying the North American market access to a low-wage workforce while avoiding some of the managerial and operational challenges associated with producing in other low-cost developing-country locations. For example, as will be discussed by Marie T. Mora and Alberto Dávila in chapter 10, U.S. nationals and their families can live in the United States, yet still work in Mexico. Also, border locations allow transportation costs and response times to be minimized for inputs coming from, and outputs going to, the United States.

In this chapter, we complement the discussion in the previous chapter by James T. Peach and Richard V. Adkisson by examining how these maquiladoras have evolved since the implementation of the North American Free Trade Agreement (NAFTA) in 1994. We first provide a broad overview of the industry, paying particular attention to the forces shaping the demand for labor. In particular, we discuss changes in maquiladora activity between 1994 and 2006. In the second section of this chapter, we present a more personal view of maquiladora operating-level employees by using information from two sets of interviews of maquiladora employees, conducted in 1992 and 2002, to gauge how employment dynamics in the industry may or may not be changing.

Maquiladora Evolution During the NAFTA Era

From 1994 to 2006, Mexican maquiladoras passed through a dramatic boom-and-bust cycle. In January 1994, maquiladora employment stood at 546,433. The electronics/electrical equipment sector (employing 190,940) and the auto parts sector (employing 126,061) were the two primary industry segments, accounting for 58 percent of all maquiladora employment (see table 4.1). The number of maquiladora jobs more than doubled over the next six years. With the exception of Agua Prieta, all border cities with a significant maquiladora community experienced strong employment growth during this period. In addition, the industry became increasingly concentrated, with the percentage of jobs in the "Big Three" sectors (electronics/electrical equipment, auto parts, and apparel) rising from 70.3 to 75.1 percent.

In policy circles and the popular press, the argument has been made that NAFTA was the driving force behind the increase in bilateral trade between the United States and Mexico, and therefore it was behind the growth in maquiladora employment, as suggested by Anthony P. Mora in chapter 1, as well as by others in this volume (see also Weintraub 1997; Romalis 2007). Whether or not this is a defensible statement largely depends on one's definition of NAFTA. For some, NAFTA is a very broad term used to describe the economic relationship between the three member countries and especially the United States and Mexico. For others, NAFTA is more narrowly defined as a complex regional free trade agreement that can help or harm individual industries and companies as the result of specific provisions of the accord. Adopting this second perspective, the evidence suggests NAFTA was the driving force underlying industry success in only one of the three major maquiladora segments. William Gruben (2001:19) concludes that "the acceleration of maquiladora employment growth from NAFTA's inception through 1999 can be explained by changes in demand factors (as expressed by changes in the U.S. industrial production index) and in supply side/ cost factors (as expressed by changes in the ratio of Mexico to U.S.

TABLE 4.1 Changes in Maquiladora Employment

City	January 1994	October 2000	December 2003	October 2006
Ciudad Juárez	129,991	264,241	196,933	242,485
Tijuana	80,506	199,428	141,938	175,925
Reynosa	34,874	67,275	72,492	97,779
Matamoros	39,126	69,989	52,201	54,640
Mexicali	19,495	65,494	49,373	54,328
Nogales	17,985	41,537	26,746	32,933
Ciudad Acuña	18,776	32,341	34,491	31,126
Nuevo Laredo	16,288	22,573	18,312	20,986
Piedras Negras	9,003	14,550	11,918	9,085
Agua Prieta	7,441	7,073	5,784	5,870
Border Total	373,485	784,501	610,188	725,157
Border Percent	68.3	58.2	58.1	59.8
Sector:				
Electronics	190,940	467,508	330,378	396,544
Apparel	67,269	293,576	195,577	168,096
Auto Parts	126,061	250,635	238,577	269,696
Big 3 Totals	384,270	1,011,719	764,532	834,336
Big 3 Percent	70.3	75.1	72.8	68.8
"Other" Sector	59,712	145,502	137,951	179,507
Industry Totals	546,433	1,347,803	1,050,210	1,212,125

Source: INEGI, Banco de Información Económica, Industria Maquiladora de Exportación

manufacturing wages and to manufacturing wages in four Asian countries)." In a later article, Gruben (2006) refines this argument, stating that NAFTA resulted in significant trade diversion in the apparel sector. NAFTA eliminated U.S. tariffs and quotas for apparel items made from regionally produced fabric and then cut and sewn in Mexico. The number of maquiladora apparel jobs increased from 67,269 in January 1994 to 293,576 in October 2000 as firms established factories in Mexico to produce within the confines of "fortress NAFTA."

The macroeconomic evidence provides one picture of how NAFTA changed the structure and functioning of Mexico's export industries and the border economy (recall also the previous chapter by Peach and Adkisson [2007]). John Sargent and Linda Matthews (2001) offer a complementary firm-level perspective. These authors propose that NAFTA has the potential to shape the actions taken by maquiladoras in four primary areas:

1) NAFTA allows maquiladoras to sell their outputs in Mexico.
2) NAFTA regional rules-of-origin requirements may result in maquiladoras increasing their use of regional rather than globally sourced inputs.
3) NAFTA Article 303 and the end of duty drawback/deferral benefits in 2001 may also result in maquiladoras increasing their use of regional rather than globally sourced inputs.
4) NAFTA allows maquiladoras and non-maquiladora producers equal access to the Mexican market. This may create pressures leading to regulatory convergence between sectors, especially with fiscal policy.

Based on fieldwork conducted in 1999 and 2000, Sargent and Matthews (2001) found that NAFTA was not having a major influence on maquiladora strategy. Very few of the plants in their sample were selling a significant portion of their output in the Mexican market. Neither the NAFTA rules-of-origin requirements nor Article 303 resulted in maquiladoras systematically increasing their use of regional inputs. Finally, during the study period, the Mexican government proposed a set of very aggressive changes designed to increase the amount of taxes paid by maquiladoras. Plant management, regional organizations, and major MNCs became very politically active and for the most part were very successful in slowing down the regulatory harmonization process.

After the success of the 1990s, the Mexican maquiladora contraction that began in November 2000 came as an unwelcome surprise. From October 2000 to March 2002, the industry shed almost three hundred thousand jobs. Employment levels stabilized during the remainder of 2002 and through 2003 before starting a slow recovery in 2004. In October 2006, total maquiladora employment remained far below the level achieved in 2000, but it was still twice the level it had been in January 1994 (see table 4.1). John Christman (2005) predicts it may be 2010 before the number of maquiladora jobs exceeds the totals reached in 2000.

There is general agreement regarding the factors contributing to the 2000–2003 contraction and the industry's lackluster job growth from 2004 to 2006 (cf. General Accounting Office 2003; Carrillo and Gomis 2003). However, there is considerable controversy regarding the relative importance of these factors. Studies consistently find that demand for Mexican exports as measured by changes in U.S. industrial production is strongly correlated with growth in maquiladora employment (Gruben 2001; Fullerton and Schauer 2001; Coronado, Fullerton, and Clark 2004). The U.S. industrial production and capacity utilization index fell from 103.3149 in December 2000 to 97.7470 in December 2001. This abrupt drop would appear to account for much of the 2001 contraction. However, this index increased from 100.4459 in December 2002 to 112.4751 in December 2006. The almost 9 percent increase in this index from 2000 to 2006 has not resulted in a similar increase in maquiladora employment.

The same studies finding a strong relationship between U.S. industrial production and maquiladora expansion also find a strong relationship between the dollar-peso exchange rate and maquiladora success. The very significant peso devaluation in 1994 and 1995 appears to have been a primary factor facilitating industry expansion in the mid and late 1990s. However, by 2000, the peso had strengthened and the dollar-peso exchange rate remained relatively stable over the 2001–2006 period. The strong peso represents a significant cost penalty for maquiladoras and a major structural impediment to employment growth.

In addition to U.S. demand and the dollar-peso exchange rate, changes in U.S. trade policy and China's ascension to full membership in the World Trade Organization (WTO) resulted in increased international competition for Mexican exporters supplying the U.S. market in two of the three primary maquiladora segments. Moreover, the 2000 Caribbean Basin Trade Partnership Act and the phase-out of the Multifiber Arrangement (MFA) in 2005 brought about a significant dilution of the unique advantages Mexico has enjoyed in the apparel sector since 1994 (i.e., duty- and quota-free entry into the United States if using regionally produced fabric) (Tafoya and Watkins 2005). In October 2000, maquiladora employment in the apparel sector reached 293,576. This number fell to 195,577 by December 2003 and to 168,096 in October 2006. With employment levels likely to continue to decline, Mexico's apparel sector is a clear example of the risks of basing a job-creation policy on regional free trade agreement-sponsored trade diversion.

The Chinese government in the 1980s adopted an export promotion framework very similar to the maquiladora program that allows firms to import raw and intermediate materials from around the world, process those goods, and then export to international markets. China's ascension to full membership in the WTO in December 2001 sharply reduced tariffs and non-tariff barriers facing Chinese producers fitting this model. The International Labor Organization (ILO) estimates that from 1997 to 2006, employment in Chinese "maquiladoras" increased from eighteen million to forty million (ILO 2007). Francoise Lemoine and Deniz Ünal-Kesenci (2004) state these producers account for more than half of all Chinese exports and 70 percent of Chinese exports to the United States.

China's WTO ascension coincided with a dramatic increase in Chinese exports. U.S. imports from China increased from $99.6 billion in 2000 to $287.1 billion in 2006 (U.S International Trade Commission 2007). Chinese exporters captured significant U.S. import share in two of the three primary maquiladora sectors. U.S. imports of electronics/electrical equipment from China increased from $29.4 billion in 2000 to $110.7 billion in 2006. U.S. imports of Chinese apparel increased from $6.2 billion to $19.9 billion over this same time period. In contrast, U.S. imports of electronics/electrical equipment from Mexico barely changed from 2000 ($44.4 billion) to 2005 ($46.7 billon) before increasing in 2006 ($54.1 billion). U.S. imports of apparel from Mexico steadily declined over the period from 2000 to 2006, dropping from $8.6 billion to $5.4 billion.

Academicians and policymakers agree that the surge in U.S. imports from China has had some effect on Mexico's manufactured exports. However, there is little agreement as to whether China's success has played a minor or a major role in the maquiladora contraction (see Cañas, Coronado and Gilmer 2004, 2007; Gilmer, Phillips, Cañas and Coronado 2004; Mollick and Wvalle-Vázquez 2006). For example, at a recent border conference, Kristin Forbes—a member of the president's council of economic advisers—argued that China's role in the maquiladora downturn has been overstated. In addition to citing the 2001 U.S. economic downturn, she cited U.S. overspending in the late 1990s, the uncertainty resulting from 9/11, and rapid increases in manufacturing productivity as factors slowing maquiladora job growth. Furthermore, a number of Asian countries are increasingly sending their intermediate products to China for final assembly rather than exporting finished products directly to the United States. This pattern may result in exports from countries such as Taiwan, Singapore, and South Korea falling and those from China increasing—but the overall percentage of U.S. imports from Asia staying relatively stable.

In strong contrast to Forbes' arguments, there is a rapidly growing number of studies finding that Chinese exports have displaced Mexican goods in a broad range of U.S. industrial and commercial markets, and hence they have reduced the demand for labor in Mexico's export industries (for a broad overview, see Devlin, Estevadeordal, and Rodríguez-Clare 2006). For example, Enrique Dussel Peters (2005) finds that China has taken U.S. market share from Mexico in low-value-added electronics and apparel segments. He also argues that "China will probably continue to compete and displace Mexico—and other countries—in additional sectors such as automobiles, chemicals, software, and pharmaceuticals in the near future" (Dussel Peters 2005:31). Sanjaya Lall and John Weiss (2005) express similar concerns. Caroline Freund and Caglar Ozden (2006) find that China's rapid export growth has had a negative effect on Mexican exports of industrial goods to the United States, that aggregate prices of Latin American exports have been depressed as a result of competition from China, and that Chinese exports are primarily competing against high-wage rather than low-wage Latin American exports. Another empirical study by Gordon Hanson and Raymond Robertson (2006:6) found that "since 1999, it appears that the impacts on Mexican exports of growth in China's exports and of the slowdown in the U.S. economy are similar in magnitude."

Discussion about China's impact on maquiladora exports and employment is not the only ongoing debate in the maquiladora literature. If one accepts that Chinese exports have played a major role in the maquiladora contraction, the next question becomes how Chinese competition will shape the activities of surviving maquiladoras as well as the profile of new export-oriented investment in Mexico. Mexico's clear comparative advantage over other low-wage locations is its geographic proximity to the United States. There is near uniform agreement that maquiladoras are specializing in industry segments where geographic proximity is important. Jesús Cañas, Roberto Coronado, and Robert Gilmer (2007); John Christman (2005); key decision makers in the Mexican government (Rocio Ruiz 2005); and others propose that Mexico's proximity advantages and China's low-cost workforce converge to create an environment favoring proximity-dependent, capital- and technology-intensive maquiladora investment requiring a highly skilled workforce.

The logic behind this argument is as follows. The maquiladora industry is composed of at least three generations: first-generation plants perform low-tech assembly operations, second-generation producers specialize in medium-tech manufacturing processes, and third-generation maquiladoras perform assembly and manufacturing tasks, utilizing capital- and technology-intensive advanced manufacturing systems (Carrillo and Lara 2005). It seems logical to propose that low wages are critically important for the survival of first-generation plants but not quite so important for second-generation producers, and that third-generation maquiladoras require a skilled rather than a lowest-cost workforce to compete. Therefore, increased competition from lower-cost China may have caused high rates of maquiladora mortality in first-generation firms, caused lower rates in second-generation plants, and created conditions favoring the survival and growth of skill-intensive third-generation producers.

Sargent and Matthews (2004, 2006, 2007) propose an alternative argument and logic for how China's success is shaping maquiladoras. They argue that China offers MNCs a significantly lower-cost structure than Mexico does, and at the same time, it is fully capable of performing on a massive scale capital- and technology-intensive, high-complexity manufacturing. Therefore, there is no a priori reason to believe that third-generation maquiladoras are better prepared to withstand Chinese competition and hence no sound basis for the hypothesis that pre- and post-China/WTO maquiladoras will differ significantly on measures of capital intensity, technology intensity, or employment quality. Based on fieldwork conducted during 2002 and 2003, Sargent and Matthews came across scattered evidence at best that established maquiladoras are systematically increasing investments in advanced technology as a strategy to compete against lower-cost international competition. In a study conducted from 2004 to 2006 at startup and rapidly expanding maquiladoras, they found that exporters making new investments in Mexico utilize production systems that vary from low to very high on measures of capital intensity, technology intensity, and human-capital investment. Finally, utilizing a data-set of 101 maquiladoras that covers the 1993 to 2006 period, after controlling for industry and plant size, they find no significant relationship between the use of advanced manufacturing technology and maquiladora survival.

Mexican policymakers fully realize that China's success places limits on job creation in the country's traditional export industries (Secretaría de Economía 2004). In response, federal, state, and local governments as well as the private sector have worked to develop nontraditional, knowledge-intensive export sectors. Targeted activities include software development, back-office services, research and development centers, and the aerospace sector (Ruiz Durán, Piore, and Schrank 2005; Ornelas 2005; Ruiz Duran 2006; Ordóñez 2006). There have been clear successes with at least some of these initiatives. For example, Mexico's Secretaría de Economía reported that as of 2007, there were at least 107 aerospace companies engaged in manufacturing, maintenance, repair and overhaul, or engineering and design activities in Mexico. Of this group, thirty-two were located on the border (fifteen in Tijuana, twelve in Mexicali, and five in Ciudad Juárez). It is not particularly surprising that companies within the aerospace cluster in Southern California would migrate some aspects of their value chain across the border to cities in Baja California. However, the fact that other border locations have not been able to attract significant aerospace investment and have made relatively little progress in other targeted, nontraditional, knowledge-intensive export sectors that require a highly skilled workforce is troubling.

Occupational data provided by El Instituto Nacional de Estadística, Geografía e Informática (INEGI), the Mexican government's statistical agency, provide another useful source of information regarding trends in the attractiveness of maquiladora employment. In 1980, 85.3 percent of the maquiladora workforce was classified as operators, 9.1 percent as technicians, and 5.6 percent as administrative employees. In January 1994, these percentages were 81.3, 11.3, and 7.3 percent, respectively; they were 78.5, 13.1, and 8.4 percent in October 2006. Consistent with the literature, the decline in the percentage of operating-level employees indicates that maquiladoras are evolving towards more capital- and technology-intensive business models that require a higher percentage of technicians and administrators. While the differences are not dramatic, there is a slight deceleration in the trend towards utilizing a lower percentage of operating-level employees during the more recent 1994–2006 period compared with the 1980–1993 period.

If Chinese competition has forced maquiladoras to adopt a complex, skill-intensive production model, there should be an acceleration in the trend towards employing individuals in higher-skill categories since 2001. To simplify the analysis, we treat January 1994 to October 2000 (eighty months) and October 2000 to October 2006 (seventy-two months) as equivalent time periods. In addition, we examine changes in operators to total employees rather than separately breaking down the analysis by technicians and staff. The percentage of operators to total employees fell slightly from 81.3 to 81.1 percent between January 1994 and October 2000, then falling to 78.5 percent by October 2006. There was little change in the apparel sector during the two time periods (a drop from 85.3 percent to 84.8 percent in period one and to 84.1 percent by the end of period two), but an encouraging acceleration in electronics/electrical equipment (from 79.2 percent to 79.3 percent in period one and to 76.5 percent by the end of period two) and auto parts (from 80.6 percent to 79.3 percent in period one and to 76.3 by the end of period two).

The Mexican government also reports on maquiladora employment in a generic "other manufacturing" category (see table 4.1). In October 2006, the number of employees in this grouping (179,507) exceeded that of the apparel sector (168,096). As the newest and fast-growing member of the newly reconstituted "Big Three," the profile of other manufacturing firms may represent an especially important indicator of maquiladora evolution. The ratio of operators to total employees in other manufacturing firms went from 81.0 to 79.8 percent in period one, and then increased slightly to 80.0 percent by the end of period two.

INEGI also reports on the gender profile of maquiladora operators. From January 1994 to October 2000, the percentage of male operators in the apparel sector increased from 26.3 to 39.0 percent. From October 2000 to October 2006, this percentage increased to 43.0 percent. There was little overall change during the two periods in the auto parts sector (a rise from 48.2 to 52.9 percent in period one and then a decrease to 48.9

percent by the end of period two). In electronics, there was an increase in the percentage of male operators in period one, but little change in period two (a rise from 33.9 to 40.2 percent in period one and to 40.7 percent by the end of period two). There was a similar pattern in the other manufacturing grouping (a rise from 41.2 to 47.4 in period one and then a decrease to 45.2 by the end of period two).

There are two additional developments directly related to the maquiladora labor market that are worthy of special attention. These include the growing presence of temporary staffing agencies and the new Industria Manufacturera, Maquiladora y de Servicios de Exportación (IMMEX) decree.

Mexican labor law has traditionally been very pro-worker. When maquiladoras hire an individual, Mexican federal law provides for a ninety-day probationary period. If the employer chooses to fire the new employee during this period, they can easily do so. After ninety days, the person is considered a permanent employee. If the maquiladora needs to reduce its workforce, it is required to pay permanent employees a significant severance package. This employment structure has traditionally been very inflexible and other arrangements (such as temporary or part-time employment) have been discouraged. In the recent past, the Mexican government has allowed maquiladoras to increase the flexibility of their workforce though the use of temporary staffing agencies. In other words, maquiladoras facing a sudden upturn in demand can contract a staffing agency to provide additional workers. These individuals are employees of the staffing agency rather than the maquiladora itself. If demand suddenly drops, the maquiladora can send the temporary employees back to the staffing agency and has no further legal obligation. In our experience, temporary staffing agencies are now being widely used, with agency employees representing one-third or more of operators at large plants.

The second development revolves around the maquiladora program itself. In the mid-1980s, the Mexican government established the Programa de Importación Temporal para Producir Articulos de Exportación, otherwise known as the PITEX program. The PITEX decree gave Mexican companies selling their products in the domestic market the opportunity to enjoy maquiladora-like import/export and tax benefits for their export sales. As mentioned, NAFTA prohibits restrictions limiting maquiladoras from supplying the Mexican market. After the phase-in of these changes, maquiladoras and PITEX companies were receiving very similar import/export and tax treatments for both their international and domestic sales. The Mexican government determined there was little rational justification to continue with two separate export promotion programs. Therefore, in November 2006, the Fox administration issued a decree that combined the maquiladora and PITEX initiatives into the Industria Manufacturera, Maquiladora y de Servicios de Exportación (IMMEX) program. This consolidation creates challenges as well as new opportunities for those studying Mexico's export industries. INEGI has for decades reported detailed information on maquiladoras but has not provided similar data on PITEX companies. INEGI provided reports on the maquiladoras utilizing its traditional methodology up to October 2006 and will begin publishing detailed information on companies registered under the IMMEX program starting in 2008 (Cañas and Gilmer 2007). Until then, the academic and policymaking communities will be somewhat blind to the latest developments in Mexico's export industries.

In this section, we have presented several of the macro- and firm-level changes in the maquiladora program since the initial implementation of NAFTA, especially as it relates to the demand for labor. In the next section, we examine the employer-employee relationship from the perspective of operating-level employees. The macro- and firm-level evidence often tends to distort what in our view continues to represent the foundation of maquiladora competitiveness, i.e., the availability of large numbers of individuals with relatively little formal education who view low-paying jobs performing highly simplified, repetitive tasks as more attractive than other opportunities in the Mexican labor market.

A Look Inside: Operating-Level Employees and the Maquiladoras

In 1992, Sargent—the first author of this chapter—interviewed fifty-one operators and eight technicians working in maquiladoras in Ciudad Juárez and Ciudad Chihuahua. The majority of the interviews were obtained through going door-to-door in neighborhoods where large numbers of maquiladora employees were known to reside. In 2002,

Melissa Najera—the second author of this chapter—interviewed seventy-five randomly selected operators at five maquiladoras located in Reynosa or Matamoros. In both rounds of data collection, respondents were asked to describe why they decided to obtain a job in a maquiladora, what kinds of jobs they had held in the past, how their jobs compared to the jobs held by friends and family, and if they planned to continue working in a maquiladora. There were also significant differences in the two rounds of data collection. For example, one of the goals of the 1992 study was to determine if operators had learned quality-control techniques consistent with the Toyota production model. The 2002 study focused on the match between worker needs and the inducements provided by maquiladora employers.

In this section, we first review worker responses in areas where similar questions were used in both 1992 and 2002. We then present especially important and interesting findings that are somewhat unique to the 2002 round of data collection. We provide quotes taken from the 2002 interviews to illustrate responses in each of the topic areas (see Sargent [1994], Sargent and Matthews [1999], and Castillo [2003] for more information regarding the research methodology and study findings).

There was considerable similarity in the profile of operators in the two studies. In the 1992 sample, the average operator was 24 years old and had completed 7.9 years of formal education. In the 2002 sample, the average operator was 24.7 years old. Of the seventy-five respondents, twelve had six or fewer years of education, forty-four had participated in—but not necessary completed—*secundaria* (nine years of school), eighteen had made it to the *preparatoria* level (twelve years), and one had attended college. There was a higher percentage of female respondents in the 2002 sample (60 percent) than in the 1992 sample (38 percent).

Shared Questions and Findings

In the 1992 and 2002 interviews, respondents were asked to describe their prior work experience. For those who had worked in non-maquiladora positions, in 1992, interviewees frequently stated that non-maquiladora jobs paid the same or more than maquiladora positions, offered very little time off, and were often unstable. In the 2002 study, comments were very similar except respondents stated that maquiladoras now paid more than non-maquiladora jobs, as indicated by the following responses (see Sargent and Matthews [1999] for earlier study information):

Why did you quit/leave your former job?

I did not want to work every day and at the boutique I would have one day off every two weeks. In the maquila they pay better and you work five days a week.

My sister told me about a maquila job. She told me that they would pay me more as compared to my sales job and also work fewer hours. I would work Monday to Sunday and my only day of rest was on Tuesday.

It's not that I wanted to work in a maquiladora but I needed to work and I was looking for something more stable than the job I had. There are really no other options here.

In both 1992 and 2002, interviewees responded to questions about why they worked in a maquiladora. Responses were similar across the two rounds of data collection, i.e., people worked because of necessity, maquiladora jobs were easy to get, and they were often the only jobs available for those who had dropped out of school. These responses are from the 2002 survey:

Why did you decide to work in a maquila?

I don't know. I only finished secundaria and I did not want to continue. There are no other jobs if you don't have more studies. School is not for me.

First of all the lack of work. There are no other jobs available. I was looking at many different jobs and plants in Matamoros but I could not find anything. I heard there was work here so I came. Thank God they gave me the opportunity to work.

Necessity. We needed more money since our children are growing. I had heard cars driving through the neighborhood announcing that maquilas needed people to work and so I decided to apply.

When asked why they were working at a specific plant, in both rounds of data collection, respondents often stated they took a position at the first maquiladora that would hire them. Others relied upon friends and family for information on the advantages and disadvantages of a particular employer. In 1992, interviewees frequently commented that there were relatively few differences in pay between maquiladoras. This was not the case in 2002.

Why did you want to work in this particular plant?

I had not heard anything about the plant. I was going plant to plant to find work. This particular plant was the first to offer me work.

This is the only job I can get that is close to my home. Plus it is the best there is around here. It has the highest salary (850 pesos per week).

What else did your friend say about the job?

My friend told me that the pay was going to be low. About 450 a week and if you work overtime you may earn more, but it's not enough. She also said, "For you that has *la prepa*. I know that you should be earning more with the education that you have. What you will earn in the plant is not enough because you have more education." But I told her, "That is not important, I prefer to work rather than be unemployed."

Other people comment that working here is better in what way?

The salary. They say that this one pays better than the others. They also give more vacation days than other plants. The friends that I talk to always want to know when they are hiring because they all want to work here.

Does the pay really differ in other plants from the pay here?

Here, the most one earns is about a thousand pesos a week. And in the other plants it is about five hundred pesos. Some make about four hundred pesos. And they also stress production. It is also more pressure in other plants. So if they want to earn more there is no other maquila that pays more, so they go to the United States to try their luck over there.

In both 1992 and 2002, interviewees responded to questions regarding whether they planned to continue with their present employer. In 2002, interviewees were also asked to describe why others had left the plant. We have combined these categories, as they provide common information regarding turnover. Respondents in both rounds emphasized that operators left in search of higher pay, more opportunities, and because they were bored with their jobs. In the 2002 round, there were also many comments emphasizing that women left due to the need to care for children.

What about the other plant you worked in? Why would people leave that job?

They just get tired. They don't like their jobs anymore, they are bored like I was.

What about some of the men who left?

Yes, it was a good plant and they did many things for the worker, but sometimes one just gets bored of the same routine, the same job and they quit to go to another plant and a different job. They anticipate the new plant pays more and they will do something different.

Do you have friends or relatives that have left this maquila?

Many, many leave due to personal family problems. Child care. Some women have someone to care for their kids and then they don't so they quit. Other times, they hear about another maquiladora offering more money so they leave. But then I see them and they say that the work is very hard and that they should not have left. Some get married and their husbands do not want them to work. Sometimes, they just do not want to work anymore once they get married. I have one kid but my mom takes care of him.

What about the other plant you were in? Why would people leave a nice plant?

Many women have left because they did not have anyone to care for their children. Usually it is related to caring for the children.

Questions and Findings from 2002 Study

As mentioned, one of the purposes of the 2002 study was to identify the major inducements characteristic of the maquiladora employer-employee relationship. Inducements are defined as job and organizational characteristics that are important to attract and retain employees. The relationship between supervisors and employees was by far the most frequently mentioned inducement. Comments about supervisors ranged from very positive to very negative.

What do you like about this plant?

I like that I can talk to my friends and even the supervisors. My supervisor talks to me, he is not yelling like others. I can talk to him about anything. He tell us when we are doing wrong but also when we are doing right. That makes us feel good. He treats us all the same. And I like to work for him.

I am very comfortable. I have friends, male and female. The work is easy and I work very comfortably here. The supervisors are very respectful to all the workers and the office people are very nice. They talk to us. We all get along.

What do your coworkers or friends complain about?

That their supervisor demands a lot from them. Above everything is the pressure. If production is going slow after an hour, the supervisor calls everyone on the line and demands to know what is going on. What is the problem. This happens every day every hour to a line. Also, when there is a product with many defects. He calls their attention again. Sometimes I think the supervisor exaggerates. Just call their attention, they don't have to yell. Some people don't like that.

As previously mentioned, pay was an extremely important inducement for employees. In addition to base pay, a factor that came out very clearly in the 2002 interviews was the importance of overtime in the total employee compensation structure. A small number of respondents complained about being required to work extra hours, but others clearly viewed the opportunity to receive overtime pay as very important.

Was it worth it to quit your prior job and move to this plant?

Another thing in the other plant is that they did not have overtime. Once in a while one wants to buy something extra and we need money. The weekly pay we get is barely enough for the necessities, so we depend on the overtime to buy things.

What don't you like about this plant?

Everything is fine, except that I need the overtime to make ends meet. If there is no overtime, I don't have enough money to live, since I have to send most back home. [This person's family stayed in Veracruz.] Right now the fact that there is no overtime really bothers me and that I am not with my family.

And your brother, what has he mentioned about working here?

My brother and I do not talk about work, but he is the one that tells me that they work us too much here, because we put in too much overtime. But we like getting overtime because we earn more money.

What could the plant do so that employees would not leave?

Since work is very slow, there is no overtime. Many people have families that need that overtime to help with the necessities. They cannot make it with the regular salary. So they are also the ones that leave to look for better opportunities in other maquiladoras.

Mexico has traditionally been regarded as a male-dominated society. But cultural strictures have loosened considerably and there are many examples of very accomplished women in the political and business worlds. Given this, we were surprised by the number of comments made by female operators regarding the presence of very traditional machismo attitudes held by their husbands. The final quote also hints at the types of social dynamics common in large plants.

Do you plan to stay?

Well, it all depends on if my husband lets me stay working here.

Why did your friend leave?

Her husband found a job in Matamoros near the beach. He is a fisherman. And she left the job to go over there. Her husband told her that she had to quit or else he was going to leave her.

You need your husband's support to continue your studies?

Yes, I know some friends that say they would like to study but that their husbands do not let them. Their husbands prefer them to work and help out financially rather than for them to go to school. They should realize that with more schooling they can eventually receive more pay.

Do you like working in the same plant as your husband?

It's OK, he supports me working and we don't have problems. I know that at one time the plant did not want married couples working here as well as family members, but that changed since there are many married couples and people that are related that work here. Also, many find their husband or wife here, so it is hard to control.

Maquiladora critics often contend that companies move to Mexico in order to avoid strict safety and environmental standards. Our experience in studying the maquiladora industry since 1992 is that the great majority of plants provide a safe work environment and have implemented world-class environmental standards. With that said, in the interviews, there were comments made by ten of the seventy-five operators stating that they were aware as a result of comments made by friends and family of health and safety concerns at plants, or that in their past or current jobs they have believed that their own health and safety was put at risk due to characteristics of the work environment.

You left the third plant because you were bored?

There was a lot of noise in that plant. We had to wear earplugs. Sometimes there were no earplugs. We would leave work and we could not hear. There was also a lot of lead. That's why we had to wear masks. We also worked with aluminum so we had to wear long-sleeved shirts. The aluminum sticks to your skin. I would go home and shower and with the sunlight you could see a lot of shine on my arms. I guess it would penetrate through the shirt. That's also why I left there.

What happened [at your prior job]?

While I was there I got pregnant. After forty days I returned to work. The thing that happened is that my baby began to have breathing problems. He is one year now, but this started when he was two months. Apparently when I was pregnant I was around humid areas where there was lead. My baby developed some allergies that prevented him from breathing well. I started being absent two days per week for more than a month. I would ask for permission, or I could be at work and they would call me that my baby was sick. It came to the point that the doctor told me that my baby needed me to be with him. He told me to ask myself what was more important, your son or your work. Your baby is still small, he told me, and your baby needs a lot of attention. So I resigned from my job or I would still be there.

Tell me ten things you do not like about this job.

I solder and it gets boring. Sometimes if it is slow, I want to fall asleep. I get very sleepy with the odor and the powder as well. Also, the area where I am I get headaches and nausea because of the smell. There are others but we don't say anything because we are afraid they may fire or lay us off. There was this girl always complaining with many symptoms and the next thing you know she was laid off.

Finally, the number of maquiladora jobs in Reynosa has increased rapidly since 1994. This growth has attracted a considerable flow of migrants from states such as Veracruz and San Luis Potosi in central Mexico. (More on internal migration will be discussed in subsequent chapters.) The migrant experience strongly shaped the attitudes and behavior of many of the respondents in the 2002 sample.

Why did you decide to leave your home and parents in Veracruz and come to Reynosa?

Some people in Veracruz told me that in Reynosa there was a lot of work. Enough for everyone. Once you get here you will find a job fast. I had gone to many other places, Mexico City and Guadalajara, but then I told my parents I was going to Reynosa.

What made you decide to come to Reynosa?

In the first place, everyone said that this is where the jobs were. I came here to work. In Poza Rica, the jobs are scarce. Also, the pay is very low. Here there is a lot of industry. That's what people were saying and that's why we came here.

What had you heard about work here in Reynosa?

Well, that finding a job is easy, the work is good, and overtime here is very well paid. Also, there is more opportunity to earn more money and save and make a better life for your family. It is easier in Reynosa to find a better job and in maquiladoras there are more opportunities to get good jobs.

Would you like to study more?

Yes, but they only help you to the prepa. But I would like to study. I don't want to be an operator forever. But at the present time I can't due to economic necessity. My mom is not here. The thing that happened was that I was going to continue my studies after I finished prepa; at that time my grandparents were seriously ill and my mom had to go to help and I had to give my money to help them. So since then I have had to save money so I can return to school. I also help my parents and sometimes I need to send money to my grandparents in Veracruz. So it becomes difficult for me to save. I am still sending money to my mom who is not here. I earn 500 pesos, and every two weeks I send her about 250 to 300 pesos. Also my sister and brother help out.

What about your coworkers here in this plant, what do they say about the work here?

They like the job here. But like me, many are tired of being without their families. I tell them that I am not making it and that I am planning on leaving soon [to Veracruz]. They tell me the same thing. The money is just not enough to sustain living and working here and then supporting a family in another state.

Was your wife OK with that decision?

We talked before making this decision, and she also felt that we were not improving our lives in Veracruz so we decided to come over here. Over there you can work all your life and never gain anything. Here we see that relatives have their own home and their own car. They have something to show for their work. Over there, it just isn't possible for what they pay. I worked for nine years, and it was just enough to live, to buy necessities. As I work here, they are paying me, more or less, but there is enough extra to save.

In this section, we have examined the maquiladora environment from the perspective of operating-level employees. Comparisons based on semi-structured interview data from 1992 and 2002 utilizing different sampling methodologies and different interviewers (one an Anglo male, the second a Hispanic female) do not enable us to make definitive conclusions regarding changes in the maquiladora employer-employee relationship. However, one general finding from the interview transcripts that stands out is the similarity in responses across the two studies. For example, in both rounds of data collection, interviewees preferred maquiladora to non-maquiladora jobs because they were easier to get, offered more time off, and provided greater stability. Furthermore, individuals who had dropped out of school often stated they had very limited opportunities in the border labor market outside of the maquiladoras.

The most profound difference between the two studies appears to be the much greater variation in maquiladora pay policies evident in the 2002 study. These differences were particularly acute for plants located in Reynosa when compared with those in Matamoros. This finding may be somewhat unique to this particular research setting and time period. For several decades, Agapito González led the primary union representing maquiladora workers in Matamoros. Due to his efforts, compensation levels in Matamoros became significantly higher than rates common in other border cities. Agapito also successfully negotiated for a forty-hour work week (a forty-five- or forty-eight-hour work week is common in other border cities). Agapito passed away in February 2001, and by 2006, compensation levels and work hours had been modified to more closely match industry standards in other border locations.

Concluding Remarks

In this chapter, we have examined the evolution of the maquiladoras during the 1994–2006 period, paying special attention to the border labor market. From a macroeconomic and firm-level perspective, border maquiladoras have clearly experienced dramatic changes during the NAFTA period. The rapid expansion of the industry during the 1990s, the contraction beginning in October 2000, the migration of production lines from Mexico to China, the rapid growth of the "other" manufacturing sector since 2003, and the combination of the maquiladora and PITEX programs in 2006 are just a few of the many developments shaping the industry. These dynamics serve to shape the demand for and the quality of jobs available on the border in Mexico's maquiladoras. We believe the macroeconomic and firm-level changes facing Mexico's export industries over the next decade will be equally as dramatic. For example, a significant strengthening of the Chinese currency will in all probability result in the return of high-volume commodity manufacturing to the border. Furthermore, Mexico has a young and rapidly growing population. Demographic trends in the United States may force proximity-dependent manufacturers serving North American markets to migrate production to Mexico simply due to the availability of labor rather than the attraction of a low-cost workforce. The trend towards the offshore outsourcing of services and a growing recognition of the advantages of near-sourcing provide U.S.-Mexico border communities another significant new opportunity.

Whether or not the border will play a major role as a producer of knowledge-intensive, nontraditional exports is an open question. Cities in the Mexican interior such as Monterrey, Guadalajara, and Aguascalientes have taken aggressive steps to attract and develop the aerospace sector, research and development centers, back-office service activities, software firms, and call centers for Spanish-speaking customers in the United States. On the border, San Diego and Tijuana and El Paso and Ciudad Juárez may also be positioned to benefit from the migration of these types of activities from the United States to the developing world. Other border cities appear to be considerably behind in their efforts to diversify beyond the traditional maquiladora sectors. Similar to leaders in the Mexican interior, border leaders in government, in the private sector, and in higher education should increase their coordinated efforts to develop the physical and human infrastructure needed to participate in the knowledge economy.

Our look inside the maquiladoras to examine the characteristics of operators and the employer-employee relationship indicates the considerable challenges involved in maquiladora upgrading. The profile, prior experiences, attitudes, aspirations, and career prospects of lower-level maquiladora workers have not changed greatly from 1992 to 2002. We want to clarify that the information presented in the second half of this chapter should not be interpreted to mean that maquiladoras do not offer lower-level employees attractive job opportunities. In Sargent and Matthews (1999), we argued that maquiladora workers themselves are capable of determining whether or not the jobs created by border maquiladoras are worthwhile. Statements made by operators who have migrated to the border from the Mexican interior provide especially powerful examples of the value of maquiladora jobs within the context of the overall

Mexican labor market. To argue otherwise "suggests a middle or upper class favoritism and a denial of the importance of the needs of the lower classes in developing countries" (Sargent and Matthews 1999:226). The work ethic that unskilled and semiskilled operating-level employees bring with them to the factory floor, which comes from the desire of individuals to improve their lives through active engagement with the global economy, will continue to make cities on the U.S.-Mexico border a very attractive location for MNCs engaged in an increasingly diverse set of manufacturing and service activities.

5

Evolution of Average Returns to Education in the Mexican Northern Border States[1]

Hector J. Villarreal

Introduction

Continuing with the focus on the Mexican side of the border, this chapter argues there are important differences between the sociodemographic characteristics, including education and salaries, of the populations living in the northern Mexican border states and the rest of the Mexican states. Moreover, these differences are correlated with two features. The first is the existence of distinct labor markets across border and non-border regions (aligned with the findings of the next three chapters in this volume). The second feature is the pattern of both internal and international migration in Mexico. This includes the fact that most Mexican migration to the United States comes from the interior of the country; this issue is discussed in more detail by Pia M. Orrenius, Madeline Zavodny, and Leslie Lukens in chapter 8 (see also Hanson 2005).[2]

A related question is whether Mexican wages differ between the border and non-border regions of Mexico because the distribution of human capital itself is highly dispersed or because of an increasing wage variance within higher levels of education (or both)(López-Acevedo 2004; Meza 1999).[3] With regards to income inequality between northern Mexico and the rest of the country, the last decade provides an interesting period to study, given a series of major events that particularly affected the border region of northern Mexico. Among them are the signing of important commercial treaties and a dramatic increase in trade, including NAFTA (recall the earlier chapter by James T. Peach and Richard V. Adkisson). Moreover, the worst economic crisis in Mexican modern history occurred in 1995 and, in 2000, the Partido Accion Nacional (PAN) assumed the presidency after more than seventy years of continued rule by the Partido Revolucionario Institucional (PRI).

Labor Demographics along the Mexican Border

Table 5.1 presents some key characteristics of the Mexican labor market during three different years: 1994 (the year when NAFTA was implemented), 2000, and 2005. This table distinguishes between the six northern border states (Baja California, Sonora, Chihuahua, Coahuila, Nuevo Leon, and Tamaulipas)[4] and other Mexican states (recall figure I.1 in the introductory chapter). Mexico City is excluded from this analysis because of its unique labor-force dynamics.

First, note that the labor-force participation rate (defined here as the labor force divided by the total population of non-institutionalized individuals sixteen years and older) increased considerably during the eleven-year period (1994–2005) in both regions; it increased by 38.5 percent in northern Mexican states and by 26.2 percent in the rest of the country. Another trend seen in table 5.1 is that women played an increasingly large role in explaining the labor-force growth. In general, however, the increasing labor-force participation rates throughout Mexico can be attributed to the impacts of the aforementioned events on the modernization of the Mexican economy.

Second, a striking increase in the average number of the years of education among the labor force is also observed in table 5.1, with an average net increase of 1.3 school years in the northern border states and 1.5 years in the rest of the country. The most dramatic changes occurred at the college level. Despite remaining small according to North American standards,[5] the share of Mexican workers possessing a college degree or equivalent doubled in both the northern border and the rest of Mexico between 1994 and 2005. Also, note the higher schooling levels among border workers versus those of workers in the country as a whole: nearly 14 percent of the labor force along the northern border had completed college, compared to less than 11 percent of Mexican workers. The higher educational attainment along the northern Mexican border may be related to this region's relatively high wealth compared with that of other Mexican states.

TABLE 5.1 Key Characteristics of the Mexican Labor Market

Characteristic		Border*			Non-Border		
		1994	2000	2005	1994	2000	2005
Labor Force	Males	66.6	65.1	62.7	68.8	65.6	61.6
(% of Total Population)	Females	33.4	34.9	37.3	31.2	34.4	38.4
	Total	9.0	9.7	10.3	7.3	8.3	8.8
Schooling	Primary	77.3	82.7	85.8	61.1	69.6	74.2
(% of Labor Force with	Junior High	49.0	57.0	64.3	34.2	43.9	50.5
Completed Degrees)	High School	19.8	23.0	32.9	14.2	19.2	25.3
	College	7.6	9.3	13.9	5.0	8.2	10.7
Self-Employed (% of Labor Force)		20.4	19.8	18.2	29.4	28.2	26.5
Formal Sector (% of labor force participating in social security)		79.1	84.6	78.4	57.8	57.7	55.1
Agricultural Workers/ Employed (%)		11.7	6.1	6.0	27.1	21.3	17.1

*Border includes those states along the northern Mexican border.

Source: Author's calculations based on Encuesta Nacional de Ingreso y Gasto de los Hogares (ENIGH) data for the years 1994, 2000 and 2005.

Third, table 5.1 shows that the self-employed represent a relatively small share of the workforce in the northern Mexican border area, where less than a fifth was self-employed in 2005, compared with more than a quarter in the rest of Mexico. In both regions, however, the share of the self-employed diminished over time. Two different forces might have led to this decline: (1) increasing paid-employment opportunities along the border (see the following chapter by Dávila, Mora, and Hales); and (2) the decline in the agricultural sector, where it is common to find workers (households) isolated. A possible explanation for the sharp drop in the agricultural sector is urban migration from Mexico's rural sector (Hanson 2005).

Finally, the relative size of the formal sector (defined in terms of participation in Social Security [Yamada 1996]) in the regions displays an interesting pattern. In the border states, the formal sector grew in relative terms from 1994 to 2000 (from 79 percent to almost 85 percent). This growth coincides with the maquiladora boom of the period, as discussed by John Sargent, Melissa Najera, and Linda Matthews in the previous chapter. Post-2000, however, the size of the formal sector declined in this region (to 78.4 percent), so that by 2005, participation in this sector was lower than in 1994, perhaps because of the declining maquiladora activity after 2000. In contrast, in the rest of Mexico, the share of the labor force in the formal sector was considerably smaller (by more than 20 percentage points) than along the border, and it remained fairly steady across this time period.

Economic Returns to Education and Inequality

Given the changes in the education and employment profiles along the northern border and in the rest of Mexico during recent years, an analysis of the evolution of the economic returns to education in the respective labor markets proves desirable. Thus, we now use regression analysis (described in this chapter's appendix) to estimate average net monthly salaries associated with different levels of schooling on the Mexican side of the U.S.-Mexico border and elsewhere in Mexico; these salaries (expressed in terms of real pesos) are contained in table 5.2.[6]

From table 5.2, it is apparent that real salaries in Mexico's northern border followed a different pattern than other states in Mexico. The

TABLE 5.2 Simulated Average Net Monthly Salaries in Mexico in Real Pesos (Base Year 2000)

		1994	2000	2005	% Change 1994–2000	% Change 2000–2005
Mexican Northern Border States	No Education	3,241	4,006	3,254	23.60	−18.77
	Primary	5,556	5,929	5,058	6.71	−14.69
	Junior High	7,000	7,014	6,110	0.20	−12.89
	High School	8,819	8,297	7,381	−5.92	−11.04
	College	24,213	23,591	17,182	−2.57	−27.17
	Graduate School	–	–	24,092		
Rest of Mexico	No Education	2,643	2,449	2,212	−7.34	−9.68
	Primary	4,985	4,472	3,486	−10.29	−22.05
	Junior High	6,543	5,789	4,237	−11.52	−26.81
	High School	8,589	7,492	5,149	−12.77	−31.27
	College	33,182	19,276	15,088	−41.91	−21.73
	Graduate School	–	–	23,194		

Notes: The calculations are for someone whose age is 35 in 1994 and who works 50 hours a week (experience is adjusted for the different years and educational levels).[6] Mexico City is excluded. See the Chapter 6 Appendix for more details.

salaries increased slightly between 1994 and 2000 in the border region for workers with less than a high school education, and they decreased slightly for the upper educational levels. In contrast, workers with all schooling levels in the rest of Mexico experienced a considerable decrease in real salaries during the same period, particularly those with a college education. College graduates in the Mexican interior in 2000 earned only 60 percent of the average salary earned by similar workers in 1994. In fact, their real salaries continued to drop between 2000 and 2005 by a greater proportion than the salary declines experienced by other workers in Mexico. It is clear that average returns to education in Mexico fell during this period once other characteristics are taken into account;[7] indeed, the decline is stronger for higher levels of education and in the interior states.

The consequences of these changes require careful analysis. Welfare impacts are difficult to infer on the basis of salaries alone because of potential changes in the cost of living and movements in relative prices across regions (Banks, Blundell and Lewbel 1996; Villarreal 2006). Moreover, some individuals may attempt to "beat" the declining average schooling returns by accumulating more human capital (years of education) to compensate for the lower payoffs associated with each year. This could be the case for workers with graduate-level education. To illustrate, in the northern border states, seven years of post-high school education (typically equivalent to a masters degree) in 2005 provided a net average salary similar to that acquired by workers who held only a college degree in previous periods (1994 and 2000). In the interior, the two extra years of graduate education provided a higher average real income than the one accrued by college graduates in 2000, but it was lower than in 1994.

Another interesting result (observed in this chapter's appendix) is that the returns to labor market experience in Mexico also declined during this time. This result is explained elsewhere in detail (Mehta and Villarreal 2005). When combining the lower experience returns with the fact that new cohorts possess substantially more years of education, it would appear that the cumulative effect of both characteristics act against older cohorts. This apparent pattern of lower average returns to education and experience in Mexico in recent years may have important welfare consequences and possible implications for public policy. For example, in a typical economic life cycle, middle-aged individuals may alter their habits of spending for children's education or saving for retirement. Moreover, the effects on public finances, such as tax revenues and the social security system, still need to be assessed.

One question that arises with the above discussion is whether these labor market dynamics have similarly impacted the earnings inequality across Mexican regions. To address this point, a standard approach to take would be to calculate Gini coefficients.[8] The Gini coefficient can take values between zero and one, where zero represents perfect equality (all the income or wealth is distributed uniformly), and one represents complete inequality. While the Gini coefficient is not the only measure of income or wealth dispersion, it is one of the most widely used (for a discussion of various inequality measures, see Deaton [1997]).

The Gini coefficients using the salaries in our sample described above are calculated here. Notice that this measure only reflects the *dispersion* of salaries. Indeed, excluding economic dependents, calculated coefficients would be lower (suggesting more equality) in comparison with Gini coefficients based on disposable income for each individual in the country.

For the northern Mexican border states, the estimated Gini equaled 0.42 in 1994, but it fell slightly to 0.41 in 2000 and 2005. As such, this improvement in wage inequality was very modest. A Gini of 0.46 was found for the Mexican interior in 1994, which indicates that the interior had more salary dispersion than the border region did. In 2000, the figure rose to 0.48, and in the following five years it fell down to 0.44. In short, salaries in the Mexican interior became more dispersed in the late 1990s, and then wage equality marginally improved in the early 2000s. Possible explanations include the human-capital dynamics described previously, and/or migration flows across the regions, as is next discussed. Dávila, Mora, and Hales in the next chapter also present more information on wage convergence in Mexico.

External and Internal Migration

To what extent have population flows altered the demographic profile of both the Mexican side of the U.S.-Mexico border and the rest of Mexico? There are two components of migration to the U.S.-Mexico border. The first refers to net international migration (most of it to the United States) and the other is the migration across Mexican states.

Consider dividing Mexico into three regions: the northern border states, Mexico City, and the other states (for ease of discussion, the latter region will be referred to as "non-border states"). Mexico City tends to be a net international migrant receiver (small in magnitude but a receiver nonetheless), while both Mexican border and non-border states have experienced net international emigration during the past few decades (for details, contact the author). However, the Mexican border states experienced a decline in the number of emigrants after 1997, so that by 2007, this negative magnitude is quite small in proportion to the region's population. The story is different for the other Mexican states: from 1990 to 2000, annual emigration doubled to more than 550,000 emigrants, and it remained high in the 2000s.

Perhaps these changes in net migration flows relate to the high inequality that persists in Mexico with respect to both human capital and income. If so, a negative selection of migrants could be expected (Borjas 1987) because moving to another region (or country) where wages are higher at every educational level (and more egalitarian overall), should bring welfare improvements to the poor. Yet, Daniel Chiquiar and Gordon H. Hanson (2005) have recently challenged this prediction by suggesting that the transaction costs of migrating (legally or illegally) may prove too high for the poorest Mexicans. Their study provides evidence that, if anything, the selection of Mexican migrants has been positive; for example, while less educated than U.S. natives, Mexican migrants to the United States tend to be more educated than the average Mexican population.

The counterfactual experience (i.e., what would have occurred had migrants remained in their home states), is difficult to estimate. However, one direct effect would be that, as migrants tend to be more educated than the average population, the actual educational average would be higher in Mexico if they had not migrated to the United States (for more discussion, see Chiquiar and Hanson 2005). If wages in real terms decline sharply for more educated workers, incentives to migrate should increase, so that positive selection among migrants occurs. Such migration not only affects the home labor market as migrants take their skills with them, but it also affects the labor market into which they migrate (e.g., Borjas 2003).

Two additional perspectives on Mexican migration to the United States need to be considered. Migration patterns vary, depending on whether they target the border region or the interior of the United States, as will be discussed in more detail in an upcoming chapter by Orrenius, Zavodny, and Lukens. Also, to the extent that U.S. labor markets become more service and information oriented, as was already noted by Thomas M. Fullerton Jr., James H. Holcomb, and Angel L. Molina Jr. earlier in this volume, the labor markets on both sides of the border may be altered by Mexican migration.

How have international migration patterns been mitigated by internal migration within Mexico? It is well known that since the mid-1980s, there have been migration outflows from Mexico City into other parts of Mexico. Across the three regions mentioned above (Mexico City, the northern border, and the rest of Mexico), net internal migration sums to zero, although it does so with considerable variance in the magnitudes of the migration flows. To illustrate, during the 1990s and the early 2000s, the border states received more net migrants than the rest of Mexico. This trend intensified after the 1995 crisis. However, starting in the late 1990s, migration to the northern border began falling, so that by 2005, the Mexican *interior* received a higher share of migrants than the border. (For more details on these migration flows, contact the author.)

These internal migration patterns may reflect changes in the economic returns to education discussed in the previous section. Recall that from 1994 to 2000, real salaries remained stable along the northern Mexican border, and they declined in the rest of Mexico. During this period, internal migration to the border region was considerably larger in magnitude than migration to other Mexican states. When real salaries began declining in the border region after 2000, however, migration to these states diminished. In this sense, this internal migration may substitute for migration to the United States. At the same time, the magnitude of the migration flows limits the extent of this substitution possibility. The actual international migration of non-northern border residents, slightly more than half a million people annually (most of them of working age), would constitute more than 2.5 percent of the population on the Mexican side of the international border with the United States. It does not seem feasible that the Mexican border region could sustain that rate of absorption.

Concluding Remarks

This chapter provides an overview of the labor market in Mexico since the 1990s, distinguishing states along the northern border from others in the country. In general, the Mexican population has been accumulating human capital (education) at an accelerated rate. The number of college graduates, while still low by North American standards, has doubled over the last decade. At the same time, real salaries in the interior of Mexico declined between 1994 and 2005, particularly for workers with higher levels of education. In contrast, real salaries in Mexico's northern border states remained stable between 1994 and 2000, but they then fell by 2005 (albeit at a slower rate than in the rest of the country).

Internal and external migration appears to be sensitive to the evolution of regional wages. When salaries along the border were stable and non-border wages were declining (from 1994 to 2000), the border region experienced higher rates of in-migration and a decline in international out-migration. After this time, both regions experienced declining wages and international migration (mostly to the United States) from the non-border states rose. It is possible that the labor force in the border states may be compensating for the falling wages by acquiring additional human capital instead of emigrating.

One unanswered question is why the average economic returns to education have been declining in Mexico. Whether it is due to poor quality of education, the lack of physical capital, or other causes, this issue remains an interesting avenue for future research. Regardless of the cause, if the economic returns to education in Mexico continue to decline, incentives for emigration to the United States should correspondingly increase.

Two policy issues stem from this chapter. First, given the strong relationship between depressed salaries and migration, the permanence of the labor force in specific areas should depend upon an adequate supply of jobs and higher salaries. The flow of financial and physical capital, as well as the provision of infrastructure, should be critical for the retention of human resources in these areas (consistent with the discussion by Dávila, Mora, and Hales in the next chapter).

Second, older populations are vulnerable to the decreasing average returns to education with likely social problems. Given that people in

Mexico usually attend school at a younger age, special education programs targeted at older cohorts may help to mitigate their declining real salaries.

Chapter 5 Appendix: Details on the Econometric Analysis

The primary specification for this study is a semi-logarithmic spline model (Hungerford and Solon 1987). In equation (1), the natural logarithm of a worker's wages is presumed to depend upon years of education and potential work experience as follows:

$$(1)\ \ln(\text{Wage}) = \alpha + \beta_Y\, \text{Years} + \beta_C\, H(\text{Years} - 13) + \varepsilon\, \text{Experience} + e$$

where Years is the number of years of education completed and H is an indicator function that takes on a value of one if an individual has completed high school (and equals zero otherwise); thirteen years of schooling corresponds to a high school diploma in Mexico. Hence, the model allows log-wages to change at a different rate for college and graduate-school education. Experience is the number of years of potential labor market experience (using the typical age – education – 5 definition); note that this specification restricts the experience effect to the linear form.[9]

While this type of earnings function has its limitations (e.g., see Mehta and Villarreal 2005), its wide use in the literature permits us to treat the Mincerian equation as a statistic and thus draw comparisons with other studies (e.g., analyses of other countries, periods of time, etc.). The β_Y, β_c, and ε coefficients may be interpreted as the percentage increase in wages statistically attributable to particular levels of education and work experience. Notice that the two β's are splines and are added together to obtain the slope of the log-wage function at a particular level of education. Thus, for individuals with a high school education or less, this slope equals β_Y; for those who attended at least some college, it equals $\beta_Y + \beta_c$.

The data employed for the analysis are from the Mexican Encuesta Nacional de Ingreso y Gasto de los Hogares (ENIGH, an income-expenditure survey, representative at the national level) for the years 1994, 2000, and 2005; see www.inegi.gob.mx for more details.

An advantage with this dataset is that its questionnaire and survey methodologies are very similar across years, facilitating comparisons over

TABLE 5.3 Estimated Parameters

Parameter	Border			Non-Border		
β_Y	0.089** (0.005)	0.063** (0.007)	0.065** (0.005)	0.102** (0.004)	0.097** (0.005)	0.069** (0.003)
β_C	0.036 (0.050)	0.090* (0.051)	0.041** (0.012)	0.078** (0.034)	0.006 (0.033)	0.081** (0.008)
ε	0.012** (0.002)	0.007** (0.002)	0.002* (0.001)	0.011** (0.001)	0.011** (0.001)	0.004** (0.001)
α	2.353** (0.070)	2.673** (0.089)	2.635** (0.067)	2.179** (0.050)	2.037** (0.060)	2.167** (0.036)

**Statistically significant at 5 percent level. *Statistically significant at 10 percent level. Standard errors are shown in parentheses.
Note: The three columns under each heading of "Border" and "Non-Border" refer to 1994, 2000, and 2005.

time. We construct our sample of interest by focusing on people between the ages of sixteen and sixty-five who were not currently enrolled in school. We also set a floor on the hourly wage equal to two pesos (currently less than $0.20). All salaries were converted to the year 2000 pesos to make comparisons possible without being contaminated by the inflation rate. Additional sample and coding details can be obtained from the author.

Table 5.3 reports the estimated parameters from equation (1). We performed a statistical test of pooling; the parameters between the regions (evaluated as a group) were statistically different for the three sample years (at a 5 percent significance level).

Earned Income along the U.S.-Mexico Border

Alberto Dávila, Marie T. Mora, and Alma D. Hales

Introduction

Earnings differentials between the border and interior regions of both the United States and Mexico have received an uneven degree of attention by existing literature. The most explored of these earnings gaps is that between paid employees along the U.S.-Mexico border and those in the U.S. interior. While this U.S. border-interior earnings gap has been partly attributed to the relatively low levels of human capital along the border region (e.g., Dávila and Mora 2000; Mora and Dávila 2006, as well as several of the contributions to this volume), some earlier research suggests that immigration serves to depress wages in the region because of an assumed abundance of Mexican labor (e.g., Sharp 1998).

The earnings gap between the self-employed along the U.S.-Mexico border and interior has also been recently investigated. The studies on this topic have found, for example, that workers have relatively high self-employment rates along the U.S.-Mexico border (Mora and Dávila 2006; Robles 2002; Flota and Mora 2001). Nevertheless, the average earnings differential between the border and U.S. interior is wider for Mexican immigrant entrepreneurs than for non-Hispanic whites (Mora and Dávila 2006). These analyses have suggested that the ethnic earnings disparity could reflect innate differences between the two populations with respect to the selection process into self-employment and reasons for locating in the border region. (More on-location decisions will be discussed in chapter 8 by Pia M. Orrenius, Madeline Zavodny, and Leslie Lukens.)

Much less is known about the respective earnings and self-employment differentials on the Mexican side of the border. Hector J. Villarreal in the previous chapter and Orrenius, Zavodny, and Lukens in chapter 8 discuss the higher wages in the northern Mexican border region relative to those in the Mexican interior. We complement their analyses by taking into account the human capital differences across the border-interior regions of *both* Mexico and the United States. In addition, to our knowledge, the border-interior earnings gap for the self-employed in Mexico has not been previously analyzed.

In this chapter, we use the Integrated Public Use Microdata Series (IPUMS)-International for both the United States and Mexico to study each one of these differentials. In so doing, we attempt to provide a "level playing field" to analyze these regional earnings differentials for the purpose of gaining insight into the labor-market dynamics of the border and interior regions in both countries. The IPUMS-International (described in more detail in the appendix chapter) is a rich dataset that allows us to identify the region of residence of workers in both Mexico and the United States.

Conceptualizing Border–Interior Wage Differentials

Before we proceed to the wage gaps between the border and interior regions in the United States and Mexico, it should be noted that, in theory, border-interior wage and salary gaps should disappear over the long run for several reasons. For one, labor from low-wage areas, in an effort to earn more, should migrate to regions with high wages. This prediction is consistent with the discussion in the previous chapter by Villarreal, who notes that in the 1990s and early 2000s, Mexican border states received more net migrants from the rest of Mexico. During this time, real salaries remained stable in the border states but had declined in the Mexican interior. This migratory process should then put downward pressure on the wages of workers in high-wage areas and the reverse would occur in those regions with low wages.

The second reason for regional wage conversion is that entrepreneurs and capital would find it more profitable to operate in regions with a relatively low cost of labor. Capital migration to the relatively low-wage areas would increase the demand for workers there at the expense of those in the high-wage region. Eventually, also, the goods in the low-wage region would be produced more cheaply than in the high-wage region, attracting more consumer demand in the former area at the expense of the latter. Recall from John Sargent, Melissa Najera, and Linda Matthews (chapter 4) that a combination of low-wage labor and the ability to circumvent managerial and operational challenges in other countries has encouraged many multinational companies to relocate to the Mexican border. These relocations have increased the demand for workers (therefore boosting employment) on the Mexican side of the border. In addition, this has led to higher employment on the U.S. side of the border, with the development of warehousing and service activities to aid in the distribution of goods produced within maquiladoras, as suggested by Thomas M. Fullerton Jr., James H. Holcomb, and Angel L. Molina Jr. (chapter 2).

This wage-conversion process, of course, requires perfect mobility of human and capital resources as well as perfect information about labor market opportunities. Arguably, not all workers operate in national labor markets. Labor mobility might be also constrained by the desire of some workers to reside in their native regions. In chapter 8, Orrenius, Zavodny, and Lukens investigate socioeconomic and demographic factors driving migrants to stay at the border. In general, these factors include preferences to stay close to a familiar culture and/or language, the lack of migrant networks, limited English-speaking ability, and limited U.S. work experience.

With regards to capital mobility, wage equality should be restored over time if workers have similar skills and are valued equally by entrepreneurs and capital owners. This assumption is problematic, as we have argued before (Mora and Dávila 2006), for border regions with expanding international trade, particularly when such trade gives rise to a comparative entrepreneurial advantage among a certain demographic group (such as Mexican immigrants on the U.S. side of the border) who might have greater insights into the language and culture in the region than U.S.-born workers. Also, the relative "quality" of labor along the border and interior regions of the United States and Mexico should be considered. If the average skills of border residents differ between the border and interior regions, workers should migrate to areas that provide the highest returns to their skills. Arguably, the U.S. border area has a higher skill shortage, given the relatively low education levels (e.g., recall the

Fullerton, Holcomb, and Molina chapter), and it should therefore attract higher-quality workers over time (e.g., Cragg and Epelbaum 1996).

Measures of Border–Interior Wage Differentials

As noted, we use decennial census data from 2000, available in the IPUMS-International. For the purposes of this chapter, we focus on civilians ages eighteen to sixty-four who report typically working a minimum of twenty hours per week. We identify the U.S.-Mexico border region as the U.S. public-use microdata areas (PUMAs) and the Mexican municipios, which are located along the international boundary. (The appendix to this volume provides more details.)

The top half of table 6.1 contains some basic average observable human-capital characteristics of paid-employment workers for the four regions in question: the U.S. interior, the U.S. side of the border, the Mexican side of the border, and the Mexican interior. With regards to age, note that paid employees in the two interior regions were slightly older than those who worked in the border regions. The relative youth implies less labor market experience, which could relate to relatively lower earnings along the border. However, the relative youth in border regions might also be attractive to firms seeking an ample source of labor, as suggested by Sargent, Najera, and Matthews in chapter 4.

There are, however, some border-interior differences between the two countries. The proportion of women along the Mexican side of the border (34 percent) slightly exceeded the proportion in this country's interior (32.7 percent). The opposite occurred in the United States, where women along the border represented 44.2 percent of workers, compared to nearly 47 percent in the interior. Women, however, had a higher representation in the U.S. labor force than women in Mexico in general. Rogelio Sáenz, Lorena Murga, and Maria Cristina Morales in the following chapter elaborate on reasons for these regional gender distributions (recall also Sargent, Najera and Matthews in chapter 4).

The importance of the maquiladora presence for Mexican employment in its northern border region can also be observed in table 6.1, where about half (51 percent) of the workers have manufacturing jobs, compared to 36 percent in Mexico's interior. The respective share on

TABLE 6.1 Characteristics of Workers in the United States and Mexico in 2000

Characteristic	Interior of Mexico	Mexican Side of Border	U.S. Side of Border	U.S. Interior
Paid Employees:				
Age (in years)	33.2	31.9	37.63	38.8
Not a high school graduate	66.9%	70.4%	17.0%	11.7%
High school graduate	15.1%	14.3%	22.0%	27.3%
College graduate	13.2%	9.6%	25.5%	28.1%
Female	32.7%	34.0%	44.2%	46.9%
Professional, managerial, executive occupation	13.1%	9.7%	29.4%	30.8%
Manufacturing occupation	36.0%	51.0%	23.8%	25.1%
Service occupation	14.0%	11.2%	15.3%	13.1%
Estimated population size	17,598,557	1,451,559	1,896,280	103,154,203
Self-employed:				
Age (in years)	39.5	39.5	43.8	44.0
Not a high school graduate	77.3%	69.3%	20.4%	11.3%
High school graduate	9.5%	12.0%	17.8%	26.1%
College graduate	10.1%	12.5%	31.1%	32.5%
Female	23.0%	21.2%	33.1%	31.4%
Professional, managerial, executive occupation	8.3%	11.9%	35.3%	38.3%
Manufacturing occupation	28.6%	37.4%	23.4%	24.9%
Service occupation	6.7%	8.5%	18.6%	15.3%
Estimated population size	5,934,331	276,135	205,101	10,313,258

Notes: Authors' estimates are from the IPUMS–International for Mexico and the United States in 2000. The samples include civilians aged 18–64 who usually work 20 or more hours per week, and who reported earned income. These figures employ the appropriated IPUMS-provided sampling weights.

the U.S. side of the border was smaller (at about 24 percent) and nearly equal to the 25 percent share of workers in the manufacturing sector in the U.S. interior.

To what extent are these differences in observable characteristics important in explaining regional earnings gaps? Consider the case of the well-researched U.S. border-interior earnings gap. Measuring earnings in terms of monthly earned income, as reported in column I in the top part of table 6.2, workers in the U.S. border region earned 13.7 percent less on average than workers in the rest of the United States. Differences in age, education, and gender between the two regions explain about 3.8 percentage points of this earnings gap, as seen in column II, and differences in regional occupational distributions account for another 0.4 percentage points, as seen in column III (for details on how these figures were estimated, see this chapter's appendix). These findings indicate that for every dollar earned in the U.S. border region, an otherwise similar worker in the U.S. interior earned an average of $1.095; this difference is statistically significant.

These results correspond with those found in extant literature: part of what appears to be regional wage differentials between the U.S. border and U.S. interior is explained by observed differences in socioeconomic and demographic characteristics. An additional part of the remaining earnings gap might be attributed to the relatively low cost of living in the U.S. border region (e.g., Dávila and Mattila 1985), as well as reflecting preferences, where workers might be willing to forgo higher wages elsewhere in exchange for residing in a given area due to its cultural and language characteristics (e.g., see the Orrenius, Zavodny, and Lukens chapter, as well as some of our previous work [e.g., Dávila and Mora 2000, 2008; Mora and Dávila 2006]).

Comparing Mexican with U.S. earnings, table 6.2 further indicates that even when controlling for observable characteristics and occupations (see column III), workers in Mexico had considerably lower wages than those in the United States. Compared with workers in the U.S. interior, workers on the Mexican side of the border earned 148 percent less, and those in the rest of Mexico earned 186 percent less. Moreover, despite being in the same geographic area separated only by the international boundary, workers on the Mexican side of the border earned *138 percent* less (147.6 – 9.5) on average than those on the U.S. side—a difference

TABLE 6.2 Earnings Differentials between the U.S.-Mexico Border and the U.S. Interior in 2000*

Region and Worker Classification	Earnings Gap (Without Controlling for Other Characteristics)	Earnings Gap (Regression Analysis Excluding Occupations)	Earnings Gap (Regression Analysis Including Occupations)
Relative to the U.S. Interior, Earnings of Paid Employees:			
In Interior of Mexico	−230.5%	−185.6%	−186.0%
On Mexican Side of Border	−189.6%	−144.8%	−147.6%
On U.S. Side of Border	−13.7%	−9.9%	−9.5%
Relative to the U.S. Interior, Earnings of the Self-employed:			
In Interior of Mexico	−355.5%	−216.0%	−184.9%
On Mexican Side of Border	−171.6%	−141.3%	−143.4%
On U.S. Side of Border	−11.5%	−7.5%	−7.1%

* See this chapter's appendix for the estimation details.

Notes: These figures indicate the earnings of workers in different regions relative to their counterparts in the U.S. interior. All of these estimates are statistically significant at the 1 percent level. These samples from the IPUMS-International include civilians aged 18–64 who usually work 20 or more hours per week and who reported earned income. These figures employ the appropriated IPUMS-provided sampling weights.

not explained by factors such as education, age, and occupation. This means that for every dollar earned by workers in the U.S.-border region, Mexican workers across the border earned the equivalent of $0.42 on average.

But what about the earnings gap between the northern Mexican border and the interior of Mexico? Without controlling for observable characteristics, the unadjusted border-interior earnings gap in Mexico stood at about 41 percent (= 230.5 − 189.6). This earnings gap remains virtually unchanged after accounting for age, education, and gender differentials between the two regions, and it declines slightly to 38.4

percent (= 186.0 − 147.6) after controlling for regional occupational differentials.

The fact that Mexican workers near the United States earned nearly 1.4 times more than otherwise similar workers in the rest of Mexico is tied to the underlying themes discussed throughout this book regarding employment, migration, and earnings. For example, recall from previous chapters that the maquiladora industry boom in northern Mexico increased the demand for workers relative to other areas, resulting in higher earnings in the Mexican border region relative to the rest of the country.

Over time, however, the relatively low wages in the Mexican interior should provide a significant incentive for Mexican labor to migrate to the northern border region of Mexico as well as to the United States, as noted by Villarreal in chapter 5, and to be discussed by Orrenius, Zavodny, and Lukens in chapter 8. Alternatively, these regional earnings differences might reflect differences in other characteristics (such as the quality of education) between workers in the northern Mexican border and those in the rest of Mexico (as the Villarreal chapter suggests), or to strong location preferences among Mexicans to live in non-border states. In either of the latter cases, this large earnings gap would not be as strong a catalyst for internal Mexican migration to the country's northern regions as expected.

Conceptualizing Border–Interior Self–Employment Earnings Differences

Do border-interior earnings gaps also occur in the self-employment sector? This question can be addressed using a "pull-push" framework, which considers whether workers who engage in entrepreneurial activities in a given region are attracted (pulled) to this sector because of potentially lucrative returns, or pushed into self-employment because of job scarcity. If pull factors are at work, we would expect entrepreneurial salaries to at least be equal to wages one would earn in the paid-employment sector. If the push factors dominate, self-employment earnings are likely to be below those observed in the wage and salary sector on the average, as workers most likely to be pushed into self-employment would be those who have the hardest time competing for jobs, such as those with relatively low skill levels.

Following this thread, Kenneth Clark and Stephen Drinkwater (1998) further argue that the selection process into self-employment has impacts on the average quality of entrepreneurs, hence their earnings vis-à-vis those in the paid-employment sector. For example, say there is a given distribution of entrepreneurial talent in the workforce, in which out of every ten individuals, one would be an excellent entrepreneur, two would be good entrepreneurs, four would be average entrepreneurs, and the rest would be bad entrepreneurs. Regions where more individuals are pushed into self-employment because of few paid-employment activities should have relatively more of the average-to-bad entrepreneurs, and thus a lower average quality and lower average earnings among the self-employed compared to workers in the wage and salary sector.

Using this logic, regional socioeconomic changes might also influence the self-employment income differences across geographic areas. For instance, recall from previous chapters that the maquiladora boom in the 1990s led to more paid-employment opportunities in the Mexican northern border region, which probably reduced the push tendencies into self-employment.[1] That is, the relative lack of paid-employment jobs in the rest of Mexico might be pushing more workers into self-employment than along the northern border states. Some evidence of this possibility, at least on the surface, can be found in the previous chapter by Villarreal as well as in our estimates based on the population sizes reported in table 6.1: self-employment rates are indeed lower along the Mexican northern border than in the rest of Mexico (16.3 percent for northern Mexican border states and 25.2 percent for the remainder of the country in 2000). We will discuss this issue in more detail below.

Measuring Border–Interior Self–Employment Earnings Gaps

Some basic human-capital characteristics of the self-employed can be seen in the bottom half of table 6.1 for the four regions discussed here. In the United States, the average age of the self-employed was about the same along the border and in the interior (about forty-four years). Compared to paid employees, the self-employed in the United States were approximately five years older in both regions, which probably reflects greater labor market experience often associated with business formation.

In the U.S. interior, however, the percentage of college graduates among the self-employed slightly exceeded those of the border region (32.5 percent versus 31.1 percent), and these percentages surpassed by about four to six percentage points the paid employees' comparable statistics. The self-employed also had a higher share of professional, managerial, and executive occupations in the U.S. interior (38.3 percent relative to 35.3 percent), but they had a lower share of service occupations (15.3 percent compared to 18.6 percent) than in the U.S. border region. Such occupational differences have implications for regional entrepreneurial earnings given that the service sector often pays less than the professional sector.

In Mexico, the self-employed had about the same average age in both regions (39.5 years), and the representation of women was about ten percentage points higher in paid-employment than in self-employment in both regions of the country. This corresponds to other work showing that women tend to be less likely to become self-employed than men. Also, the occupational distribution in the Mexican border region was particularly skewed towards manufacturing, as should be expected given this region's relatively strong industrial structure from the maquiladora industry.

Border-interior educational differences among the self-employed in Mexico are also apparent in table 6.1. The northern border region had a higher share of college graduates among this group (12.5 percent versus 10.1 percent). Also, college graduates represent a higher share of the self-employed than paid employees (by about three percentage points) in the border region, while the opposite pattern occurs in the Mexican interior. This observation is consistent with the border region providing "pull" opportunities into self-employment, while many workers in the Mexican interior might be pushed into self-employment because of the lack of labor market opportunities.

As noted above, these differences in observable characteristics between regions in both countries, as well as possible unobservable differences related to "push-pull" reasons for self-employment, could give rise to regional earnings gaps in the entrepreneurial sector. To address this issue, consider the border-interior self-employment earnings gap in the United States presented in the bottom part of table 6.2. Without adjusting for observable characteristics, the self-employed on the U.S. side of the border earned about 11.5 percent less than their counterparts in the rest of the United States. This earnings gap falls by four percentage points when accounting for education, age, and gender differences between the regions (column II), and it falls a bit more (to 7.1 percent) when occupational controls are used (column III). These findings are consistent with those reported by Chrystell Flota and Marie T. Mora (2001) and Mora and Alberto Dávila (2006) in that self-employment earnings in the U.S. border region are less than those in the U.S. interior.

Two observations about these results deserve more attention. First, the magnitude of the adjusted self-employment earnings gap is close to that for paid-employment workers. As such, this earnings gap might generally reflect a regional cost-of-living differential and other factors, such as residential preferences, as reported in other chapters in this volume. Second, given that the self-employment rate along the U.S.-Mexico border (9.8 percent, based on the population sizes from table 6.1) slightly exceeds that of the interior (9.1 percent), this earnings difference could also be capturing variations in unobservable characteristics between these two regions generated from the self-employment selection process discussed above. For example, the lower wages and the higher unemployment rates in the U.S. border region versus the nation as a whole could be related to a disproportionate pushing of workers into self-employment along the border.[2]

Turning to the self-employment earnings gap in Mexico—again, reported in table 6.2—the unadjusted measure in column I indicates that the self-employed in the interior of Mexico earned 183.9 percent less (= 355.5 − 171.6) than their northern-border counterparts. However, this difference shrinks to 74.7 percent after accounting for age, education, and gender (column II) and to 41.5 percent after further accounting for variations in occupational distributions (column III) in these two regions.

Unlike the comparable self-employment earnings gap for the United States, the magnitude of the border-interior gap in Mexico suggests that it cannot be reasonably explained by cost-of-living differences between the two regions in question. As reported in Villarreal, outside of the northern border area, self-employment in the informal sector is relatively widespread. One explanation for this earnings penalty's magnitude, then, could be that informal self-employment pays considerably less than self-employment pays in the formal sector, and these workers find it difficult to compete in the formal sector. Douglas Marcouiller, Veronica Ruiz de Castilla, and Christopher Woodruff (1997) report (with some caveats), however, that both of these sectors offer comparable earnings in Mexico. Recall also the 38 percent adjusted border-interior earnings differential among paid-employment workers in Mexico, which is a figure close to the one found here for the self-employed.

A Note on the "Quality" of the Self-Employed in Mexico

According to the conceptualization we presented above of the self-employment process, areas where individuals are pushed into self-employment might have entrepreneurs with lower average entrepreneurial talent, who would thus earn relatively less. Regions with lucrative business opportunities might pull talented individuals into self-employment, so that their entrepreneurial earnings would be relatively high.

In this section, we test for this quality proposition as an explanation for the large difference between the earnings of the self-employed in Mexico's northern border region and the earnings of those in the rest of Mexico. Specifically, we consider factors related to the likelihood that an individual is self-employed. For example, prior work has shown that socioeconomic and demographic characteristics such as education, work experience, being married, and being male tend to enhance self-employment propensities (e.g., Mora and Dávila 2006; Sanders and Nee 1996; Borjas and Bronars 1989). When controlling for these factors and re-examining self-employment earnings, our results indicate that Mexican workers in the interior appear to be pushed (i.e., negatively selected) into self-employment.[3] In contrast, we find evidence of attractive entrepreneurial activities in the Mexican northern border region by observing a positive selection (consistent with pull factors) among the self-employed. In a related study (see note 2), we also find evidence of pull factors among self-employed Mexican immigrants on the U.S. side of the border, suggesting that the border region in general provides entrepreneurial opportunities among Mexicans living on either side of the border.

It appears that the self-employed in the Mexican interior have fewer formal labor market opportunities, so that they become self-employed to avoid being unemployed. A disproportionate presence of low-skilled workers among the self-employed would be consistent with their relatively low average earnings. In the border region, however, the positive selection implies the presence of self-employment pull-factors among Mexican business owners. As such, the considerable self-employment earnings differential between the interior and border regions of Mexico seems to partly reflect underlying differences behind why individuals might become self-employed in the two regions.[4]

Concluding Remarks

This chapter provides an integrated approach to the study of border and interior earnings gaps in both Mexico and the United States. While much of the literature on border-interior wage differentials focuses on the United States, these differentials are vastly smaller than those observed in Mexico.

Focusing on Mexico, it appears that the northern border region has experienced a rapid increase in the demand for labor, as suggested by the increase in maquiladora activity following NAFTA, pushing up wages in that region relative to the rest of Mexico. If labor and capital face mobility barriers, this can prevent short-run wage convergence in the country. A related explanation for these large earnings gaps is that workers in the Mexican interior are relatively attached to this area, or perhaps they possess lower average unobservable characteristics related to reduced labor mobility and labor earnings. A policy that would promote labor and capital mobility might help promote wage conversion in Mexico if the former explanation holds; however, these types of policies would be ineffective, or indeed counterproductive, if the latter scenario occurs.

Beyond the wage and salary sector, the significantly large self-employment earnings gap between border and interior entrepreneurs in Mexico is also striking. We find evidence that the industrialized Mexican border region has created relatively profitable entrepreneurial opportunities in the area, while the comparative weakness of labor markets in Mexico's interior appears to be pushing individuals into self employment. The policy implications from these findings might well depend on the relative health of the labor markets in the interior of Mexico vis-à-vis its northern border region. If regional wage convergence in Mexico improves labor-market opportunities in the interior of Mexico, this, in turn, should help alleviate the "push" conditions into the informal sector in the region.

Chapter 6 Appendix: Details on the Empirical Results in Table 6.2

Table 6.2 provides three different estimates of earnings differentials between the U.S. interior and other regions. The first estimate represents the difference in the mean natural logarithm of monthly earned income (the sum of wages, salaries, and self-employment income, expressed in U.S. dollars) between workers in the different regions and those who work in the U.S. interior. T-tests indicate that all differentials are statistically significant at the 1 percent level.

The remaining two columns report the earnings differentials estimated using regression analysis based on a standard Mincer-type earnings function (see Mincer 1974 for more details). Specifically, using the method of ordinary least squares (OLS), we combine workers in the U.S. interior with those in a particular region (e.g., the Mexican interior) and thrice estimate (once for workers in the Mexican interior, another time for workers on the Mexican side of the border, and the last for workers on the U.S. side of the border):

(1) $\text{Ln(Income)} = (\text{Region})\beta + XB + e$

where Ln(Income) represents the natural logarithm of monthly earned income. The binary variable Region equals one for individuals residing in a particular region and equals zero for workers in the U.S. interior. The coefficient β reflects the estimated earnings differential between the given region and the U.S. interior.

The term X is a vector containing standard human capital and demographic characteristics generally used in earnings functions, including education, age, age squared, gender, a set of occupational categories, and a constant term. The vector B contains coefficients for the variables in X to be estimated, while e denotes the normally distributed error term.

We estimate two versions of equation (1), with and without the occupation controls. The earnings differentials in the last two columns of table 6.2 are based on the estimated β coefficients, all of which are statistically significant at the 1 percent level. The full set of regression results can be obtained from the authors.

7

Wage Determinants of Mexican Immigrant Women along the U.S.-Mexico Border

Rogelio Sáenz, Lorena Murga,
and Maria Cristina Morales

Introduction

In chapter 1 of this volume, Anthony Mora describes how the historical construction of the U.S.-Mexico border represents a heavily contested politicized region between border residents and federal governments. As his introductory chapter notes, the meanings of the border have shifted through time, with the pendulum swinging in favor of some groups of people and capital. Furthermore, the border is conceptualized differently across international settings. For instance, while border communities on the Mexican side are commonly among the most economically prosperous areas in Mexico, their counterparts on the U.S. side are among the ranks of the poorest places in the nation (see Anderson 2003; Fong 1998; Hansen 1981; Hardesty, Holmes, and Williams 1988; Mora and Dávila 2006; Sáenz and Ballejos 1993; see also Mora 2006).

Nonetheless, for Mexican immigrants, these communities represent the gateway into the United States. It is here where many immigrants locate employment, and for many others, the border is a stopover from which they launch their sights to interior regions of the country. Because of the proximity of maquiladoras and the border's expanding service sector (recall the Sargent, Matthews, and Najera chapter), Mexican immigrant women are especially attracted to the region (see Marquez and Padilla 2004). Indeed, women are increasingly represented among the flows of Mexican immigrants in general (Cerrutti and Massey 2004; Donato 1993; Donato and Patterson 2004; Donato and Tyree

1986; Hondagneu-Sotelo 1994, 2001; Lozano Ascencio 2002; Massey, Durand, and Malone 2002; Tyree and Donato 1985). Moreover, the analysis of survey data by Pia M. Orrenius, Madeline Zavodny, and Leslie Lukens in the next chapter shows that migrants to border cities are consistently more likely to be women. In addition, despite suggestions concerning the continuation of traditional sex roles among Mexican women and Mexican-origin women in the United States, they are increasingly working outside of the home (Driskell and Embry 2007; Greenlees and Sáenz 1999; Kanaiaupuni 2000; Morelos 2005; Parrado and Zenteno 2001; Tiano 1984; Vega Briones 2003); research also shows that married women, although not daughters, migrate to the United States for family-related reasons—as opposed to work (Cerrutti and Massey 2001).

An important aspect of the labor market experiences of Mexican immigrant women, especially along the border, concerns Mexican immigrant jobs (occupations that are disproportionately overrepresented by Mexican immigrant men and women). Roger Waldinger (1996:317) suggests that "the new immigrant phenomenon is largely the story of the ethnic niche" or occupations and industries saturated by members of the same ethnic/racial group. These jobs are partly attributed to the continuous use of migrants as sources of low-wage labor in the United States that has made ethnicity the crucial mechanism sorting groups of people into identifiable sets of jobs. It is precisely these jobs that lure Mexican immigrant women, particularly in the border region, but that also place great limitations on their upward mobility due to occupational segregation and gender inequality.

Unfortunately, relatively little research has examined the labor market outcomes of the most vulnerable segment of the Mexican immigrant population—immigrant women—working in the most economically vulnerable region of the United States (exceptions include Dávila and Mora 2000; Flota and Mora 2001; Hardesty, Holmes, and Williams 1988; Marquez and Padilla 2004; Pisani and Yoskowitz 2002). Illustrating the importance of region in shaping sociopolitical outcomes, recent research based on the U.S.-Mexico border has focused on how region intersects with race, class, and gender/sexuality. Pablo Vila (2000, 2003), for instance, describes a "regionalization of gender" in which region intervenes with social constructions of ethnicity and gender. Maria Cristina Morales and Cynthia Bejarano (2008), who coined the term "border sexual conquest," explain how the feminicides and other forms of sexual violence on the U.S.-Mexico border are partly attributed to the intersection of multiple oppressions (of gender, race, and class), along with the border's regional marginality at the global, national, and local levels. These studies suggest that region does more than provide context to societal behavior and ideology—it has a unique influence.

This chapter seeks to examine the influence of border residence and employment in immigrant niche occupations on the earnings of Mexican immigrant women in the four U.S. border states (Arizona, California, New Mexico, and Texas). As does the previous chapter by Alberto Dávila, Marie T. Mora, and Alma D. Hales, this chapter seeks to determine the extent to which workers pay a penalty for living along the border (on the U.S. side only in this chapter). However, it adds two features. First, this chapter focuses on Mexican immigrant women. Second, the analysis also examines the wage returns for doing work that is typically associated with Mexican immigrants. The examination of such structural economic factors on wage disparities will illuminate the influence of regionalism and help explain the low socioeconomic standing of this group.

Comments from the Literature

The understanding of the inequality that Mexican immigrant women experience is enhanced by viewing labor market institutions and processes as gendered and racialized (see Hondagneu-Sotelo and Cranford 1999; Pessar 1999). Historically in the United States, both paid and unpaid work have been divided along gender lines (Sayer, Cohen, and Casper 2005) with occupational sex segregation representing "one of the most enduring features of the U.S. labor market" (Reskin and Roos 1990:4). Even today, women's work remains devalued (Dill, Cannon, and Vanneman 1987; Reid 1998). In the case of Mexican-origin women, Chicana feminists have illustrated how this group occupies an especially vulnerable position, as they are subject to both sex and racial/ethnic discrimination (Moraga and Anzaldúa 1984; Segura and Pesquera 1999). Indeed, women of color are clustered in female-dominant jobs (e.g., service occupations) and paid lower wages compared to those of their white counterparts (Reid 1998). In the border region, labor markets have shifted from a prominence of employment in agricultural and goods-producing services to service-sector, sales-related, and information-oriented jobs, as discussed elsewhere in this volume (e.g., see the earlier chapter by Fullerton, Holcomb, and Molina, as well as the following chapter by Orrenius, Zavodny, and Lukens).

Yet, within the category of women of color, it is Mexican immigrant women who experience additional vulnerabilities in the U.S. job market. Mexican-born women face discrimination associated with their gender, their race/ethnicity, their immigration status, and, for many, their lack of naturalized citizenship and lack of English proficiency. Moreover, Mexican immigrant women tend to be disproportionately clustered in jobs and areas that are predominantly Mexican. Thus, inevitably, the participation of female Mexicans in the U.S. labor market is reduced to a notion of "cheap labor" (Fernández-Kelly 1983) providing a reserved work force (see Piore 1979; Rodriguez 2004) laboring in jobs such as domestic work, service occupations, and positions in maquiladoras (Fernández-Kelly 1983; González 2000; Pisani and Yoskowitz 2002).

The literature shows that the low wages of persons of Mexican origin, including immigrant women, is associated with low levels of human capital (e.g., education, skills, and experience) and characteristics associated with "otherness" (e.g., dark skin, accented English, limited English proficiency, immigration status, etc.) (Dávila, Bohara, and Sáenz 1993; Telles and Murguia 1990, 1992). Yet, of particular interest, there is a literature that goes beyond these individual-level explanations to focus on structural-level factors that affect the labor market outcomes for persons of color, including Mexican immigrant women. For example, in the following chapter of this book, Orrenius, Zavodny, and Lukens observe that "border migrants earn less on average because they are more likely to be female than migrants to the interior."

Border Location

As noted throughout this book, despite being among the fastest-growing places in the country, areas on the U.S. side of the border continue to be among the poorest (see also Sáenz and Ballejos 1993). Research comprehensively documenting the low wages on the U.S. side of the U.S.-Mexican border extends back to the work of Alberto Dávila and Peter Mattila (1985). Furthermore, reflecting the lack of opportunities in traditional labor markets, Mora and Dávila (2006) observe that Mexican immigrants living in metropolitan statistical areas (MSAs) along the U.S.-Mexico border tend to have greater levels of self-employment but lower earnings than their counterparts in MSAs in the interior (see also Flota and Mora 2001). Moreover, André Varella Mollick, in a later chapter (chapter 11), indicates that border counties, from the 1990s to 2005, have experienced generally higher unemployment rates compared to the rest of the nation.

For the most part, the little research that has examined the labor market experiences of Mexican immigrants on the U.S.-Mexico border has focused on Texas (Hardesty, Holmes, and Williams 1988; Marquez and Padilla 2004; Pisani and Yoskowitz 2002) or on MSAs (Dávila and Mora 2000; Flota and Mora 2001). In this respect, our analysis presented below, based on the earnings of Mexican immigrant women across the border and interior regions of the four states on the U.S.-Mexico border, contributes to the development of a broader portrait of their employment conditions, as does the work of Dávila, Mora, and Hales in chapter 6, which additionally examines border states on the Mexican side of the border.

Job Clustering

Aside from location, the types of jobs that minorities and immigrants hold also tends to affect their wages. In particular, people of color employed in minority-concentrated jobs continue to suffer wage and/or pay penalties (Catanzarite and Aguilera 2002; Kmec 2003). For instance, jobs identified as predominately Black and Hispanic pay less per hour compared to similar jobs that are identified as White (Kmec 2003). Indeed, as Lisa Catanzarite and Michael Bernabé Aguilera (2002:121) suggest, "pay penalties associated with Latino jobsite composition constitute a structural feature of employment with powerful consequences for individuals' pay."

Furthermore, social science research examining "brown-collar" jobs, which are identified as those in which Hispanic immigrant workers experience occupational segregation and earnings disparities (Catanzarite 2000), provide additional insights into the links between job clustering and earnings. Indeed, Catanzarite (2002:332) notes that workers in brown-collar occupations are "increasingly concentrated in low-paid fields" and that "occupational prospects are bleaker than in the past, and long-term earnings gains are likely to remain out of reach for both recent and earlier immigrant Latinos because pay levels appear to be exacerbated precisely by the employment of coethnic newcomers in brown-collar jobs."

The establishment of homogeneous ethnic workplaces, or work environments filled with members of the same ethnic group, has stimulated the development of theories, research, and terminology identifying the participation of ethnics in the labor market. For instance, social scientists have explored the participation of people of color in the labor market (see Bailey and Waldinger 1991; Bonacich 1976, 1987; Catanzarite 2000; Light et al. 1994; Valdez 2006), and more recently, a merging of the literature has explored the interaction of gender, ethnicity, niches, and labor market segregation (Schrover, van der Leun, and Quispel 2007). However, debates among social scientists researching ethnic enclaves and ethnic economies, for instance, have occurred within the literature. Our own analysis contributes to this discussion as it seeks to assess the relationship between women holding a Mexican immigrant job and wages. Particularly instructive will be the extent to which this relationship holds across border and interior regions in the United States.

Methods

Data for the analyses were obtained from the 2000 Five Percent Public Use Microdata Sample (PUMS); more information about PUMS data can be found in this volume's appendix. The sample used here includes 55,767 foreign-born Mexican women living in four southwestern states bordering Mexico who worked and had earnings in 1999. For comparative purposes, the analysis also examines 106,896 Mexican immigrant men. Note that our sample includes both full-time and part-time workers.

Our variable of interest is the logged form of the hourly wage (obtained by dividing the worker's annual earnings by the total number of hours worked during the year). The analysis includes two primary independent variables, along with a variety of other factors used as control variables (see this chapter's appendix for a list of the control variables). The first of the independent variables is border (versus interior) location. The border variable is a binary variable in which a value of "one" is assigned to persons who live in one of the eighty-four Public Use Microdata Areas (PUMAs) bordering Mexico, with everyone else receiving a value of "zero" (interior location). Given that Mexican immigrants tend to cluster in work designated as "Mexican immigrant jobs" (see Douglas and Sáenz 2008), the second independent binary variable represents a measure of the disproportionate concentration of Mexican immigrant workers in certain occupations. This sector of the economy tends to be harsh, low-paying, and does not offer benefits or internal ladders for advancement. We identify "Mexican immigrant jobs" as those in which Mexican immigrants are disproportionately represented relative to their presence in the overall workforce across the four states.[1] This procedure identifies twenty-five Mexican immigrant occupations among women and twenty-four such occupations among men. Half of employed Mexican immigrant women and men worked in this set of occupations in 2000. The list of occupations representing the Mexican immigrant jobs is presented in table 7.1.

We use regression analysis to examine how border residence and working in a Mexican immigrant job affects earnings.[2] The main analysis focuses on women, with the analysis based on men included when appropriate for comparison purposes. Furthermore, we conduct the analysis separately by location (state and border/interior) to obtain a more in-depth understanding of the relationship between the independent and dependent variables.

Results

We start our analysis with a descriptive overview of Mexican immigrant women in the labor market across the four border states. Overall, women represent a greater share of the Mexican immigrant workforce in the border area (37.9 percent) of the four-state region than they do in the interior (33.3 percent), as seen in figure 7.1. This is also the case in each of the states except Arizona. Yet women command the greatest representation in the Mexican immigrant workforce of the Texas border. For example, they account for 43 percent of Mexican immigrant workers in the region, a greater share than that of any of the other three states. In addition, women are 1.5 times more likely to be part of

TABLE 7.1 List of Occupations Comprising "Mexican Immigrant Jobs"

Code	Occupation

Mexican Immigrant Jobs Held by Both Men and Women

402	Cooks
403	Food Preparation Workers
413	Dining Room and Cafeteria Attendants, Bartender Helpers, and Miscellaneous Food-Preparation and Serving-Related Workers
414	Dishwashers
422	Janitors and Building Cleaners
605	Miscellaneous Agricultural Workers, Including Animal Breeders
775	Miscellaneous Assemblers and Fabricators
781	Butchers and Other Meat- Poultry- and Fish-Processing Workers
832	Sewing Machine Operators
896	Other Production Workers, Including Semiconductor Processors and Cooling and Freezing Workers

Mexican Immigrant Jobs Held by Women but not Men

423	Maids and Housekeeping Cleaners
460	Chefs and Head Cooks
561	Shipping, Receiving, and Traffic Clerks
604	Agriculture Products Graders and Sorters
770	First-Line Supervisors/Managers of Production and Operating Workers
772	Electrical, Electronics, and Electromechanical Assemblers
822	Other Metal Workers and Plastic Workers, Including Milling, Planing, and Machine-Tool Workers
830	Laundry and Dry-Cleaning Workers
831	Pressers, Textile Workers, Garment-Material Workers and Related Workers
835	Tailors, Dressmakers, and Sewers
874	Inspectors, Testers, Sorters, Samplers, and Weighers
880	Packing and Filing-Machine Operators and Tenders
961	Cleaners of Vehicles and Equipment
962	Hand Laborers and Freight, Stock, and Material Movers
964	Hand Packers and Packagers

Mexican Immigrant Jobs Held by Men but not Women

425	Miscellaneous Grounds Workers
622	Brickmasons, Blockmasons, and Stonemasons
623	Carpenters
624	Carpet, Floor, and Tile Installers and Finishers
626	Construction Laborers
633	Drywall Installers, Ceiling-Tile Installers and Finishers
642	Painters, Construction and Maintenance Workers
651	Roofers
814	Welding, Soldering, and Brazing Workers
881	Painting Workers
960	Industrial Truck and Tractor Operators
961	Cleaners of Vehicles and Equipment
964	Hand Packers and Packagers

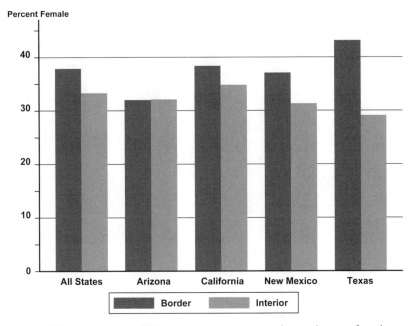

Percent Female

FIGURE 7.1 Percentage of Mexican immigrant workers who are female by geographic area. *Source:* Authors' estimates using 2000 PUMS data.

the Mexican immigrant workforce in the Texas border region than in the Texas interior.

Alongside their greater presence in U.S. border labor markets as compared with interior labor markets, female Mexican immigrants have lower earnings along the border. Indeed, Mexican immigrant women along the border of the four-state region had a median hourly wage of $7.06 in 1999, about 6 percent lower than the median hourly wage of their counterparts in the interior ($7.50) (see "All Workers" in figure 7.2). In addition, while this border-interior wage gap also exists in the case of Mexican immigrant men, the gap is somewhat smaller (3.3 percent). Furthermore, the gender gap (female/male) in earnings is slightly greater along the border (where immigrant women have median earnings that are 21.2 percent lower than those of men) than in the interior of the border states (where they are 18 percent lower).

Mexican immigrant women's wages vary not only by region but also by the type of job held. Regardless of location (border/interior)—or gender, for that matter—workers with a Mexican immigrant job earn less

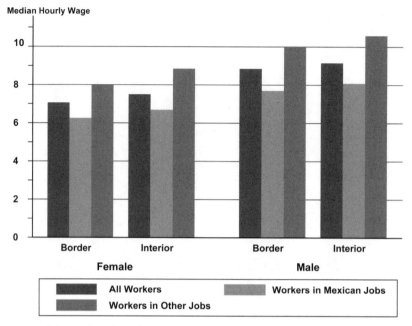

Median Hourly Wage

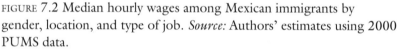

FIGURE 7.2 Median hourly wages among Mexican immigrants by gender, location, and type of job. *Source:* Authors' estimates using 2000 PUMS data.

than those who have other types of jobs (see figure 7.2). Still, however, the hourly wages of Mexican immigrant women are the absolute lowest ($6.25) if they live in the border area and they have a Mexican immigrant job. In contrast, wages are the highest among Mexican immigrant women who live in the interior and do not have a Mexican immigrant job. Similar trends exist in the case of Mexican immigrant men.

The descriptive analysis suggests that Mexican immigrant women pay a cost for living on the U.S. side of the border as well as for working in jobs where Mexican immigrants are clustered. However, to examine the relationship between location and type of job and hourly wages, we need to shift the analysis to a multivariate context in which important control variables are introduced.

The first part of table 7.2 shows the empirical results using the entire four-border-state region. In the case of Mexican immigrant women, the independent and control variables explain approximately 11 percent of the variance in the logged hourly wages. Moreover, the results confirm the patterns observed in the descriptive analysis. In particular, women living in the border area have hourly wages that are 8.3 percent lower than those of their counterparts living in the interior. In addition, women who hold Mexican immigrant jobs earn 14.4 percent less than women in other jobs. Note that similar results exist in the case of Mexican immigrant men.[3]

Further Explorations

To gain deeper insights into the dynamics of the relationship between border location, type of job, and hourly wages, we conduct two additional sets of analyses. First, we conduct the analysis separately for each of the four border states, as seen in the last four columns of table 7.2. The results suggest that while women working in Mexican immigrant jobs pay a penalty, the cost associated with living on the border only exists in New Mexico and Texas. Mexican women in the Texas border region have wages that are 16.1 percent lower than their counterparts in the interior of the state, while the border-interior wage differential is 12.8 percent in the case of women in New Mexico. Similar results also exist for Mexican immigrant men (results not shown to conserve space). While men who hold Mexican immigrant jobs have lower wages than those with other types of jobs across the four states, the border earnings penalty only exists for those living in New Mexico and Texas when controlling for other observable characteristics. Indeed, Mexican immigrant men along the Arizona-Mexico border earn significantly *higher* wages (8.7 percent higher) than their otherwise similar peers in the interior of the state.

Second, we examine the interaction between border location and holding a Mexican immigrant job to assess the variations in the strength of the association between such jobs and wages across the two geographic locations, as seen in table 7.2. The results reveal significant interaction effects in the case of Mexican immigrant women, but not for immigrant men. In particular, all else equal, those women who hold a Mexican immigrant job and live on the border receive an increase in wages of 4.9 percent compared to both (1) women holding these jobs in the interior, and (2) those in non-Mexican jobs along the border.[4] Nonetheless, this interaction effect is being driven almost exclusively in Texas. Indeed, as table 7.2 shows, the interaction effect is not statistically significant in

TABLE 7.2 The Effect of Border Residence and Holding a Mexican Immigrant Job on the Hourly Earnings of Mexican Immigrants in 2000

Characteristic	By Entire Region		By State (Females Only)			
	Female	Male	Arizona	California	New Mexico	Texas
Model A:						
Border Residence	-8.3%**	-8.5%**	1.4%	-1.9%	-12.8%**	-16.1%**
Holds a Mexican Immigrant Job	-14.4%**	-12.5%**	-14.2%**	-15.1%**	-14.4%**	-12.8%**
Model B:						
Border Residence	-10.5%**	-8.5%**	-1.1%	-3.3%*	-13.2%	-18.2%**
Holds a Mexican Immigrant Job	-15.6%**	-12.5%**	-18.4%	-15.5%***	-14.8%*	-14.2%**
Border Residence × Mexican Immigrant Job	4.9%**	-0.1	4.5%	3.2%	0.8%	4.5%#

** Statistically significant at 1 percent level. * Statistically significant at 5 percent level.

Statistically significant at 5.6 percent level.

Notes: The list of control variables for models A and B are included in the appendix to chapter 7; the difference between the two models is that model A does not include the interaction between border residence and holding a Mexican immigrant job, while model B does. The full set of regression results can be obtained from the authors. The analyses are based on 55,767 Mexican immigrant women and 106,896 Mexican immigrant men who lived in one of the four U.S. border states and who reported earnings. The adjusted R-squared values for model A are 0.107 for women and 0.128 for men.

Arizona, California, and New Mexico. In the case of Texas, the interaction effect is significant at the 5.6 percent level. Mexican women working in a Mexican immigrant job along the Texas-Mexico border have a 4.5 percent earnings advantage over other women in the same region and over those in the interior with similar jobs. Background analysis focusing on Mexican men, moreover, reveals that this interaction effect is also only significant for men in the case of Texas, but the association occurs in the opposite direction than that of women. Mexican-born men with Mexican immigrant jobs in the Texas border area have wages that are 3.8 percent lower than either men along the border with non-Mexican jobs or those with Mexican jobs in the interior of the state.

Thus, this exercise suggests that Mexican immigrant women living in the border region, especially in Texas, are not penalized as severely for working in jobs where Mexican immigrant women cluster as are those in the interior. This could be for two reasons. First, it could be that there is a strong demand for Mexican immigrant women workers along the border, especially because of the many maquiladoras in the region (recall the discussion by Sargent, Najera, and Matthews earlier in this volume). Despite being located on the Mexican side of the border, many U.S. residents work in the industry. Second, wages are uniformly low in the border region, resulting in the lack of an economic advantage for employment in occupations where Mexican immigrants are not clustered. The predicted logged hourly wages of the various categories of Mexican immigrant workers in the Texas border region based on the model containing the interaction effects give us some hint concerning why women are not as severely penalized along the border for working in jobs with a disproportionate share of Mexican women.

As seen in figure 7.3, the predicted logged hourly wages of women and men are the lowest among the two groups of workers in the border region, with those in Mexican immigrant jobs having the lowest wages. Moreover, consistent with the pattern associated with the findings from the interaction effect analysis, the logged hourly wages of Mexican immigrant women employed in Mexican immigrant jobs and living along the border are only 6.6 percent lower than those of women in other jobs. In contrast, this gap is larger in the interior among Mexican immigrant women (8.8 percent). Furthermore, the pattern is reversed in the case of Mexican immigrant men—the earnings disadvantage of men working in

Predicted Logged Hourly Wage

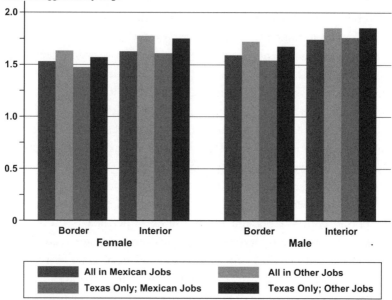

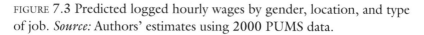

FIGURE 7.3 Predicted logged hourly wages by gender, location, and type of job. *Source:* Authors' estimates using 2000 PUMS data.

Mexican immigrant jobs is greater near the border (8.6 percent) than in the interior (5.4 percent).

Thus, we suggest that foreign-born women along the border, especially in Texas, are part of a homogeneous labor market with uniformly low wages regardless of the type of work. The disproportionate representation of Mexican immigrant women in the border labor force represents a large reserve army of workers who satisfy employers' demands for cheap labor. Of particular importance is that the positive interaction effect between border residence and holding a Mexican immigrant job only exists among women (in the entire border region and in Texas). This suggests that while the attainment of a job not typically associated with Mexican immigrants represents a stepping stone for upward mobility (in the form of wages) for Mexican immigrant men, this is not the case for women, as they do not gain as much economically from moving out of the Mexican immigrant niche.

Concluding Remarks

Although women have increased their presence in the Mexican immigrant workforce along the U.S.-Mexico border, relatively little research has specifically examined their labor market outcomes. The scant research examining the labor market conditions of Mexican immigrant women along the border has tended to focus on the Texas border or on a few selected larger metropolitan areas across the Southwest. This study serves to fill the gap in the literature by assessing the earnings of Mexican immigrant women across the four U.S. states located along the U.S.-Mexico border.

A major finding is that border residence has a negative effect on the wages of Mexican immigrant women—more than it does on men's wages. Especially disturbing is that it occurs in the border region where Mexican immigrant women represent a relatively large share of the Mexican immigrant workforce compared with the interior areas of the four states. As such, the disproportionate share of Mexican immigrant women in the region's labor force suggests that their large-scale presence (labor oversupply) represents a "buyer's market" for employers who rely on cheap Mexican female labor and have a ready and steady supply of easily disposable workers if workers make demands for better wages and work conditions. Furthermore, the results point to New Mexico and Texas as places where border women pay a cost for living in the border region.

A second major finding is the influence of occupations saturated by co-ethnic immigrants on the wages of Mexican immigrant women. We used the term "Mexican immigrant jobs" to describe occupations in which Mexican immigrant women (and men, for that matter) are over-represented. The examination of labor market outcomes of Mexican immigrants holding Mexican immigrant jobs is important given their reliance on ethnic- and/or immigrant-concentrated work environments (Sáenz, Morales, and Ayala 2004). The results of this analysis showed that there is a wage penalty associated with working in Mexican immigrant jobs for both Mexican immigrant women and men. Hence, as in the case of Catanzarite's (2000, 2002) research, we find that there is a pay penalty associated with brown-collar occupations (those that over-represent Hispanics), although our own research extends this observation to the case of women.

A third major finding concerns the interaction between border residence and Mexican immigrant jobs on wages among Mexican immigrant women. Specifically, the pay penalty associated with employment in Mexican immigrant jobs is not as severe in the border region as it is in the interior of the border states. However, the state-specific analysis shows that this finding is only present in Texas. This result suggests that regardless of their occupation, women living on the border, especially in Texas, are uniformly paid low wages. Thus, while Mexican immigrant men along the border achieve economic gains for leaving the immigrant niche, Mexican immigrant women do not reap as great a benefit from a similar shift in employment.

These findings have important policy implications related to the socioeconomic standing and labor market conditions of Mexican immigrant women in the border region. As Mexican immigrant women represent a larger share of the labor market of border areas in the Southwest than in the interior, they will need to be better incorporated into formulae for improving the social and economic standing of the communities where they toil. Given their marginalized position in the labor market, Mexican immigrant women have major needs related to education, health care, and childcare. Scholars, along with grassroots organizations, have certainly addressed the need for a critical examination of the experiences of women of color residing in the U.S.-Mexico border region. For example, Morales and Bejarano (2008)—as we note in the introduction of this chapter—point to the roots of structural sexual violence experienced by women living along the U.S.-Mexico border. Although their discussion largely focuses on the feminicides in Ciudad Juárez, they point to the direct effects of intersecting oppressions (e.g., of race, class, gender, and nativity) resulting from structural, economic, and political forces found in the border region.

While our analysis in this chapter focuses on the labor market outcomes of Mexican women along the U.S.-Mexico border, a growing literature addresses other social costs affecting these women. In particular, Gabriela F. Arredondo et al. (2003) challenge traditional hegemonic discourse in their discussion of the historical and contemporary social status of Latina and Chicana women. This literature points to the intersecting social factors affecting women of Mexican origin. Living on the fringes of the borderlands requires a re-centering of the voices of women of Mexican origin, along with the re-examination of the dominant (e.g., white, masculine, heterosexual) paradigms traditionally used in analyses of these women (Arredondo et al. 2003). Finally, there is a major need for the enforcement of basic human rights for this group of women, who represent the most vulnerable segment of one of the most imperiled work forces (Mexican immigrants) living in one of the most impoverished regions of the richest country in the world.

Chapter 7 Appendix: List of Control Variables Included in the Analysis

A) *Age*: Five binary variables consisting of (1) ages twenty-five to thirty-four, (2) ages thirty-five to forty-four, (3) ages forty-five to fifty-four, (4) ages fifty-five to sixty-four, and (5) age 65 and older. Persons from sixteen to twenty-four years of age represent the reference category.

B) *Education*: Three binary variables consisting of (1) some high school education (completed nine to eleven years of schooling), (2) high school graduates, and (3) post-high school education. Persons with eight or fewer years of schooling represent the reference category.

C) *Year of Immigration*: Three binary variables consisting of (1) immigrated before 1970, (2) immigrated between 1970 and 1979, and (3) immigrated between 1980 and 1989. Persons who immigrated between 1990 and 2000 represent the reference category.

D) *English Proficiency*: One binary variable for persons who speak English at home or who speak a non-English language at home but speak English "well" or "very well." Persons who speak English "not well" or not at all represent the reference category.

E) *Naturalized Citizen*: One binary variable for persons who are naturalized citizens; persons who are not naturalized citizens represent the reference category.

F) *Self-Employment*: One binary variable for persons who are self-employed; those who are not self-employed represent the reference category.

G) *Experience*: One interval-level variable based on Age – Years of Education – 6; this measure estimates the number of years of labor-force experience among workers.

H) *Experience Squared*: One interval-level variable representing the squared form of experience.

I) *Married*: One binary variable for persons who are currently married; those who are not represent the reference category.

J) *Presence and Age of Children*: Three binary variables consisting of (1) children ages newborn to five only present, (2) children ages six to seventeen only present, and (3) children ages newborn to five and ages six to seventeen present. Persons who do not have children in their home represent the reference category. Note that this information is only available for women.

K) *Nonmetropolitan Residence*: One binary variable for persons living in a PUMA that does not contain a metropolitan area; persons in PUMAs that are exclusively or partly metropolitan represent the reference category.

L) *State of Residence*: Three binary variables identifying Arizona residents, New Mexico residents, and Texas residents; persons living in California represent the reference category.

Differences between Mexican Migration to the U.S. Border and the Interior

EVIDENCE FROM MEXICAN SURVEY DATA[1]

Pia M. Orrenius, Madeline Zavodny, and Leslie Lukens

Introduction

While quite a bit is known about Mexican migration to the United States, most research has examined migrants' experiences in traditional gateway destinations. These include the states of California, Texas, and Illinois—specifically the Los Angeles, Chicago, and Houston metropolitan areas.[2] Much less is known about Mexicans who choose to migrate to the U.S. border. The research that has been done suggests that border migrants are quite different from interior migrants.[3] Alberto Dávila and Marie T. Mora (2000) use census data to compare the labor market characteristics of Mexicans across border and interior cities and find that they differ in many respects, including English fluency, education, occupational distribution, and earnings.

There are many reasons why border migration *should* be distinct. The border economy is unique, and there are not one but two dominant languages, a binational culture, and a large Hispanic labor force; in addition, the area is geographically accessible to Mexico. This accessibility is key—Mexicans with proof of employment and residence in Mexico have typically been able to apply to the U.S. State Department for a border-crossing card, which grants them permission to cross the border regularly and visit U.S. border cities for several days at a time.

This chapter uses a unique data set, the Mexican Migration Project (MMP), to study how border migrants differ from other Mexican migrants with respect to their sociodemographic characteristics and migration patterns. We also consider whether these differences can explain why migrants who work along the U.S. side of the border earn significantly lower wages than those in the U.S. interior and why, despite this, they remain there. The results are consistent with a scenario in which fewer migrant networks (family and friends with migration experience) and strong geographic preferences underlie border migrants' willingness to settle for lower wages close to Mexico rather than seeking higher wages in the U.S. interior.

The Border Economy: A Framework for Migration

Border economy characteristics help shape the region's labor demand and supply, which together hold important clues about what migrants to the region might look like. First of all, because of its location, the U.S. border likely attracts Mexican migrants who prefer to stay close to home, perhaps because they have family in the northern Mexican states or because they are unwilling to leave a relatively familiar cultural and language environment and risk venturing into the U.S. interior. They may also lack the funds to pay for a longer trip; it is easier and less costly to cross legally (or illegally) into the border region than to continue into the U.S. interior. The latter requires that legally admitted foreigners fill out additional immigration forms (specifically, USCIS Form I-94) and that illegal entrants circumvent Border Patrol checkpoints along all major roads and highways.[4]

Mexican migrants might also prefer border cities over interior destinations if they lack migrant networks, do not speak English, and have little U.S. work experience. They may be skilled in occupations that are disproportionately common on the border, such as service and sales occupations, or in skilled occupations for which native (U.S.-born) labor is scarce in the border region and hence wages are relatively high—such as professional jobs in architecture, engineering, technology, vocational teaching, and college professorship.

Moreover, because of the border's high concentration of Border Patrol and other immigration and customs officials, the region likely attracts migrants who can cross the border legally, such as those who have temporary visas, including tourist visas and border-crossing cards.[5] There are also likely spillover effects from the dynamics of labor supply on the Mexican side of the border. For example, by attracting workers to the border from other parts of Mexico, the maquiladora industry acts as an initial stage in the migration process that often leads to workers going to the United States (Kopinak 2005; Rivera-Batiz 1986).[6]

Historical Background

Mexico has a long history of migration, both internally and to the United States. The Bracero Program, investments in irrigation in the north, and later the establishment of the maquiladoras along the border spurred internal migration from the impoverished south to the more-developed north. Deportations from the United States, such as those of "Operation Wetback" during the 1950s, also boosted the population along the Mexican side of the border as workers opted to stay in the north instead of return to the south (Hewitt de Alcantara 1976; Lorey 1999). Internal migration continues in large numbers to this day, as discussed by Hector J. Villarreal in chapter 5.

Migration from Mexico to the United States has existed since the border was drawn. As discussed by Anthony P. Mora in chapter 1, hundreds of thousands of Mexicans migrated to the United States between 1900 and 1929. These immigrants lived primarily in the Southwest, although enclaves existed in Midwest manufacturing centers. The Bracero Program brought millions of temporary workers into the country from 1942 to 1965 and set the stage for later chain-migration from the main areas in which Bracero permits were allocated. These immigrants eventually settled across the United States in both agricultural and urban areas.

Key Determinants of Migration Patterns

Economic conditions in both the home and host regions drive changes in migration over time, so wages and employment are likely critical factors.[7] Gordon H. Hanson and Antonio Spilimbergo (1999) find that Border Patrol apprehensions, a measure against illegal immigration, are sensitive to both Mexican and U.S. wages. They find, for example, that a 10 percent decline in the real Mexican wage leads to a 7 to 9 percent increase in apprehensions, and the effect is very precisely estimated and conditional on the level of border enforcement. Using the MMP, Pia M. Orrenius and Madeline Zavodny (2005) find that Mexican agricultural production and the real interest rate can better explain migration patterns than can Mexican manufacturing wages, although U.S. wages do positively and significantly impact migration northward. To the extent that it is easier to cross into the border than into the U.S. interior, we expect border migration to be more sensitive than interior migration to economic conditions.

Migrant networks have long been identified as another key factor in Mexican migration decisions. Migrant networks are made up of family and friends with prior migration experience, including those living abroad, and they are a form of migration-related social capital. Networks can provide information on employment, housing, and border-crossing opportunities to potential migrants. In fact, because a group's migration experience can have such a large impact on individuals, sociologists sometimes refer to the "social process of migration" (Massey et al. 1987). In addition, as illegal border crossings have become more dangerous and expensive in recent years (Orrenius 2001), networks have become an important means by which migrants raise funds to pay their smugglers. Because it is easier for Mexicans both to enter U.S. border cities than interior cities and to obtain border housing and employment information, we expect networks to matter less for border migration than for interior migration.

Data and Methods

We use the Mexican Migration Project (MMP114) to investigate border migration and wages.[8] The MMP dataset, although not representative of all Mexican migrants to the United States, is one of the few sources on the characteristics and time-varying migration behavior of undocumented and return migrants from Mexico. We focus on first and last U.S. trips made by males and females ages twelve and older who migrated to the United States for purposes of work between 1980 and 2005 and were not missing data on key variables such as place of destination. Survey participants reported on many dimensions of their migration, including where they were in the United States and for how long, their occupation and wage, and their legal status. Household heads were also asked about their English fluency and their family's migration experience. Fourteen percent of all individuals surveyed had at least one qualifying trip, yielding a sample of 17,144 trips.

The majority of MMP migrants are from western states, including Jalisco, Guanajuato, Michoacán, Colima, and Aguascalientes, which make up a region which has traditionally contributed large numbers of migrants to the United States (e.g., North and Houston 1976). The other MMP states and their regional designations are Baja California Norte, Chihuahua, Nuevo León ("border" states);[9] Sinaloa, Durango, Nayarit, Zacatecas, and San Luis Potosí ("northern" states); and Oaxaca, Puebla, Guerrero, Hidalgo, Tlaxcala, Veracruz, and the state of México ("central" states).

To identify the U.S. border region, we follow the metropolitan statistical area (MSA) approach.[10] During our sample period, 7.4 percent of the trips made by Mexican migrants were to the U.S. border. The remainder were to the U.S. interior. Top destinations for migrants to the interior United States included Los Angeles (26.7 percent), Chicago (10.7 percent), Houston (4.5 percent), Dallas (4.1 percent), Orange County (3.6 percent), and Fresno (3.1 percent).

Our analysis of Mexican migration to a U.S. border destination is modeled using a simple ordinary least squares (OLS) regression, where migration is a function of migrant characteristics, economic conditions in Mexico and the United States, U.S. immigration policy, and time trends. Immigration policy variables include the number of temporary visas issued to Mexicans and the intensity of Border Patrol enforcement as measured by its hours spent patrolling the border (linewatch hours). The regression specification and the variables are described in more detail in this chapter's appendix.

Summary Statistics: Characteristics of Border Migrants

Mexican migrants to U.S. border cities differ significantly from Mexican migrants to other U.S. destinations during our sample period (see table 8.1). They have more years of education, are more likely to be female, and tend to come from slightly smaller families. They are less likely to report that they speak no English. These summary statistics (and those below) are consistent with the results of Dávila and Mora (2000), who also find that Mexicans on the border are more educated and have greater English fluency.

According to table 8.1, Mexican migrants on the border are much more likely to be from northern Mexico—with 53 percent from northern non-border states and 22 percent from border states—and from communities with less migration experience as evidenced by fewer migrant networks. This is consistent with the findings of Villarreal, the author of chapter 5 in this volume, who documents that the majority of Mexican migrants do not come from the northern *border* states. Migrants to the U.S. interior, meanwhile, tend to be from central and western Mexico and from communities with significantly more parent and sibling networks.[11]

Table 8.1 also shows that border migrants are significantly less likely to cross into the United States illegally and are more likely to have a history as domestic migrants, migrating within Mexico before deciding to work in the United States. Once in the United States, border migrants are much more likely to hold service and sales sector jobs. Migrants to the U.S. interior are much more likely to be employed as production and farm workers. Overall, during the sample period, border migrants earn $1.61 less per hour (in 2006 dollars) on average than those in the U.S. interior. This finding is consistent with Rogelio Sáenz, Lorena Murga, and Maria Cristina Morales, who in the previous chapter find that Mexican immigrant women along the border receive lower wages than their counterparts in the U.S. interior. There is a slightly higher concentration of professionals among border migrants as compared with interior migrants. An important subgroup among Mexican professionals on the border are factory owners, managers, and executives, many of whom are likely working in maquiladoras in Mexico while living on the U.S. side of the border (see chapter 10, by Mora and Dávila).[12]

The nature of the MMP allows for changes in migration patterns to be observed over time. To illustrate, figure 8.1 shows a rising share of trips to U.S. border cities vis-à-vis the U.S. interior between 1989 and 1997. The spike in border migration in 1995 is particularly striking. Dubbed the "Tequila Crisis," the 1995 downturn saw the value of the peso drop by 49 percent and Mexican gross domestic product (GDP) contract 7.1 percent. During this time, the border was an escape valve for

TABLE 8.1 Average Characteristics of Mexican Migrants
by Border Versus Non-Border Destination

	Trip Destination	
Characteristic	Border	Non-Border
Age (in years)	29.60	29.60
	(10.70)	(10.50)
Education (in years)	7.08**	6.61
	(3.53)	(3.56)
Female	0.21**	0.16
Married	0.76	0.75
Family Size	8.37*	8.60
	(3.81)	(3.78)
Originated in Central Mexico	0.05**	0.16
Originated in Western Mexico	0.20**	0.52
Originated in Northern Mexico	0.53**	0.29
Originated along U.S.-Mexico Border	0.22**	0.04
Number of U.S. Trips	3.42*	3.69
	(4.00)	(4.68)
Does not Speak English	0.29*	0.33
Illegal Crossing (without Documentation)	0.53**	0.63
Migrant Parent Network	0.18**	0.26
Migrant Sibling Network	0.39**	0.48
Domestic Migration	0.25**	0.22
On First U.S. Trip	0.36	0.37
Months of U.S. Experience	72.80	75.80
	(66.90)	(72.40)
Wage (in 2006 U.S. Dollars)	7.47**	9.08
	(4.59)	(5.86)
Professional Occupation in United States	0.04**	0.02
Agriculture Occupation in United States	0.14**	0.25
Skilled Production Occupation in United States	0.07**	0.15
Unskilled Production Occupation in United States	0.11**	0.25
Construction Occupation in United States	0.04**	0.07
Service Occupation in United States	0.35**	0.19
Sales Occupation in United States	0.20**	0.04
Other Occupation in United States	0.06**	0.03
Sample Size	1266.00	15878.00

** Statistically different between border and non-border migrants at 1 percent level.
* Statistically different between border and non-border migrants at 5 percent level.
+ Statistically different between border and non-border migrants at 10 percent level.
Notes: The first eight variables are reported at the time of the survey; the remaining refer to the first or last trip in question. These estimates are based on a sample size of 17,144, with the exception of the U.S. wage (based on 8,208 observations because of missing data) and English fluency (based on 5,854 observations, as it is only reported for household heads and applies to the last trip.)
Source: Authors' estimates using the Mexican Migration Project 114.

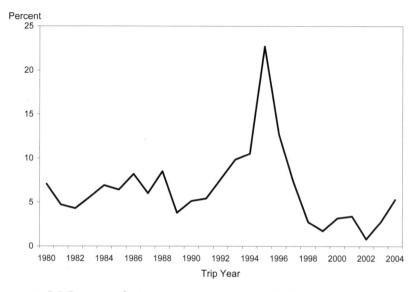

FIGURE 8.1 Percent of migrant workers going to U.S. border cities (three-year moving average). *Source:* Mexican Migration Project 114.

Mexicans hurt by the recession. Not as much can be made of the drop-off in border migration after 1997, since it is likely an artifact of the way the MMP data are collected; the sample sizes become smaller towards the end of the time period as communities fall out of the sampling frame. The decline is particularly severe among border migrants since they were a much smaller sample initially.

With respect to gender, female migrants made up a disproportionate share of migrants to U.S. border cities during the entire sample period (see figure 8.2). This likely stems from the border-related migration factors discussed above, including the nature of border labor markets (recall the previous chapter by Sáenz, Murga, and Morales). For example, maquiladoras have traditionally relied on a predominately female workforce and have acted as a magnet for such migrants from other parts of Mexico. (For related anecdotal evidence, see chapter 4 of this volume; Alberto Dávila, Marie T. Mora, and Alma D. Hales also note in chapter 6 that women are overrepresented along the Mexican side of the border relative to the Mexican interior.) Also, female migrants have always found plentiful work opportunities along the U.S. side of the border in domestic service and, more recently, in retail and hospitality-related

Percent

Trip Year

——Border City   —■—Non-Border City

FIGURE 8.2 Percent of migrant workers who are female (three-year moving average). *Source:* Mexican Migration Project 114.

industries. It may also be the case that female migrants prefer to remain close to their families and cultural roots—more than male migrants—and so they are reluctant to venture into the U.S. interior. Sáenz, Murga, and Morales in chapter 7 point out that Mexican immigrant women in the United States generally tend to cluster in jobs and areas that are predominately Mexican.

Regarding illegal migration, figure 8.3 indicates that the share of illegal entries into the United States has generally been lower among migrants to border cities than among migrants to the U.S. interior. The only exception to this pattern is the immediate aftermath of the 1986 amnesty (the Immigration Reform and Control Act), when the share of illegal immigration going to the U.S. interior hit a historic low. As the share of legal Mexican migrant workers going to U.S. border cities rose, the average real wages of migrants in the region also increased, as seen in figure 8.4. In fact, the average wages of border migrants reached the level of those earned by non-border migrants in 1999, at approximately $8.20 per hour (in 2006 dollars), and they remained above the non-border wages until 2002.[13]

Percent

FIGURE 8.3 Percent of migrant workers illegally entering the United States (three-year moving average). *Source:* Mexican Migration Project 114.

U.S. Dollars per Hour

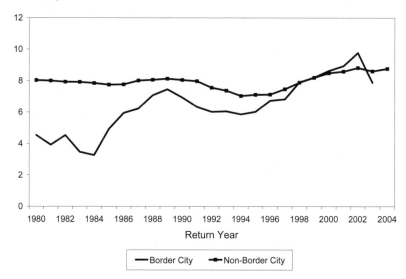

FIGURE 8.4 Average migrant worker wage (three-year moving average). *Source:* Mexican Migration Project 114.

Additional characteristics related to occupation (not shown here to conserve space) are consistent with the transformation of the border economy discussed above and elsewhere in this volume. For example, the percentage of migrants to U.S. border cities who worked in agriculture declined from 60 percent in 1980 to less than 10 percent in 2004. During the same time period, the share of border migrants working in sales occupations nearly tripled to reach 33 percent.

Results

Migrant Choice of Destination

Table 8.2 presents the results from estimating how observable characteristics affect the probability of migrating to a U.S. border city; details for this regression analysis can be found in the appendix to this chapter. Many of the differences between border and interior migrants discussed above are borne out by these results. Focusing on column I, it is apparent that border migrants are much more likely to be female and to first have migrated domestically (within Mexico) than other migrants. They also have significantly fewer migrant networks and are less likely to be on their first trip than are non-border migrants.

The picture that emerges is one in which border migrants come from communities with a shorter migration history and less migration overall than migrants to the U.S. interior. As a result, Mexican migrants to U.S. border cities appear to be less vested in U.S. migration and are likely to also try migrating within Mexico. Because their time is more divided between the United States and Mexico, the border migrants have made slightly fewer U.S. trips and have less U.S. experience than do migrants to the U.S. interior (as shown in table 8.1). In essence, border migration appears to be slightly less structural in nature, and perhaps more circular and less permanent, although average U.S. trip durations are not shorter among border migrants than among interior migrants.

These differences hold up across the various specifications in table 8.2 as we add more control variables for region of origin (column II), economic conditions (column III), and U.S. immigration policy (column IV—our preferred specification). The results from column II confirm that border migrants are much more likely than migrants to the U.S. interior to be from Mexican border states and from northern Mexican

TABLE 8.2 Mexican Migration to the U.S. Border (Dependent Variable = 1 if Migrated to the U.S. Border; = 0 Otherwise)

	(1)	(2)	(3)	(4)
Age	-0.0003	-0.0005	-0.0005	-0.0004
	(0.0004)	(0.0004)	(0.0004)	(0.0004)
Education	0.0013	0.0000	0.0002	0.0002
	(0.0009)	(0.0009)	(0.0009)	(0.0009)
Female	0.0283**	0.0305**	0.0304**	0.0306**
	(0.0086)	(0.0082)	(0.0081)	(0.0081)
Family Size	-0.0003	0.0013	0.0011	0.0009
	(0.0011)	(0.0011)	(0.0010)	(0.0010)
Illegal Crossing	-0.0280**	-0.0040	-0.0045	-0.0054
	(0.0081)	(0.0076)	(0.0074)	(0.0074)
Migrant Parent Network	-0.0559**	-0.0385*	-0.0323*	-0.0329*
	(0.0159)	(0.0155)	(0.0155)	(0.0155)
Migrant Sibling Network	-0.0233*	-0.0311**	-0.0321**	-0.0311**
	(0.0119)	(0.0121)	(0.0119)	(0.0119)
Domestic Migration	0.0165*	0.0125†	0.0133†	0.0131†
	(0.0077)	(0.0074)	(0.0074)	(0.0074)
First U.S. Trip	-0.0103	-0.0212**	-0.0189**	-0.0179*
	(0.0080)	(0.0072)	(0.0070)	(0.0070)
Time Trend		0.0053*	0.0529**	0.0147
		(0.0021)	(0.0087)	(0.0101)

	(1)	(2)	(3)
Time Trend Squared	-0.0002**	-0.0002	0.0010**
	(0.0001)	(0.0002)	(0.0003)
Central Mexican State Origin	-0.0095	-0.0114	-0.0128
	(0.0084)	(0.0089)	(0.0091)
Northern Mexican State Origin	0.0886**	0.0838**	0.0817**
	(0.0100)	(0.0092)	(0.0090)
Border Mexican State Origin	0.2877**	0.2827**	0.2803**
	(0.0245)	(0.0244)	(0.0244)
Ln Border Employment		-0.7596**	-1.0396**
		(0.2894)	(0.2651)
Ln U.S. Employment		-0.0249	1.4722**
		(0.4107)	(0.4857)
Ln Mexican Real GDP		-1.0693**	-0.4304**
		(0.1585)	(0.1533)
Ln Mexican Interest Rate		-0.0110	0.0454**
		(0.0076)	(0.0123)
Ln Visas Issued to Mexicans			0.0240†
			(0.0138)
Ln Linewatch Hours			-0.2662**
			(0.0445)

** Statistically significant at 1 percent level. * Statistically significant at 5 percent level. + Statistically significant at 10 percent level.

Notes: Standard errors in parentheses. Coefficients are from linear probability model regressions of border versus U.S. interior destinations (N=16,208). Female, legal status, domestic migration, first trip, and origin variables are all binary variables taking either the value 1 or 0. Economic variables are expressed in natural logs of their value. See the chapter 8 Appendix for more details.

states. Adding the region-of-origin control variables renders the coefficient on illegal status insignificantly different from zero. This suggests that migrants to the border are less likely to make illegal crossings, largely because of their northern Mexican origins. Residents of northern Mexico are more apt than are Mexicans in the center and south of the country to have border-crossing cards or other temporary visas, and hence they are more likely to cross the border legally. However, this does not mean that they have legal permission to work, which typically requires a work-based visa, a green card, or U.S. citizenship.

Economic conditions also influence border migration in much the same way as we predicted. The lone exception is border employment (defined as Bureau of Labor Statistics county-level household employment), which takes on the wrong sign (see columns III and IV in table 8.2). Clearly, one would expect border employment growth to attract, not repel, Mexican migrant workers. In our preferred specification (column IV), labor demand appears to be better captured by U.S. employment as a whole; that coefficient is strongly positive and suggests that a 10 percent increase in employment leads to a 15 percent increase in migration to border cities. It is possible that our measure of border employment has the wrong sign because it is picking up the effect of Mexican employment growth. The U.S. border economy is strongly influenced by Mexican conditions, suggesting high correlations between employment in U.S. border cities and employment on the Mexican side.

Other findings in column IV of table 8.2 further suggest that border migration is much more sensitive than migration to the U.S. interior to U.S. and Mexican economic conditions. In addition to the large coefficient on U.S. employment, there is also a very large significant effect of Mexican GDP and interest rates on border migration. According to the results, a 1 percent decline in Mexican GDP leads to a 0.4 percent rise in migration to the U.S. border region relative to the U.S. interior. A 10 percent rise in short-term interest rates leads similarly to a 0.4 percent rise in border migration vis-à-vis migration to the U.S. interior.

Column IV also shows that the immigration policy variables affect migration patterns as one would predict. Visa issuances are correlated with worker migration to the border—significantly more than with migration to the interior. This is despite the fact that these visas are overwhelmingly for tourists, not workers. While visas attract border migration, Border Patrol enforcement repels it. The coefficient on line-watch hours is large and negative, suggesting that a 10 percent increase in linewatch hours reduces border migration relative to interior migration by 2.7 percent. This result is consistent with studies that have documented a pronounced increase in border relative to interior enforcement during the sample period, particularly in the years following the passage of the Immigration and Reform Control Act (IRCA) (Dávila, Pagán, and Grau 1999).

Wages

As we saw above, border migrants are distinct in many ways, but it is unclear how these differences play out in terms of the rewards to migration—their wages. From table 8.1, we know that border migrants earn significantly less on average than migrants to the U.S. interior. (More generally, all workers—not just Mexican immigrants—tend to earn less along the border than in the interior, as shown by Dávila, Mora, and Hales in chapter 6.) What factors underlie this border-interior earnings differential? To address this question, we estimate simple wage regressions of real hourly wages (in natural logs) that migrants report earning in the United States. The regressions have many of the same covariates as in table 8.2. Table 8.3 contains the regression results, with column II adding control variables for region of origin and column III adding interactions of certain key variables with a border binary variable.[14]

Wages are substantially lower for border workers, older workers, females, and workers with illegal status. At first, there appears to be a border wage penalty of 16 to 20 percent, as seen in the negative and significant coefficient on the border destination variable in columns I and II. However, once interactions of border with other key variables are included in column III, the border wage penalty appears to be largely related to the nature of the border labor supply and border skill prices. Border migrants earn less on average because they are more likely to be female than migrants to the interior. Also, illegal immigrants on the border earn significantly less than those in the U.S. interior, presumably because they have to compete with a large binational pool of workers, many of whom have skills and backgrounds similar to those of the undocumented workers but can work legally in the United States.

TABLE 8.3 U.S. Wage Outcomes for Mexican Migrants
(Dependent Variable = Natural Logarithm of Real Hourly Wages)

	(1)	(2)	(3)
Border	−0.1952**	−0.1569**	−0.0326
	(0.0976)	(0.0340)	(0.0979)
Age	−0.0028**	−0.0027**	−0.0027**
	(0.0008)	(0.0008)	(0.0008)
Education	0.0113**	0.0116**	0.0112**
	(0.0025)	(0.0026)	(0.0027)
Female	−0.2581**	−0.2667**	−0.2513**
	(0.0230)	(0.0228)	(0.0232)
Illegal Crossing	−0.1390**	−0.1445**	−0.1322**
	(0.0186)	(0.0190)	(0.0194)
Migrant Parent Network	0.0513	0.0564	0.0586
	(0.0423)	(0.0439)	(0.0440)
Migrant Sibling Network	0.0518	0.0678†	0.0683†
	(0.0368)	(0.0362)	(0.0362)
US Experience	0.0011**	0.0011**	0.0011**
	(0.0001)	(0.0001)	(0.0001)
Central Mexican State		0.0199	0.0199
		(0.0272)	(0.0272)
Northern Mexican State		−0.1000**	−0.0985**
		(0.0190)	(0.0190)
Border Mexican State		−0.0640	−0.0756
		(0.0500)	(0.0529)
Education × Border			0.0080
			(0.0088)
Female × Border			−0.1598†
			(0.0945)
Illegal × Border			−0.1575*
			(0.0703)
U.S. Experience × Border			−0.0007
			(0.0005)

** Statistically significant at 1 percent level. * Statistically significant at 5 percent level.
+ Statistically significant at 10 percent level.
Notes: Standard errors are in parentheses. Coefficients are from regressions of real hourly wages on person and trip characteristics (N = 7,708).

Migrants with more years of education earn significantly more than other workers, although an additional year of education is only associated with a 1 percent rise in wages. Despite the fact that education is relatively scarce on the border, the interaction term between education and the border is not statistically significant, suggesting that returns to education are not higher on the border after all—at least not for Mexican migrants.

Female migrants earn 25 to 27 percent less than otherwise similar men, a gap that is substantially larger for females who work on the border. The coefficient on the interaction between female and border in column III suggests an additional 16 percent deficit for women who stay close to Mexico. Sáenz, Murga, and Morales in the previous chapter find a smaller border wage penalty for Mexican women, about 8.3 percent, but they limit their analysis to the four border states and only include Mexican workers who are living in the United States at the time their sample was surveyed. Some of the earnings differential is due to the type of jobs Mexican immigrant women tend to hold, particularly on the border, such as those of nannies, housekeepers, and retail workers. Dávila and Mora (2000) also note that occupational sorting of Mexican females along the border into the low-paying service sector has suppressed their earnings.

Illegal immigrants earn about 14 percent less than otherwise similar workers who crossed legally. This gap is over twice as large along the border, as indicated by the large negative coefficient on the interaction of illegal and border in column III. U.S. work experience is also an important determinant of wages, although the coefficient on the border interaction suggests that U.S. experience is less valued on the border than in the interior (it is not statistically significant, however).

Concluding Remarks

This study uses unique Mexican household survey data to look at how border migration differs from Mexican migration to the U.S. interior. The transformation of the U.S. border economy since the 1980s provides a fascinating backdrop to explore how border migration has changed over time and how it is different vis-à-vis migration to the U.S. interior. Some long-standing patterns of border migrants remained unchanged during this period while others underwent drastic changes. For example, border migrants are consistently more likely to be female, to have migrated within Mexico, and to lack migrant networks compared to Mexicans who migrated to the U.S. interior. Meanwhile, the occupational profile of border migrants has changed from predominately agricultural work to being largely made up of service-sector and sales-related work.

Border migration has remained highly sensitive to Mexican and U.S. business cycles, much more so than migration to the U.S. interior. And while the data suggest that raw border migrant wages caught up to other migrants' wages by the early 2000s, wage regressions indicate that border migrants who are female and/or undocumented continue to earn far less than migrants who choose to work in the U.S. interior. It is likely that access to fewer migrant networks and strong geographic preferences driven by a desire for proximity to Mexico outweigh the wage penalty in the minds of these migrants and help account for their settling along the border. Costs of living are also lower along the border, which further shrinks the real wage gap in relation to the interior.

Policy Implications

Understanding why Mexican (and other) immigrants choose a particular destination is clearly important, both to areas seeking to attract workers and to those anxious to avoid increases in government expenditures related to permanent influxes of less-educated migrants and their families. Immigrants typically have more children than natives, which can strain public school districts. Relatively low rates of private health insurance among Mexican immigrants can also drain public coffers via higher Medicaid or uncompensated care costs. Although this chapter does not directly examine government expenditures (for a discussion of such issues, see the following chapter by Catalina Amuedo-Dorantes and Cynthia Bansak), the findings here indicate that more Mexicans are likely to migrate to the interior as the number of Mexicans in the United States— and hence the size of networks—grows.

Border migration has many desirable attributes from a policymaker's perspective. It provides a disproportionate number of opportunities for women, particularly when the Mexican economy is doing poorly. It has historically been more temporary and less structural than migration to the interior, with many migrants maintaining permanent residences in Mexico while working in the United States. Border migration, in contrast to interior migration, has also been made up of predominately legal crossings. The post-9/11 increases in border security have disrupted some of these longstanding patterns of migration; more enforcement has endangered the sensitivity of border migration to changing economic conditions and its circular and more transitory nature. Long lines at crossing points, shorter authorized stays for border crossers, and more stringent rules on visa issuances have all made it more difficult for Mexicans to cross over into the U.S. side. More generally, increases in border security will reduce the likelihood that Mexican migrants go to the border. There will be fewer employment opportunities and slower economic growth. There may even be greater incentives to migrate to the interior under the more restrictive border regime, although that depends on whether interior enforcement measures also increase.

An interesting extension of our findings is to ask whether the border migration pattern discussed in this chapter is along the lines of what one would expect if a guest-worker program were implemented to allow for the legal, temporary migration of Mexican workers to the United States. Similar to border migration, guest-worker migration would be highly cyclical, largely temporary, and attractive to Mexican workers who desire short-term employment in the United States. Conditional on having an employment offer, guest workers would face much lower migration costs than illegal immigrants to the interior, much like many border migrants today. The result would be flexible migration and less public burden associated with permanent settlement, but also more female and less-educated migrants.

Chapter 8 Appendix:
Regression Model Details

In order to estimate the migration equation using regression analysis, we merge economic and immigration policy data with the MMP data on migration. Annual national and county-level total personal income (deflated using the U.S. CPI-W and expressed in 2006 dollars) are from the Bureau of Economic Analysis Regional Economic Information System (BEA REIS). National as well as county-level employment is based on the Bureau of Labor Statistics (BLS) household data. We use ninety-one-day yields on Mexican Treasury certificates from Banco de México for the nominal interest rate, which is a proxy for the cost of short-term debt, such as credit card rates. Real Mexican GDP (in millions of 1993 pesos) is from El Instituto Nacional de Estadística, Geografía e Informática (INEGI). We also include the total number of non-immigrant visas issued to Mexicans abroad to control for border accessibility; the visa data are from the U.S. Department of State Bureau of Consular Affairs. Border enforcement is measured by the annual total of Border Patrol linewatch hours from the Department of Homeland Security. Linewatch hours are a count of the time Border Patrol agents spend patrolling the border to apprehend and deter undocumented migrants (versus the time they spend doing paperwork or other tasks); they are a good measure of enforcement intensity and have been used in a number of studies (see Bean, Edmonston, and Passel 1990 for papers using enforcement statistics).

To explain border migration in a multivariate setting, we estimate the following linear probability model of trip i at time t:

(1) Border Destination$_{it}$ = $\alpha + \beta X_{it} + \gamma Z_i + \sigma \text{Econ}_t + \rho \text{Imm}_t + \tau T_t$
$+ e_{it}$

where the dependent variable, Border Destination, takes on the value of 1 if the migrant chooses a border destination and zero otherwise.[15] The covariates include both time-varying variables, X_{it}, and time-invariant variables, Z_i. Time-varying controls include a migrant's age in the year of the start of the trip, a binary variable equal to 1 for an illegal crossing (and zero for a legal crossing), a binary variable equal to 1 for it being a migrant's first trip (instead of last, since we examine both first and last trips), and a binary variable for domestic migration (equal to 1 in cases in which the person first migrated within Mexico). Migrant networks are also time-varying and measured by the share of households in the home community that have a household head with a parent or sibling who has migrated to the United States previously. Time-invariant covariates are measured at the time of survey and include the number of years of education, a female binary variable (equal to 1 if the migrant is female, zero for males), family size, and binary variables for three of the four places of origin (which we classify into west, north, central, and border states, as noted above).

TABLE 8.4 Economic and Immigration Policy Conditions,
Annual Means

Border:	
Border Employment	2013641.00
	(310238.10)
Border Income Per Capita (in 2006 dollars)	25641.58
	(1965.77)
U.S.:	
U.S. Employment	118357633.92
	(10327877.07)
U.S. Income Per Capita (in 2006 dollars)	29537.51
	(2671.62)
Mexico:	
Real Mexican GDP (in millions 1993 pesos)	1196225.00
	(185404.80)
Mexican short-term interest rate (nominal)	39.35
	(24.32)
U.S. Immigration Policy	
Border Patrol Linewatch Hours	3441048.00
	(2157916.00)
Visas Issued to Mexicans	57044.04
	(17651.30)

Notes: The sample period is from 1980–2004. The total sample size is 17,051. The border city totals reflect sum across all cities. Standard deviations are in parentheses. See the text for the data sources.

In addition, certain specifications include the economic control variables described above, including logged values of border employment, U.S. employment, real Mexican GDP, and Mexican short-term interest rates. Two controls for immigration policy (the log of the number of temporary visas issued to Mexicans and the log of Border Patrol linewatch hours) are also added to certain specifications. Means of the aggregate variables are reported in table 8.4. Lastly, a linear time trend and its square are included to control for the common trend in the aggregate variables, such as employment and GDP.

9

How Do Mexican Migrants Affect Public Coffers?

CHANGES IN THE UTILIZATION OF
AND CONTRIBUTION TO PUBLIC BENEFITS
IN U.S. BORDER STATES

Catalina Amuedo-Dorantes and Cynthia Bansak

Introduction

The rapid growth of the immigrant population in the United States has not only brought the topic of immigration reform to the spotlight, but it has also raised concerns that low-skilled immigrants might be a drain on public coffers (Smith and Edmonston 1997). Although undocumented migrants are not eligible for public assistance (other than emergency health care), a variety of studies show that immigrants became more likely to receive public assistance during recent decades than they were before (e.g., Blau 1984, Borjas and Hilton 1996). This finding has raised fears of the United States becoming a "welfare magnet" attracting immigrants wanting to receive public benefits (Bartel 1989; Buckley 1996; Borjas 1999; Dodson 2001).

Concern about immigrants' overuse of public services led, in fact, to the enactment of the Personal Responsibility and Work Opportunity Reconciliation Act (PRWORA) on August 22, 1996, limiting the extent to which immigrant households can receive public assistance. In particular, while the PRWORA gives states significant leeway in defining their eligibility rules, the act clearly specifies three key provisions that affect legal migrants' usage of public services. Most non-citizens arriving before August 22, 1996, are (1) to be excluded from supplemental security income (SSI), food stamps, and Medicaid within a year; (2) to be excluded from most types of public assistance during the first five years after arrival; and (3) subject to stricter eligibility requirements by an inclusion of their sponsors' assets within the immigrants' assets when applying for public aid during the first ten years in the United States. Perhaps owing to fear, stigma, or tougher eligibility rules, some studies have reported a lower rate of welfare participation in immigrant households after the PRWORA, i.e., the so-called "chilling effect" (Borjas 2001; Fix and Passel 1999).

Yet despite the concern by some about immigrants becoming a drain on public coffers, some researchers have argued that most immigrants come to the United States in search of employment, work, have taxes withheld from their paychecks, and—as a whole—do not seem to be responding to the availability of public services when deciding on their destination within the United States (Zavodny 1997, 1998; Kaushal 2005). This is particularly true of undocumented migrants, who despite paying taxes at a lower rate than their legal counterparts, have always been excluded from receiving most types of aid. In sum, to date, there has been little consensus on the "net effect" of undocumented immigration on public budgets.

In this chapter, we revisit this topic focusing on a sample of Mexican migrants who had visited a U.S. border state over the past twenty years. Mexican migrants tend to be overrepresented among lower-paid workers (Capps, Fix, Henderson, and Reardon-Anderson 2005) and comprise the largest share of recent, as well as undocumented, immigrants (Passel 2004, 2005, 2006). Furthermore, as noted in the previous two chapters by Pia M. Orrenius, Madeline Zavodny, and Leslie Lukens, as well as Rogelio Sáenz, Lorena Murga, and Maria Cristina Morales, recent migrants to the U.S. border region appear more likely to lack important networks, which can serve as safety nets, and earn significantly less than their counterparts in the interior of the United States, possibly raising their need for public assistance. Therefore, using data from the Mexican Migration Project (MMP114, as with the previous chapter by Orrenius, Zavodny, and Lukens), we first examine the determinants of Social Security and federal income tax payments by Mexican migrants in U.S. border states over the past two decades. We then look at usage of some public services, such as public schools, unemployment insurance (UI), food stamps, and doctor visits, over the same time span.

Specifically, we address the following questions: Have tax payment rates among immigrants in border states risen over the twenty-year period under consideration? Does the utilization of the aforementioned public benefits by Mexican immigrants vary according to the likelihood of paying taxes or legal status? And, if so, does it vary in a fashion that would contribute to the draining of public coffers? Finally, has there been a generalized drop in the utilization of public benefits after the passage of the 1996 welfare reform? We address these questions with the purpose of gaining a better understanding of the net effect of Mexican migration on government coffers. Given our distinction between legal and undocumented migrants' payment of taxes and usage of public services, our findings provide some insight into the potential impact of future amnesty and work programs on federal and border state budgets.

Data Description

We use data from the MMP114 to characterize the utilization of public benefits, payment of government taxes, demographic characteristics, job characteristics, and legal status of Mexican migrants upon their return to Mexico.[1] The MMP114 is particularly useful for the study at hand, as it contains information on three of the key variables in our analysis: immigrants' legal status as of their last U.S. entry, use of public services, and tax withholding during their last U.S. trip.[2]

Despite being unable to make inferences on the entire universe of Mexican migrants with U.S. experience, the MMP114 provides reasonable data on authorized and unauthorized Mexican migrants (Massey and Zenteno 2000; Munshi 2003).[3] For the purpose of this study, we use the information collected from approximately two thousand migrating household heads who report having resided in one of the four U.S. border states, were interviewed between 1982 and 2006, and had nonmissing information on our variables of interest.

Table 9.1 displays some of the personal and job-related characteristics of our sample overall and by legal status. More than 90 percent of the full sample was married and 94 percent of our sample was male. This finding is not surprising, given that our sample includes household heads who had migrated to a U.S. border state. On average, immigrants in the sample were thirty-nine years old when they last migrated to the United States, and they possessed limited human capital. Average educational attainment was six years of schooling, and only 33 percent of immigrants were fluent in the English language. Furthermore, only 43 percent of the immigrants in our sample were documented during their last U.S. trip.

TABLE 9.1 Average Characteristics of Mexican Migrants

Characteristics	All Migrants	Undocumented	Legal	Do Undocumented Differ from Legal Migrants?
Personal:				
Married	0.91	0.92	0.89	Yes*
Male	0.94	0.95	0.93	No
Age (in years)	39.05	37.24	41.46	Yes**
Years of Education	6.13	5.97	6.35	Yes*
Illegal	0.57	1.00	0.00	
Speaks English	0.33	0.23	0.46	Yes**
Job Related:				
Working	0.93	0.94	0.91	Yes**
Professional	0.01	0.00	0.02	Yes*
Technical	0.00	0.00	0.00	No
Agricultural	0.25	0.22	0.29	Yes**
Manufacturing	0.48	0.51	0.45	Yes*
Services	0.26	0.27	0.24	No
Duration of Last Trip (in months)	23.25	21.66	25.38	Yes*
Number of Observations	2219	1267	952	

** Undocumented migrants are statistically different from legal migrants at 1 percent level, according to t-tests.
* Undocumented migrants are statistically different from legal migrants at 5 percent level, according to t-tests.
Note: The remaining differences are not statistically significant at the 10 percent level.

Regarding job-related characteristics, the vast majority of our sample (93 percent) worked while in the United States. In terms of specialty, about one-fourth worked in agriculture, 48 percent in manufacturing, and another one-fourth worked in services occupations. Very few worked in technical or professional jobs and the average length of their stay in the United States was close to two years.[4]

Legal versus Undocumented Mexican Migrants

Table 9.1 also compares the characteristics of Mexican immigrants in U.S. border states by legal status. There are sizable differences between immigrants with a legal status and those without. Therefore, it is important for policymakers to note that the characteristics and behavior of these two groups should be assessed separately—and that is how we proceed in our analysis in this book chapter.

In terms of personal characteristics, undocumented migrants in U.S. border states are more likely to be married than those who legally migrated. Furthermore, compared to their legal counterparts, undocumented migrants tend to be younger, usually have fewer years of schooling, and are considerably less likely to be able to speak English. Job characteristics also vary for these two groups. Undocumented immigrants were more likely to have a job, despite the slightly shorter duration of their trips relative to those of the legal group. By industry, the undocumented group was more likely to be concentrated in manufacturing and services jobs, while legal migrants were more likely to be working in agriculture.

Preliminary Statistics on Mexican Immigrants' Usage of Public Services

Despite numerous claims in the media that immigrants do not significantly contribute to public coffers, the data suggest otherwise. The majority of Mexican migrants in border states have both Social Security and federal taxes withheld from their paychecks, regardless of legal status. As shown in the last column of table 9.2, about 55 percent of undocumented migrants had taxes withheld and more than 80 percent of legal migrants directly paid federal taxes. Furthermore, usage of public services among Mexican immigrants between 1986 and 2006 appeared relatively low, particularly among undocumented immigrants. Over that time span, only 9 percent of undocumented migrants had children in public schools, 4 percent received welfare or food stamps, and only 2 percent received unemployment insurance.

Legal migrants were more likely to have children in public school (26 percent), receive unemployment insurance (24 percent), and receive welfare or food stamps (7 percent and 9 percent, respectively) than their undocumented counterparts. Therefore, while undocumented immigrants were less likely to pay taxes, they were also significantly less likely to use public services. This low usage rate may be attributed to the fact that undocumented immigrants were not eligible for many services (Kaestner and Kaushal 2005). Additionally, they may have been unwilling to come "out of the shadows" to attempt to utilize public services. Finally, it is possible for these figures of migrants' utilization of public services to be driven by changes in eligibility rules across states or by the familiarity of undocumented migrants with such rules. Therefore, in what follows, we will account for migrants' specific state of residence as well as for the time spent in the United States during their last trip.

Within the various types of public services being examined, medical services are of special interest. After all, usage of health care by undocumented immigrants and the rapid increase of health care costs have been topics of heated debate, as it is often believed that taxpayers bear the burden of these expenses for low-income individuals (U.S.-Mexico Border Counties Coalition 2006).[5]

Table 9.2 suggests that less than a third of our undocumented sample visited a doctor or hospital while in the United States, compared to half of legal migrants. Furthermore, most health expenses incurred by migrants (regardless of legal status) are not covered by the government through public health insurance or other programs. For the undocumented group, almost half reported having paid for health care themselves and almost 20 percent were covered by their employer. Private insurance paid for 3 percent of our respondents who had medical expenses, and 24 percent were covered by public insurance or other forms of payment. For the legal group, 60 percent covered their own medical costs, 11 percent were paid by their employer, 5 percent had private insurance, and 16 percent were covered by public insurance or other programs.

TABLE 9.2 Usage by Year of Entry and Legal Status

Characteristics	1986–1990	1991–1995	1996–2000	2001–2006	Average
Undocumented Migrants					
Social Security Taxes Withheld	0.57	0.51	0.54	0.47	0.55
Federal Taxes Withheld	0.53	0.49	0.53	0.45	0.52
Children in Public Schools	0.12	0.09	0.05	0.00	0.09
Received Unemployment Insurance	0.03	0.03	0.01	0.00	0.02
Received Food Stamps	0.06	0.04	0.03	0.04	0.05
Received Welfare	0.04	0.04	0.04	0.04	0.04
Visited a Doctor	0.37	0.27	0.18	0.30	0.30
Visited a Hospital	0.29	0.23	0.18	0.19	0.25
Means of Health Care Payment:					
Self	0.47	0.45	0.40	0.42	0.45
Employer	0.14	0.22	0.17	0.16	0.17
Private Insurance	0.03	0.03	0.02	0.16	0.03
Public Insurance	0.08	0.09	0.21	0.05	0.10
Other	0.17	0.12	0.08	0.11	0.14
Number of Observations	574	356	223	49	1202

Legal Migrants

Social Security Taxes Withheld	0.85	0.80	0.73	0.65	0.81
Federal Taxes Withheld	0.83	0.76	0.70	0.70	0.79
Children in Public Schools	0.33	0.20	0.17	0.05	0.26
Received Unemployment Insurance	0.28	0.28	0.07	0.00	0.24
Received Food Stamps	0.14	0.06	0.05	0.09	0.09
Received Welfare	0.08	0.06	0.08	0.05	0.07
Visited a Doctor	0.64	0.53	0.27	0.23	0.54
Visited a Hospital	0.54	0.45	0.31	0.30	0.47
Means of Health Care Payment:					
Self	0.64	0.64	0.27	0.22	0.60
Employer	0.10	0.11	0.10	0.33	0.11
Private Insurance	0.03	0.03	0.31	0.11	0.05
Public Insurance	0.05	0.02	0.22	0.11	0.06
Other	0.12	0.10	0.04	0.00	0.10
Number of Observations	421	300	127	23	871

By Time Period

We also show time trends in the usage of public services and payment of taxes by Mexican migrants in U.S. border states over the period from 1986 to 2006 in table 9.2. We aim to address the following two questions: (1) Have tax payment rates among immigrants risen over the 20 year period under consideration? and (2) Has there been a generalized drop in the utilization of public benefits after the passage of the 1996 welfare reform?

To begin, usage of public services by undocumented immigrants in U.S. border states fell over this time period. For example, the share with children in public schools fell from 12 percent in the earliest period (1986–1990) to zero percent in the most recent period (2001–2006). Meanwhile, the share receiving unemployment insurance fell from 3 percent to zero percent, and the share receiving food stamps fell from 6 percent to 2 percent. Although it appears that the decline began before the welfare reform legislation (PRWORA) passed in 1996, the decline continued at a similar or faster rate after 1995. Given that the PRWORA only continued to prohibit illegal immigrants from receiving most types of aid, it is not clear whether this trend is a result of the spillover effects of the more stringent legislation, an increased fear of deportation, or confusion created by the PRWORA. Alternatively, it is possible that changes in demographic characteristics of migrating Mexicans over the time period under consideration may be driving the observed decline in their usage of public services. Regression analysis will help us gauge this possibility.

What about legal migrants? We see a similar pattern of declines in their usage of public services over this period, which suggests that concerns over eligibility or the fear and stigma associated with the PRWORA may have had a "chilling effect," causing immigrants who were eligible for the services to not seek them (Fix and Passel 1999). Indeed, the share with children in public schools fell dramatically from 33 percent to 5 percent. In addition to the restrictions imposed by the PRWORA on the receipt of public assistance by legal immigrants entering the United States after August 22, 1996, the observed pattern may also reflect the change in demographics and reasons for migrating of recent legal migrants (Jasso, Rosenzweig, and Smith 2000). It is possible that recent migrants are more likely to be younger or have left more of their family members back in Mexico. The share receiving unemployment insurance also fell significantly—dropping from 28 percent to essentially zero in the most recent period. Again, this may be indicative of the characteristics of more recent migrants in addition to the effects of the PRWORA. Lastly, the share receiving food stamps declined over this period, as did the share receiving welfare.

We observe a similar pattern with regards to the usage of doctor services or hospital visits in border states. For both groups (undocumented and documented), we see a sizable decline, on net, over this twenty-year period. While the share receiving such services in the United States declined over this period, we do find an increase in the share relying on public health insurance conditional upon the receipt of health care up to the year 2000. The increase may be due to the outreach efforts and public health care expansions made by some states during this period (Kaushal 2005).

Lastly, table 9.2 also presents time trends in the payment of taxes for Social Security and to the federal government. For undocumented migrants, the share paying Social Security taxes held steady at about 50 percent over the period, while the share having federal taxes withheld also remained virtually unchanged. For legal migrants, there was a slight decline over this period. The percent with Social Security taxes withheld fell from 85 to 65 percent and the proportion with federal taxes withheld fell from 83 to 70 percent. Once more, this trend may be reflecting changing demographics and employment patterns over the time period under consideration. To address this possibility, we proceed to the estimation of simple multivariate probabilistic models.

Mexican Immigrants' Likelihood of Paying Taxes

Which migrants are more likely to pay taxes? Have immigrants in U.S. border states become more or less likely to contribute to public coffers over time? And, in particular, are undocumented migrants more likely to take advantage of the fiscal system by avoiding paying taxes? Table 9.3 addresses these questions with the results (specifically, the marginal effects) from estimating simple probit models of the likelihood of paying Social Security taxes, federal taxes, or any taxes.[6] Given the gender composition of our sample and the prominence of the male household

TABLE 9.3 Regression Results (Marginal Effects) for the Likelihood of Paying Taxes

Independent Variables	Paid Social Security Taxes	Paid Federal Taxes	Paid Any Taxes
Illegal	−0.247***	−0.252***	−0.239***
Trend	−0.002	−0.001	−0.003
Married	−0.076	−0.098*	−0.070
Male	0.281***	0.294***	0.269***
Age	−0.001	−0.001	−0.001
Years of Education	0.000	0.000	0.000
Speak English	0.062***	0.051***	0.066***
Time in U.S. Last Trip	0.002***	0.002***	0.002***
Number of Observations	2009	2009	2009

*** Statistically significant at 1 percent level. ** Statistically significant at 5 percent level. * Statistically significant at 10 percent level.

Notes: All regressions include a constant term, occupation binary variables, and binary variables corresponding to the various border states where migrants resided. The estimated coefficients, standard errors, and other empirical details can be obtained from the authors.

head as principal breadwinner in Mexican families, it is not surprising to find men as more likely to pay taxes than their female counterparts.

Perhaps more crucial to our study is the fact that undocumented Mexican migrants in border states are twenty-five percentage points less likely to pay Social Security and/or federal taxes than their legal counterparts when controlling for other observable characteristics. This finding supports the often common public perception of undocumented migrants taking advantage of the fiscal system, as this result is conditional on the migrant being at work. What are other traits of tax-paying migrants? In addition to being male and legal, tax-paying migrants are more likely to be fluent English speakers, possibly a by-product of their longer U.S. stays. Finally, the time trend suggests that their contribution to public coffers did not change significantly over time.

Usage of Public Services by Mexican Immigrants

Did Mexican migrants, nonetheless, become less likely to use public services in border states post-welfare reform? Has there been a drop in the utilization of public benefits after the passage of the 1996 welfare reform? And, in general, how has the utilization of public benefits changed according to immigrants' legal status and likelihood of paying taxes? The figures in table 9.4 address these questions with the results from various probit models examining the likelihood, among Mexican migrants, of using a variety of public services, such as public schools, unemployment insurance, food stamps, and medical services.

There are some common determinants of the usage of all these public services worth discussing. In particular, despite being less likely to pay taxes, undocumented migrants are also eleven percentage points less likely to use public schools, sixteen percentage points less likely to receive unemployment insurance, three percentage points less likely to get food stamps, and twenty-one percentage points less likely to visit a doctor.[7] In fact, Mexican migrants in general became significantly less likely to make use of most of these public services post–welfare reform, regardless of their legal status at last entry.

As such, the passage of welfare reform in 1996 appears to have been accompanied by a sort of "chilling effect" that does not seem to have been generally driven by a significant reduction in the usage rate of public services by undocumented migrants; in fact, usage of unemployment insurance as well as doctor/hospital visits increased for undocumented migrants after 1996. The reduction in the use of public services primarily among legal migrants is not surprising, as they were the ones whose eligibility rules for public services were effectively changed by the PRWORA. In fact, in all instances, perhaps contrary to the general public perception, tax-paying Mexican migrants and those fluent in English (possibly due to their longer time in the United States) are the ones who consistently appear more likely to make use of public schools, unemployment insurance, food stamps, and medical services in U.S. border states.

The figures in table 9.4 also underscore other demographic determinants of public benefit usage of the aforementioned services. For instance, public schools are, not surprisingly, more likely to be used by older, married, female Mexican migrants, who are perhaps more likely to have a larger number of children than younger, single, and male migrants. Likewise, less-educated migrants are more likely to receive unemployment insurance (perhaps due to their greater intermittency in the labor market) and, along with married migrants, more likely to use medical services in the United States. Lastly, married Mexican migrants are four percentage points more likely to receive food stamps than their nonmarried counterparts, other things the same.

TABLE 9.4 Regression Results (Marginal Effects) for the Likelihood of Receiving Services

Independent Variables	Children in School	Unemployment Insurance	Food Stamps	Visited a Doctor	Receiving Public Health Insurance Coverage (If Visited a Doctor/Hospital)
Paid Taxes	0.078***	0.043***	0.023*	0.162***	0.019
Illegal	-0.107***	-0.158***	-0.033***	-0.212***	0.024
Post 1996	-0.052*	-0.064***	-0.024	-0.260***	0.270***
Post 1996* Illegal	0.015	0.099**	0.030	0.181***	-0.040**
Married	0.068***	-0.021	0.036*	0.088	0.016
Male	-0.235***	-0.038	-0.029	-0.296***	0.019
Age	0.004***	0.000	0.000	-0.001	-0.001*
Years of Education	-0.003	-0.005***	0.002	-0.008**	0.000
Speak English	0.110***	0.043***	0.029***	0.174***	-0.041***
Time in U.S. Last Trip	0.001***	0.000	0.000***	0.002***	0.001***
Number of Observations	1973	1982	1970	1977	946

*** Statistically significant at 1 percent level. ** Statistically significant at 5 percent level.

* Statistically significant at 10 percent level.

Notes: All regressions include a constant term, occupation binary variables, and binary variables corresponding to the various border states where migrants resided. The estimated coefficients, standard errors, and other empirical details can be obtained from the authors.

Differences in Trends by Legal Status

We also considered the possibility that trends in the payment of taxes and in the usage of public services in border states vary by legal status. As suggested by the figures in table 9.3, tax payment rates do not appear to have significantly changed over time for either legal or undocumented migrants.[8] Yet usage rates fell for legal and undocumented migrants after the passage of the 1996 PRWORA. As shown in table 9.4 through the coefficient on the interaction term of *Post 1996* and *Illegal*, in only two instances did we find a significant difference in the usage of public services by legal status, i.e., a higher rate of unemployment insurance and doctor/hospital visits by undocumented migrants after 1996.

What may be driving this trend in doctor/hospital visits? To answer this question, table 9.4 also displays the results from a simple multivariate probability model of the likelihood of receiving public health insurance coverage for medical services.[9] It is interesting to note that, in addition to married, female, more educated, and tax-paying migrants, undocumented migrants in border states were, indeed, about eight percentage points more likely to have their medical services covered by public health insurance once they sought care. If undocumented migrants are more reticent to seek medical help unless in urgent need, the percentage of them having their medical needs covered by public health insurance may end up being higher.[10]

Concluding Remarks

The rapid growth of the immigrant population, particularly the undocumented immigrant population, has raised concerns about the net impact of this new immigrant inflow on public budgets, particularly those in U.S. border states. Focusing on Mexican migrants, who comprise the largest share of recent—as well as undocumented and lower-paid—immigrants (Capps et al. 2005; Passel 2004, 2005, 2006), we ask ourselves the following policy-related questions: Have tax payment rates among immigrants in border states risen over the twenty-year period under consideration? Does the utilization of the aforementioned public benefits by Mexican immigrants vary according to the likelihood of paying taxes or legal status? And, if so, does it vary in a fashion that would contribute to the draining of public coffers? Finally, has there been a generalized drop in the utilization of public benefits after the passage of the 1996 welfare reform?

After examining the trends and determinants in the payment of government taxes and in the usage of public services by this population, we find that the majority of Mexican migrants in border states have both Social Security and federal taxes withheld from their paychecks regardless of legal status. However, undocumented Mexican migrants are twenty-four to twenty-five percentage points less likely to pay Social Security or federal taxes.

Focusing on the usage of public schools, unemployment insurance, food stamps, and medical services, we find that Mexican migrants, as a whole, became significantly less likely to make use of these services in border states over time. For illegal migrants, who were never eligible for many services (Kaestner and Kaushal 2005), this trend may be due to increased fear of deportation. For legal migrants, however, the reduced usage of public services may have been a by-product of the stricter eligibility rules imposed by PRWORA or the confusion created by the new legislation, which may have led some eligible migrants to not seek help (i.e., the "chilling effect"). In any event, it is worth noting that tax-paying migrants are, in fact, the ones exhibiting a greater likelihood—between two and sixteen percentage points higher—to make use of public services.

In sum, despite the existing concerns regarding the possibility that recent immigrants are a drain on public coffers through their lower likelihood of paying government taxes and their increasing usage of public services over the past decades, the analysis of the MMP114 data suggests otherwise. In all instances, contrary to the general public perception, immigrants in U.S. border states appear more likely to pay government taxes and less likely to use public services. In fact, tax-paying Mexican migrants are the ones who consistently appear as more likely to make use of public schools, unemployment insurance, food stamps, and medical services in the United States, casting doubt on public claims that immigrants constitute a burden to the U.S. economy and calling for further analyses on this topic.

The Earnings of U.S.-Resident Cross-Border Workers in 2000 and 2005

Marie T. Mora and Alberto Dávila

Introduction

Most studies on international migration flows between the U.S. and Mexico focus on Mexican immigrants in the United States (as with the three previous chapters). However, there are also thousands of U.S. residents who cross the international border on a daily basis to work in Mexico. Given the U.S. border region's relatively low income levels, the ability of U.S. residents to find lucrative employment and entrepreneurial opportunities across the border could alleviate some of the pressure in U.S. labor markets. In related studies, we have found that many U.S. resident "cross-border" workers earned significantly more on average than their counterparts who worked on the U.S. side of the border in 2000, but not in 1990 (Mora and Dávila 2007; Mora 2006). The development of this cross-border earnings premium could reflect (1) the growing number of employment opportunities for high-skilled workers that occurred with the boom in the Mexican maquiladora industry and the expansion of trade during the 1990s,[1] and (2) the demands of these workers to be better compensated for having to cross into the Mexican side of the border on a daily basis.[2]

What remains unclear is whether the cross-border earnings premium has been stable in the presence of sociopolitical and economic events that have occurred since 2000. Arguably, this premium might have increased in the early 2000s, considering (1) the impact that the terrorist attacks in the United States on September 11, 2001, had on border-security issues and border crossings (recall the discussion by Pia M. Orrenius,

Madeline Zavodny, and Leslie Lukens in chapter 8); (2) rising transportation costs (e.g., higher gasoline prices); and (3) concerns over growing violence in Mexican border cities since 2000. From the perspective of a compensating-wage differential framework (Rosen 1974), cross-border workers might have bargained for higher earnings to compensate for these additional costs and the stress associated with crossing the border.

However, recall from the chapter by John Sargent, Melissa Najera, and Linda Matthews that employment in Mexican maquiladoras declined in the early 2000s, potentially reducing the demand for cross-border workers and possibly reducing their earnings. Also, recent technologies designed to ease cross-border movements (including the SENTRI program described in the next section) might have reduced border-crossing time, perhaps reducing the need for workers to request relatively high wages. As such, recent changes in the cross-border earnings premium are theoretically ambiguous.

This chapter analyzes the earnings of U.S. residents who worked in Mexico in 2000 and 2005. Since little is known about this population outside of the border region, we first provide an overview of some basic logistics pertaining to cross-border employment for U.S. residents. We then discuss socioeconomic and demographic differences between U.S. residents who work in Mexico and those who work in the United States. Finally, accounting for these differences, we compare the cross-border earnings premium in 2000 with the one in 2005 to observe whether this premium changed in the early 2000s.

Overview of Cross-Border Employment Logistics

Literally thousands of U.S. residents cross the southern international border into Mexico on their way to work. These workers need a business visa, even if they work for a U.S.-owned maquiladora. Following the provisions of chapter 16 of the North American Free Trade Agreement (NAFTA), U.S. residents whose primary places of employment are located in Mexico must have an FM3 business visa, which allows for multiple entries within a year and is renewable for up to four additional years. The FM3 visa can be obtained at Mexican embassies and consulates within the United States and Canada, or from Mexican immigration Officials at the ports of entry.[3]

Besides obtaining the visa, cross-border workers must pay a toll to drive across many of the international bridges (generally ranging between two and three dollars when leaving the United States and between twenty and twenty-four pesos [about $1.80–$2.20] when leaving Mexico), although not all of the bridges have tolls (including the Bridge of the Americas—one of the major bridges connecting El Paso and Ciudad Juárez). We note, however, that even when tolls are charged, they do not always represent a direct cost to the worker because employers often pay for them. In addition, recent technological advances have been developed to reduce the amount of time it takes frequent border crossers to pay tolls on the bridges that charge them. For example, workers can acquire an Identificación Automática Vehicular (IAVE) pass, which includes a transponder (to be attached to their vehicle's windshield) that is scanned when crossing, automatically deducting the toll.

While crossing into Mexico involves clearing Mexican immigration and customs, the process often takes less time than entering the United States because the random screening process (generally through a stoplight system) allows many personal vehicles to enter Mexico without their occupants being interviewed by immigration or customs officials. In contrast, screening by U.S. immigration and customs officials (currently under the U.S. Customs and Border Protection [CBP] agency) usually involves direct contact between all entering vehicles' occupants and the CBP officials. Consequently, north-bound traffic on the U.S.-Mexico international bridges often moves more slowly than south-bound traffic. The CBP inspection time usually takes thirty to forty seconds, but the time that passenger vehicles spend reaching the inspection booth varies considerably—from less than a minute to more than an hour, depending on the bridge location and the time of day (U.S. CBP 2006).

To reduce this waiting and processing time, some frequent border crossers now have the option to apply for the Secure Electronic Network for Travelers Rapid Inspection (SENTRI) pass. According to the U.S. CBP (2006), SENTRI participants face a ten-second average inspection time versus thirty to forty seconds without it, and they have shorter waiting times to reach the primary inspection booths. Passenger vehicles crossing at noon from Ciudad Juárez into El Paso on the Paseo del Norte bridge wait an average of thirty seconds to reach the inspection booth in SENTRI lanes, compared to seventy-five *minutes* for non-SENTRI vehicles (U.S. CBP 2006). To apply for a SENTRI pass, individuals undergo a background check, and then are fingerprinted and interviewed by a U.S. CBP officer. If approved, they receive a radio frequency identification card and decal for their vehicle. Upon approaching the inspection booth in the special SENTRI commuter lane, the system automatically identifies the vehicle and its occupants, and the data are then verified by a CBP officer.

Demographic and Socioeconomic Characteristics of Cross-Border Workers

We use data from the 2000 U.S. decennial census and the 2005 American Community Survey in the Integrated Public Use Microdata Series to study the earnings of U.S.-resident cross-border workers.[4] These detailed datasets (described in this volume's data appendix) contain information on the primary location of work that can be used to identify workers who live in the United States but work outside the country. Our sample includes individuals between the ages of twenty-five and sixty-four who resided in public-use microdata areas (PUMAs) containing those counties adjacent to Mexico (see the appendix chapter for details). The relatively large military presence in certain border cities such as El Paso, Texas, and San Diego, California, means that some border residents who work abroad do so on military bases in the rest of the world, and not in Mexico; we therefore exclude from our sample individuals serving in the military.

Our discussion here highlights some of the socioeconomic and demographic characteristics of the cross-border workers. In particular, figure 10.1 provides the real (inflation-adjusted) and nominal (non-adjusted) average annual earned income (defined as wage and salary income plus self-employment income) for U.S. residents living close to Mexico in 2000 and 2005.[5] Cross-border workers earn substantially more on average than their counterparts who live and work on the U.S. side of the border.[6] To illustrate, U.S. residents who worked in Mexico earned nearly $50,500 on average in 2000, compared to $37,100 earned by their peers employed on the U.S. side of the border. Adjusting for inflation, figure 10.1 indicates that these real incomes (in 2007 dollars) were equivalent to $61,100 (for cross-border workers) and $44,900 (other workers). Moreover, figure 10.1 shows that the average earnings advan-

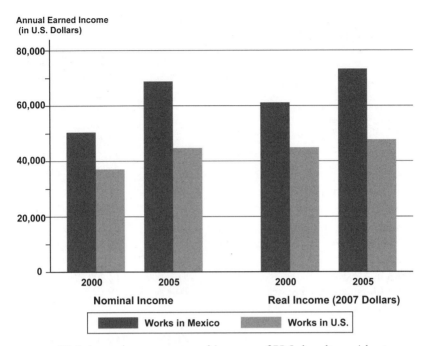

FIGURE 10.1 Annual average earned income of U.S. border residents in 2000 and 2005, by work location. *Source:* Authors' estimates using 2000 PUMS and 2005 ACS data in the IPUMS.

tage enjoyed by the cross-border workers rose between 2000 and 2005. To illustrate, the average real income (in 2007 dollars) rose by nearly $3,000 (to the equivalent of $47,800 in 2007) among individuals who lived and worked on the U.S. side of the border in 2005, but it increased by more than $12,000 (to the equivalent of $73,300 in 2007) among cross-border workers during this time.

Of course, part of the earnings premium associated with employment on the Mexican side of the border presumably reflects differences with respect to observable socioeconomic and demographic characteristics between cross-border and domestically employed workers. As we have reported in other studies (Mora and Dávila 2007; Mora 2006), U.S. residents who primarily work in Mexico tend to represent high-skilled labor. Table 10.1, which provides some key average characteristics for these groups, indicates that this tendency strengthened between 2000 and 2005.

TABLE 10.1 Mean Characteristics of Workers Residing on
the U.S. Side of the Border in 2000 and 2005

Characteristic	Resides in U.S. and Works in Mexico		Resides and Works on U.S. Side of Border	
	2000	2005	2000	2005
Years of Education	14.04	15.05	13.04	13.21
	(3.53)	(2.59)	(3.38)	(3.25)
Age (in years)	41.34	43.71	41.60	42.70
	(9.29)	(8.13)	(9.94)	(10.33)
Commute to Work	34.87	30.31	19.70	19.07
(in minutes)	(22.20)	(13.72)	(18.36)	(15.63)
Manufacturing Industry	40.2%	41.8%	11.3%	9.1%
Manager, Professional, Executive	49.3%	51.0%	30.5%	31.6%
Born in Mexico	41.6%	51.7%	17.5%	20.2%
Born Outside United States & Mexico	11.4%	10.4%	9.0%	9.4%
Female	16.0%	17.9%	42.3%	42.3%
Hispanic	56.9%	71.3%	40.0%	45.0%
Sample Size:	520	94	94,750	21,080
Estimated Population Size:	11,571	10,484	1,968,844	2,140,526

Notes: The parentheses contain robust standard errors for the continuous variables. These samples, based on IPUMS data, include civilian non-student workers between the ages of 25 and 64 who: (1) resided on the U.S. side of the border, (2) reported earned income (wages, salaries, and self-employment income), and (3) worked at least 20 hours per week for 32 or more weeks in the year prior to the survey. The sampling weights provided in the datasets are employed. The sample size refers to the number of observations in our sample, while the estimated population size reflects the size of the population the sample captures.

For example, cross-border workers have considerably higher average levels of education than workers living and working on the U.S. side of the border, and this education differential widened during this time period. The average schooling of cross-border workers increased by an entire year (from fourteen to fifteen years) during these five years, while it remained the same (at thirteen years) for workers employed on the U.S. side of the border. Moreover, the standard deviations (provided in parentheses in table 10.1) show that the variance in education narrowed among cross-border workers, while it remained virtually unchanged for

U.S. workers between 2000 and 2005. Given the rising importance of education for labor market earnings in recent years (e.g., Welch 2000), and given the tightening of the education distribution among cross-border workers, these schooling differences might be responsible, at least in part, for the apparent increase in the cross-border earnings premium observed in figure 10.1.

Table 10.1 also shows that cross-border workers have longer commutes (of an average of thirty-five minutes in 2000) than those living and working on the U.S. side of the border (less than twenty minutes), as would be expected. The higher average salaries of cross-border workers might then be partly attributed to transportation costs and compensating wages for their relatively long commutes and potential stress (e.g., McQuaid, Greig, and Adams 2001; Gabriel and Rosenthal 1996; Zax 1991).

As noted above, however, recent technological advances have been made since 2000 to ease border-crossing times, particularly for frequent border crossers. Evidence that such advances have been working can be observed in table 10.1: the average commuting time fell to 30.3 minutes (a 4.5 minute drop) for cross-border workers by 2005, compared to a decrease of 0.7 minutes (about 42 seconds) for other workers along the border. Of further interest, the *variance* of the commuting time also fell during this time (see the standard deviations), reflecting reduced uncertainty (and potential stress) of arriving on time to work and returning home. It therefore appears that technological advances for frequent border crossers reduced border-crossing times between 2000 and 2005, despite rising security and immigration concerns. Another possibility is that the cross-border workers in 2005 moved closer to the international border than their counterparts had lived five years earlier, perhaps purposely selecting their residential locations to reduce their total commuting time. We cannot test for this latter possibility.

Regardless of the cause, other border-crossing costs increased during this period. For example, average gasoline prices nearly doubled in real terms from about $1.50 to $3.00 a gallon between 2000 and 2005 (zfacts.com 2007). This price increase effectively raised the average transportation costs of cross-border workers relative to those of their U.S.-employed counterparts, given their longer commutes. Moreover, tighter border security, independent of crossing time, might have led to an increase in the nonmonetary costs (such as stress) of crossing the border, given the additional enforcement scrutiny by U.S. immigration and customs officials.

Also increasing psychic costs (stress) associated with working in Mexico is the rising rate of violence and kidnapping incidences on the Mexican side of the border in recent years. To illustrate, an Associated Press report from January 27, 2005, notes that the U.S. State Department issued an alert that "U.S. citizens should be aware of the risk posed by the deteriorating security situation" in Mexico's northern border region. The same report also mentions that the U.S. ambassador to Mexico, Antonio Garza, sent a letter to Mexican officials about his concern that growing drug-related violence and kidnappings could have a "chilling effect" on cross-border trade and tourism (see also Thompson 2005a, 2005b). It follows that the 4.5-minute reduction in the average border-crossing time might not have been enough to offset these other rising costs associated with employment in Mexico.

Other characteristics in table 10.1 worth mentioning include the shares of (1) Mexican immigrants (who represented more than half of the cross-border workers in 2005, compared to just more than a fifth of other border workers); (2) women (representing 18 percent of cross-border workers but 42 percent of other workers); (3) managers, professionals, and executives (who comprised half of the cross-border workers but less than a third of other workers); and (4) workers in the manufacturing industry (42 percent among cross-border workers, compared to 9 percent of the U.S.-employed in 2005). The disproportionate presence of U.S.-resident cross-border Mexican immigrants probably reflects their comparative advantage in securing employment in Mexico, given their inherent knowledge of the language, culture, and business practices.

The relatively large increase (of ten percentage points) of Mexican immigrants among the cross-border workers between 2000 and 2005 could be partly driven by growing concerns about rising violence on the Mexican side of the border. Indeed, some supporting evidence of this can be found in work by Ignacio Alvarado (2008), who discusses how El Paso's housing market has been prospering partly due to an increase in the number of Mexican buyers who are leaving Ciudad Juárez because of fears over safety. Many of these buyers are teachers and small-business owners who continue to work in Juárez, but who want their children to attend El Paso schools. The sharp increase in the presence of the self-employed among cross-border workers (from 16 to 26 percent between 2000 and 2005) echoes this phenomenon.

It is not surprising that women represent such a small share of U.S. residents working in Mexico because of the longer commute times involved with cross-border employment. Other studies have found that women tend to commute shorter distances to work and are less likely to find employment outside their local communities (e.g., Hanson, Kominiak, and Carlin 1997). Finally, the relatively high percentage of cross-border workers in the manufacturing industry observed in table 10.1 provides evidence that many are employed in the maquiladoras.

Before turning to a more detailed analysis of cross-border earnings, we should note that the size of the cross-border workforce is not large (around 10,500 in 2005) compared to the two million workers who live and work on the U.S. side of the border. Also, the decline in the number of cross-border workers between 2000 and 2005 indicates that some jobs were lost during this time. Part of the decline probably relates to the reduction in maquiladora employment that occurred during this time (recall the Sargent, Najera, and Matthews chapter earlier in this book). It could also reflect the growing concerns over safety, in which some U.S. residents became unwilling after 2000 to expose themselves to the rising violence on the Mexican side of the border.[7] Regardless, many of the 10,500 cross-border workers in 2005 held lucrative employment in a region that hosts some of the highest unemployment rates and lowest per-capita personal income levels in the United States (e.g., recall chapters 2 and 3). It follows that policies affecting border-crossing propensities could impact a nontrivial number of U.S. residents in close proximity to Mexico.

Measures of the Cross–Border Earnings Premium

Table 10.2 provides three different measures of the wage premium associated with cross-border employment; see the chapter 10 appendix for how these measures were estimated. Because some of the differences in the annual income measures observed in figure 10.1 relate to differences in the number of work hours, we focus on hourly wages. The premium in the first column represents an "unadjusted" premium; that is, the cross-border wage premium without accounting for such factors as education

TABLE 10.2 The Earnings Premium of Cross-Border Workers in 2000 and 2005

Cross-Border Earnings Premium	Earnings Premium without Controlling for Other Characteristics	Earnings Premium from Regression Analysis (Excluding Commuting Time)*	Earnings Premium from Regression Analysis (Including Commuting Time)*
Premium in 2000	18.7%	12.0%	7.5%
Premium in 2005	21.2%	14.1%	9.5%
Does the 2005 Premium Significantly Differ from 2000?*	No	No	No

* See the chapter 10 appendix for details.

Notes: These premiums indicate the average earnings advantage that U.S. residents working in Mexico had over their counterparts living and working on the U.S. side of the border. These samples, based on IPUMS data, include civilian non-student workers between the ages of 25 and 64 who: (1) resided on the U.S. side of the border, (2) reported earned income (wages, salaries, and self-employment income), and (3) worked at least 20 hours per week for 32 or more weeks in the year prior to the survey. The sampling weights provided in the datasets are employed.

or commuting time. This premium was 18.7 percent in 2000 and 21.2 percent in 2005. That is, for every dollar in hourly wages earned by U.S. residents employed on the U.S. side of the border, those who worked in Mexico earned an average of $1.19 in 2000 and $1.21 in 2005. Despite the increase in the face-value of this premium, it was not significantly different between 2000 and 2005.

The remaining columns in table 10.2 contain additional estimates of the cross-border earnings premium obtained using regression analysis (see this chapter's appendix). These estimates are smaller than in column I, indicating that part of the border-crossing premium stems from differences in observable socioeconomic and demographic characteristics between cross-border workers and those employed in the United States. As seen in column II, the cross-border workers earned 12 percent more on average in 2000, and 14 percent more in 2005, than otherwise similar workers employed on the U.S. side of the border, when ignoring the time it takes to commute. As with the unadjusted premium, the seeming rise in this premium during the early 2000s is not statistically significant.[8]

When considering the time involved to travel to work, the cross-border premium falls in magnitude to 7.5 percent in 2000 and to 9.5 percent in 2005, indicating that some (but not all) of the higher compensation observed for cross-border workers is related to their relatively long commutes. We further note that controlling for commuting time caused about the same reduction in the cross-premium (of 4.5 percentage points) in 2000 as in 2005. This finding is of interest because we would have expected commuting time to be a less important determinant of cross-border earnings by 2005, given that the average commute declined more for cross-border workers than for those employed in the United States in the early 2000s.

In short, it appears from these results that the sociopolitical events occurring in the early 2000s did not significantly affect the cross-border earnings premium. What remains an issue is why this premium exists when controlling for other characteristics, including commuting time. One explanation is that cross-border workers have higher average observed skills than their counterparts, the returns to which have increased in recent times (e.g., Welch 2000). While we control for factors such as education, such workers could have higher *unobserved* skills or traits as well, such as innate ability, motivation, and risk-taking preferences. Perhaps with the slowdown in maquiladora employment, the workers who kept their jobs possessed even higher levels of these unobserved characteristics.

Another explanation is that the commuting time measure does not capture all of the costs associated with crossing an international border on the way to work, as described above. According to the hedonic wage theory in labor economics (Rosen 1974), individuals maximize their expected happiness and firms maximize profits when determining the optimal combination of wages and other job characteristics. This theory can be expanded to include cross-border employment decisions made by these economic agents, as they relate to perceived community amenities such as geographic location and distance to work (Mora and Dávila 2007). Even though many residents view the twin city across the border as part of the same community as the one on their side of the border, as we noted in the introductory chapter, perhaps a significant share of U.S. residents prefer to work in the United States because of the nonmonetary costs associated with border-crossing (such as the stress from being investigated by immigration officials or safety concerns). If so, some U.S. residents would only accept employment on the Mexican side of the border if firms provide an economic incentive, independent of the amount of the time it takes to get to work.

Concluding Remarks

This chapter focuses on the thousands of U.S. residents who work on the Mexican side of the border. These cross-border workers earn significantly more on average than their counterparts employed on the U.S. side of the border, even after controlling for a variety of socioeconomic and demographic factors. Moreover, despite a slowdown in Mexican maquiladora employment and a decrease in the average commuting time for cross-border workers between 2000 and 2005, our results show that this cross-border premium, while positively related to commuting time, did not significantly change during this time. Perhaps potentially greater stress associated with more intensive contact with U.S. immigration officials as well as safety concerns offset the expected wage-dampening effects that the maquiladora slowdown and shorter commuting time should have had.

These findings have policy implications, given the prevailing sociopolitical climate in the United States to further restrict labor flows between Mexico and the United States. One possibility is that intensified border security would significantly increase commuting time and other border-crossing costs, compounding the potential effects that concerns over violence have on U.S. border residents' willingness to work in Mexico. As a result, maquiladora employers might have to offer cross-border workers an even larger premium, but these additional labor costs could drive some of these plants elsewhere. Arguably, such an outflow of maquiladoras would have a detrimental effect on the economic development of the northern Mexican border *and* the southern U.S. border. The latter region would likely lose a pool of high-skilled workers who contribute to its economic base as they sought employment elsewhere. This loss, of course, would be in addition to the potential loss of *billions* of dollars per year if even a small share of Mexican nationals decided to stop visiting U.S. border communities because of a reduction in the ease of border-crossing.[9]

Given the economic interdependence of border communities, it is not surprising to observe widespread opposition by the U.S. communities that would be directly affected by further restrictions on labor flows between Mexico and the United States. For example, on June 1, 2007, the Texas Border Coalition (which represents the mayors, counties, and economic development entities leaders from El Paso to Brownsville) launched a summer-long campaign to rally growing opposition to the federal government's planned fortified fence along the Texas-Mexico border (Diaz 2007). Regardless of the outcome, policymakers should be aware of the potential unintended consequences for U.S. residents from restricting labor flows or increasing border-crossing costs (including psychic costs) between the United States and Mexico.

Chapter 10 Appendix: Details on the Empirical Results in Table 10.2

Table 10.2 provides three different estimates of the cross-border earnings premium for 2000 and 2005. The first estimate represents the difference in the mean natural logarithm of hourly earnings between U.S. residents who work in Mexico and those who work in the United States for each year.[10] A t-test (t-statistic = 0.76) indicates that the premiums do not significantly differ at conventional levels between 2000 and 2005.

The remaining two columns report the premiums from regression analysis, obtained by estimating a standard Mincer-type earnings function (see Mincer 1974 for more details). Specifically, using the method of ordinary least squares (OLS) and pooling the 2000 and 2005 samples, we estimate:

(1) $\text{Ln(Wage)} = (\text{Cross})\beta_1 + (\text{Cross} \times 2005\text{ACS})\beta_2 + X\,B_1 + (X \times 2005\text{ACS})B_2 + e$

where Ln(Wage) represents the natural logarithm of hourly earnings. The variable Cross is a binary variable for workers engaged in cross-border employment (equal to 1 for U.S. residents employed in Mexico and zero otherwise), and (Cross × 2005ACS) represents the interaction between Cross and a binary variable for individuals in the 2005 ACS (equal to 1 for the 2005 ACS and zero for 2000). The coefficient β_1 reflects the estimated earnings premium associated with cross-border employment, while β_2 shows the change in the premium between 2000 and 2005.[11] Therefore, the t-statistic for β_2 reveals whether the cross-border premium significantly differed between 2000 and 2005, and the sum of β_1 and β_2 provides the magnitude of the premium in 2005.

The term X is a vector containing standard human capital and demographic characteristics generally used in earnings functions, including education; experience; experience-squared; self-employment; gender; race/ethnicity (Hispanic, African American, non-Hispanic white [base], and "other" [a composite category for individuals not fitting these other descriptions]); birthplace (Mexico, non-Mexico/non-United States, and United States [base]); the U.S. tenure of immigrants; limited English-language proficiency (a binary variable equal to 1 for individuals who do not speak English "well" or better; equal to zero otherwise); commuting time; and a constant term. The vector $(X \times 2005\text{ACS})$ includes all of the variables in X interacted with the 2005ACS binary variable. The vectors B_1 and B_2 contain coefficients for the variables in X and $(X \times 2005\text{ ACS})$ to be estimated, while e denotes the normally distributed error term.

We estimate equation (1) twice, with and without commuting time and its interaction with the 2005ACS variable. The cross-border earnings premiums in the last two columns of table 10.2 are based on the estimated β coefficients. When excluding commuting time, the estimated β_1 coefficient (standard error) equals 0.1196 (0.0373), and β_2 is 0.0216 (0.1122). Note that $\beta_1 + \beta_2 = 0.1412$, or 14.1 percent—the 2005 cross-border premium listed in table 10.2. The F-test statistic for the combined β_1 and β_2 equals 6.04. When including commuting time in equation (1), the estimated β_1 and β_2 coefficients (standard errors) equal 0.0748 (0.0370) and 0.0206 (0.1112), and the F-test statistic for the combined β_1 and β_2 equals 2.45. The coefficients (standard errors) on commuting time and its interaction with the 2005ACS variable are 0.0030 (0.0002) and 0.0012 (0.0004). The full set of regression results can be obtained from the authors.

We realize that a potential problem with estimating equation (1) is the underlying assumption that observable characteristics similarly affect labor market earnings on both sides of the border. However, when using wage decomposition analysis (e.g., Oaxaca 1973) to predict what U.S. residents who primarily work in Mexico would have earned if they faced the same earnings structure as workers on the U.S. side of the border, the results change little from the "standard" regression results. For example, the 2000 cross-border earnings premium (standard error) from the wage decomposition technique when including commuting time is 0.0741 (0.037)—nearly identical to the β_1 estimated from equation (1). We therefore only report the cross-border earnings premiums from equation (1) in table 10.2.

Comparing U.S.-Mexican Border Unemployment Rates to Non-Border Large MSAs

André Varella Mollick

Introduction

Areas along the U.S.-Mexico border tend to have higher unemployment rates than the national average. Figure 11.1 shows the local unemployment rates for the five largest U.S. metropolitan statistical areas (MSAs) located directly along the U.S.-Mexico border, along with the national unemployment rate, from 1990 to 2005.[1] Other than the San Diego MSA, these border MSAs had higher unemployment rates than the nation over this period, with that of the McAllen MSA in Texas hovering at more than 20 percent in the early to mid-1990s. However, in line with the economic boom of the late 1990s, the border MSAs showed a visible decline in their unemployment rates in 2000, seemingly following the decline in the national unemployment rate of that year.

Given the relatively high unemployment rates of these border regions (with the exception of San Diego), this chapter compares the unemployment rates in border MSAs with the corresponding rates of the largest non-border MSAs in the same states (specifically Dallas and Houston in Texas, and Los Angeles and San Francisco in California) between 1990 and 2005. In addition, an explanation for these relatively high unemployment rates along the U.S.-Mexico border that depends on the level of industrial composition of a region is given in this chapter.[2]

To create a backdrop for what follows, it should be noted that previous studies document that national unemployment rates vary substantially in their explanatory power of local unemployment conditions (see Mollick 2008b for a review). The rationale behind this view is that when

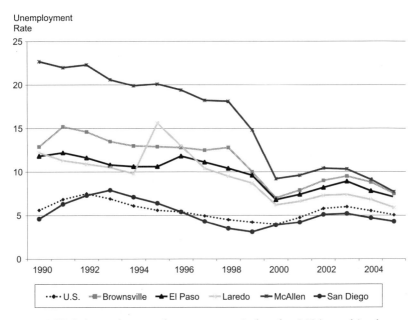

FIGURE 11.1 Annual unemployment rates in border MSAs and in the United States from 1990 to 2005.

a region's workers are highly concentrated in one (or a few) industrial sector(s), an economic downturn in the dominant industrial sector will, of course, disproportionately increase the unemployment rate of that region. While some displaced workers will find employment in other sectors of the region's economy, this would occur after substantial retraining and acquisition of sector-specific knowledge. Depending on the difficulty of acquiring the necessary skills for employment in other sectors, relatively high rates of unemployment in certain industrial sectors could be long-term.

Basic Unemployment Trends

Several observations regarding unemployment rates along the border versus the interior are worth noting. First, as seen above in figure 11.1, the nation's unemployment rate seemingly served as the lower bound of the Texas border MSAs' local unemployment rates between 1990 and 2005, while San Diego's unemployment rate closely followed the

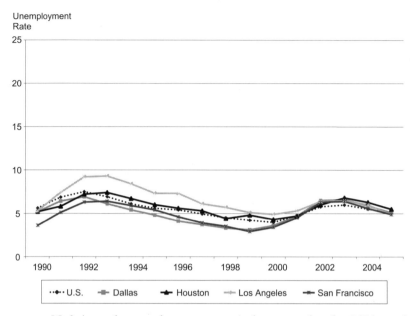

Unemployment
Rate

FIGURE 11.2 Annual unemployment rates in large non-border MSAs and in the United States from 1990 to 2005.

national figures (staying below or above the national unemployment rate within a one-percentage-point margin). Second, the unemployment rate of the Laredo MSA in 1995 edged higher, while the rates in the other border MSAs declined. Perhaps employment in Laredo was more sensitive to the recession in Mexico after the 1994–1995 currency crisis.[3] This event was mostly confined to this border MSA. Moreover, with the exception of San Diego, after the economic slowdown during 2001 and 2002, the border MSA unemployment rates moved slightly higher along with the national unemployment rate, although they were still well below their rates in the early 1990s.

When considering unemployment in the largest non-border MSAs in Texas and California over the 1990–2005 period, a clear convergence with the national unemployment rate is observed (see figure 11.2). However, contrary to the border city trends, there was not a "clean" distinction between Texas and California in that the Houston and Los Angeles MSAs persistently displayed higher unemployment rates than the U.S. average, while the Dallas and San Francisco MSAs were systematically below it—at least until 2001. After 2001, the unemployment rates in these four cities remained above the national unemployment rate, with the exception of the San Francisco MSA in 2005 (4.9 percent compared to the national rate of 5.1 percent). Comparing figures 11.1 and 11.2 therefore indicates that the relatively high unemployment rates observed in Texas-Mexico border MSAs do not appear to be driven by economic conditions in Texas alone. The next section examines employment concentrations in specific industries to determine whether the differences in the local unemployment rates relate to employment changes in the MSAs' dominant industrial sectors.

An Explanation through Industry Composition

The simplest way to measure a city's specialization in a given industrial sector is to estimate the share of the sector in total employment. Looking at the employment share of each city's largest sector, the specialization index can be defined as the largest share of an industry in a particular region. Because certain sectors account for a larger share of national employment than others, Gilles Duranton and Diego Puga (2000) propose an alternative estimate—the *relative specialization index* (RSI), measured by dividing the share of each sector in local employment by its share in national employment.[4] Observing RSIs over time can be used to determine whether the change in employment in a city's most important industrial sector occurred at a rate greater than, less than, or the same as the change in the nation's share of employment in the given sector.

For the cities studied here, ten industrial sectors were considered: (1) natural resources, mining, and construction; (2) manufacturing; (3) trade, transportation, and utilities; (4) information; (5) financial activities; (6) professional and business services; (7) education and health services; (8) leisure and hospitality; (9) other services; and (10) the government. Of these ten, the sectors with the highest share of employment were two: government (in San Diego, Brownsville, El Paso, and McAllen) and trade, transportation, and utilities (in Dallas, Houston, Los Angeles, San Francisco, and Laredo). The fact that Laredo differs from the other border MSAs with respect to its largest employment concentrations in trade and transportation is not surprising, given that it serves as

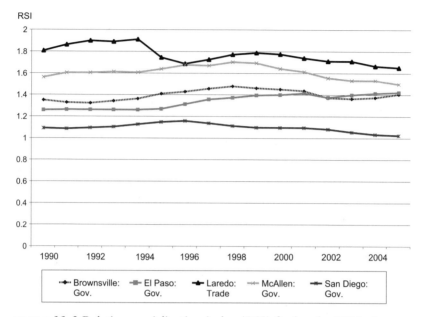

FIGURE 11.3 Relative specialization index (RSI) for border MSAs from 1990 to 2005.

a major transportation hub from Mexico into the United States through the I-35 highway; it is also a major shopping destination for Mexican consumers.

Figures 11.3 and 11.4 provide the relative specialization indices for the border MSAs (figure 11.3) and the large non-border MSAs (figure 11.4). The highest of all the RSIs out of the nine MSAs studied was for trade, transportation, and utilities in Laredo, although it fell from 1.807 in 1990 to 1.651 in 2005. The RSI value of 1.807 means that the trade employment share in Laredo was 1.807 times higher than the employment share in trade in the United States overall in 1990. By 2005, the RSI of 1.651 indicates that Laredo's trade employment share was 1.651 times higher the United States' share that year. The fact that Laredo's RSI fell between 1990 and 2005 shows that the trade sector's industrial employment dominance fell by a greater proportion in Laredo than for the United States as a whole.

Although of a smaller magnitude than for Laredo, the border MSAs of McAllen and San Diego also experienced declines in their RSIs dur-

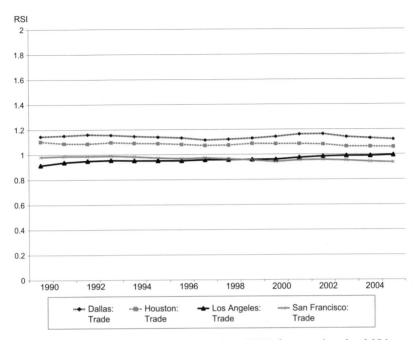

FIGURE 11.4 Relative specialization index (RSI) for non-border MSAs from 1990 to 2005.

ing this time (falling from 1.563 to 1.498 in McAllen and from 1.091 to 1.026 in San Diego). In contrast, between 1990 and 2005, the RSIs increased in Brownsville (going from 1.350 to 1.406) and El Paso (from 1.259 to 1.422), suggesting an intensification of employment in their dominant industries of a greater magnitude than what occurred in the United States overall. Evidence for the border region is thus mixed on how the industrial employment dominance of this region changed vis-à-vis the nation.

Of interest, figure 11.4 shows that Los Angeles and San Francisco were the only MSAs considered here with RSIs below 1, meaning that employment in these cities was more diversified than in the United States overall. Moreover, figure 11.4 provides evidence of a decrease in the RSIs between 1990 and 2005 for the largest non-border MSAs in Texas and California—except for Los Angeles, which had its RSI increase from 0.915 to 0.993. It therefore appears that employment generally became more diversified in the interior of these states than directly along the border.

It should also be noted that when comparing figures 11.3 and 11.4, the border MSAs have higher RSIs than other large MSAs in the interiors of their respective states. This finding indicates that employment in cities along the U.S.-Mexico border is less diversified than in other large MSAs in the same state.[5]

How do these employment concentrations relate to unemployment? According to the specialization thesis, two forces are at play. First, the regional specialization thesis associated with the Marshall-Arrow-Romer view establishes that the concentration of an industry in a city helps knowledge spillovers between firms and then the growth of employment within the city. That is, if the specialization thesis is correct, all else constant, cities that have their index increase over time should have their local unemployment rates decrease. Edward Glaeser et al. (1992), however, find that urban variety—but not regional specialization—encourages employment growth in industries in U.S. cities. Similarly, other studies (using alternative measures of employment concentration) have shown that higher degrees of concentration relate to higher unemployment rates in a city (e.g., Mizuno, Mizutani, and Nakayama 2006; Izraeli and Murphy 2003; Simon 1988). There is thus not much support for the regional specialization view across U.S. MSAs.

On the other hand, recall that an increase in the RSI index reflects more employment concentration in a single sector relative to the national average. When a negative shock to the sector occurs, employers lay off workers, who then wish to migrate to other sectors, seeking employment. Therefore, using the Laredo example, the reduction in its trade-sector RSI may help explain the disproportionate decline in its local unemployment rate, which fell from 12.2 percent in 1990 to 5.9 percent in 2005, compared to the change from 5.6 to 5.1 percent in the nation as a whole (recall figure 11.1).

Given the two conflicting forces (knowledge spillovers within an urban area versus too much employment in a single industry, making the region particularly vulnerable to demand fluctuations), additional analysis is needed. When controlling for local fixed effects, national unemployment, diversity indexes, and population density, André Varella Mollick (2008b) provides empirical evidence that an increase in RSI for the border cities panel led to a decrease in their unemployment rates over time, a result not observed for the panel of non-border MSAs in the same states.

This finding supports the specialization thesis for the border cities. In a study of two interesting cases of heavily concentrated employment figures in two Mexican cities (tourism in Cancún versus manufacturing in Ciudad Juárez), Christopher R. Tamborini (2007) reports that, in 1998, urban Mexico recorded an overall unemployment rate of 3.1 percent, versus the rates of Ciudad Juárez (0.9 percent) and Cancún (1.6 percent). While unemployment and industry composition was not directly examined by Tamborini, these numbers would be consistent with the specialization thesis for these two cities south of the border. The specialization thesis did not, however, seem to be applicable to the other large cities in Texas and California examined in this paper; unemployment in these interior MSAs closely follows the national unemployment patterns [see Mollick 2008 for more details].

Based on the above calculations for the specialization index, trade/transportation/utilities as well as the government were the sectors with the highest share of employment adjusted by national shares. The government sector was the major one for the border cities of San Diego, Brownsville, El Paso, and McAllen, while trade/transportation/utilities was the most important sector for Dallas, Houston, Los Angeles, San Francisco, and the border city of Laredo. For the border cities examined here, only in Brownsville was there an increase in the specialization index for government. For all others, there was a movement towards less concentration. To the extent that government activities are relatively labor intensive, this suggests that unemployment is not likely to be worsening in the future. While the analysis does not support the idea that the dynamic sectors in each border MSA are capital intensive and thus labor displacing, one long-term implication is that border cities should develop dynamic areas of economic activity other than government.

Concluding Remarks

This chapter shows more variation in unemployment and higher degrees of employment concentration for the five largest U.S. border cities relative to other large MSAs in the same state. Following Mollick (2008b), the relative employment specialization has a powerful impact on the local unemployment in U.S. cities close to Mexico. Conversely, for the large non-border metro areas, local unemployment is well explained by the national unemployment rate. This research documents that the government sector was the major employer for the border cities of San Diego, Brownsville, El Paso, and McAllen, while the trade, transportation, and utilities sector was the most important for Dallas, Houston, Los Angeles, San Francisco, and the border city of Laredo. For the border cities, only in Brownsville was there an increase in the specialization index for government. For all others, there was a movement towards less concentration.

In view of the relatively low per-capita income levels and large educational gaps for the border area as described earlier by Thomas M. Fullerton Jr., James H. Holcomb, and Angel L. Molina Jr. in chapter 2, this chapter posits that the structural component of unemployment is the driving force of the higher unemployment rate along the border. An important issue for further study is the fact that some workers live in border metros but work across the border, as Marie T. Mora and Alberto Dávila discuss in chapter 10.

At least two extensions are worth mentioning at this juncture. First, measurement errors in the unemployment statistics form an avenue for further work. Second, it is well known that areas along the U.S.-Mexico border have been popular destinations for many North Americans wishing to escape the cold weather of winter (e.g., Simpson and LeMaster 2006). If these residents have a considerable impact on the local economy, the seasonality explanation for local unemployment commonly found in agricultural areas may also be important systematically in border areas.

Some Policy Implications
for the U.S.-Mexico
Border Region

Alberto Dávila and Marie T. Mora

WE STARTED THIS BOOK CONSIDERING a series of themes, and the intersection of these, as a means to frame the discussions on labor market issues along the U.S.-Mexico border contained throughout this volume. These themes include migration, trade, gender, education, earnings, and employment. Most of the chapters explore these themes in the context of a series of policy-related events. For example, Anthony P. Mora discusses the historical progression of events that eventually industrialized northern Mexico, led to the establishment of the Bracero Program in August 1942, and set forth a dynamic between migration and trade in the region. The Bracero Program initiative allowed for the legal recruitment of temporary Mexican labor into the United States for more than two decades. It was followed by the trade-related Border Industrialization Program in 1965 that gave birth to the maquiladora industry, fundamentally changing the underlying economic structure of both sides of the U.S.-Mexico border. These historical events in turn seem to have had ironic unintended consequences. Pia M. Orrenius, Madeline Zavodny, and Leslie Lukens suggest that one of many policies could have promoted internal migration to northern Mexico and undocumented immigration to the United States.

Moreover, these events might have been responsible for more recent policies. For example, U.S. immigration reform, such as the 1986 Immigration Reform and Control Act and the failed immigration-policy proposals of 2007, is designed to stem undocumented flows. Orrenius, Zavodny, and Lukens note, however, that increases in border security reduce the likelihood that Mexican migrants will go to the border, arguably reducing the employment opportunities and stifling economic growth in the region, given the interdependence of U.S. and Mexican border twin cities. In our chapter on cross-border workers, we further suggest that stress created by more intensive border-security measures in reaction to the events of September 11, 2001, might compound the concerns over the rising violence in Mexican border cities; if so, these rising psychic costs could reduce the willingness of U.S. residents to accept potentially lucrative employment in Mexico. Policies designed to reduce labor flows across the U.S.-Mexico border could therefore unintentionally dampen labor market outcomes on both sides of the border.

Of course, an additional line of debate used to fuel further immigration reform has been the belief that Mexican immigrants—particularly the undocumented—in the southern border states are a drain to public goods and therefore reduce socioeconomic outcomes in the region. However, when analyzing Mexican migrants' propensities to pay taxes and use public goods in U.S. border states, Catalina Amuedo-Dorantes and Cynthia Bansak do not provide evidence to support this talking point.

The themes of employment, trade, and migration are at the heart of many recent policy debates. For example, policies leading to increased trade opportunities have often been cited as panacea to stimulate employment. Certainly NAFTA has been a trade agreement that professes this philosophy, although James T. Peach and Richard V. Adkisson provide mixed evidence for the U.S. side of the border. Regarding the Mexican side, John Sargent, Melissa Najera, and Linda Matthews discuss the large growth in employment in the maquiladora industry that occurred between 1994 and 2000 because of NAFTA. Another advantage associated with cross-border trade is noted by Thomas M. Fullerton Jr., James H. Holcomb, and Angel L. Molina Jr. in their findings that commerce from Mexican nationals keeps sales-to-income ratios in many U.S. border communities at or above U.S. national averages. We also argue (with Alma D. Hales) that the unique geographic location and the economic and cultural dependence of border communities stimulate small-business formation and employment on both sides of the border.

Another example of the intersection of themes in this volume is that among the employment, earnings, and migration. Hector J. Villarreal documents that the returns to education are higher in Mexico's northern border region than in the rest of the country, possibly affecting migration flows within Mexico and between Mexico and the United States. We illustrate (with Hales) that workers—both paid employees and the self-employed—in the U.S. border region earn less than those in the U.S. interior, but considerably more than those on the Mexican side of the border. Sargent, Najera, and Matthews further provide ethnographic evidence of the relatively weak labor-market conditions in the interior of Mexico versus those in the border region. Combined, these large regional economic disparities raise the likelihood that workers from Mexico's interior will continue to migrate northward over time.

The intersection of the migration, gender, and employment themes gains policy prominence when an account is made of the steady rise in the population of Mexican migrant women in the workforce on both sides of the border. On the Mexican side, this demographic pattern owes at least partly to maquiladoras' disproportionate hiring of women in their labor forces (although a reversal of this trend has been noted by some [e.g., Tiano 2006]). Orrenius, Zavodny, and Lukens indicate that women represent a larger share of Mexican migrants in the U.S. border region than in the U.S. interior, although they seem to lack the networks of their counterparts in the U.S. interior. Sáenz, Murga, and Morales further point out that while women represent a greater share of the Mexican immigrant workforce along the U.S. border versus the interior, issues remain with regards to how this population has been incorporated into their host communities in terms of education, health care, and childcare. Policymakers may therefore wish to consider gender-specific issues when framing policies designed to stimulate economic growth and well-being in the border region.

This volume also provides insights into the issue of education as an engine for economic development along the U.S.-Mexico border regions. Fullerton, Holcomb, and Molina provide a relatively bleak assessment of the education levels on the U.S. side of the border compared with those of the rest of the country. An implication of this assessment is that, given the increasing returns to education in the United States, the U.S. border region's relatively low average education levels will continue to drag down the economic development of the U.S. side of the border region. As for the Mexican side of this region, while Villarreal finds evidence that college graduation rates have increased there, he notes these still lag behind those of the Mexican interior. Moreover, he reports declining returns to education in Mexico, which could lead to some emigration from Mexico into the United States, thus sustaining the border region's relatively low average levels of education.

This said, to better acknowledge the role of education to the economic development of the U.S.-Mexico border regions, an implicit argument made here is that a broader context should be used to include the education *quality* and the type of education (e.g., formal schooling versus job-training programs) of border residents. Villarreal notes that the returns to education might be falling in Mexico because of a declining schooling quality in that country. Also, André Varella Mollick identifies structural unemployment as a source for the higher average unemployment along the U.S. side of the Mexican border, observing that workers might need retraining to obtain employment. Sargent, Najera, and Matthews further note that to compete with Chinese manufacturers, Mexican maquiladoras have begun to shift their production into more high-tech and capital-intensive ventures, so that they will need a more skilled workforce to fill these positions. Peach and Adkisson add that trade policies tend to benefit those who have the education and skills to adjust to rapidly changing labor and product markets. It follows that policies designed to promote human capital development in the border region may do best to consider those mechanisms related to enhancing formal education opportunities, as well as those related to improving the quality of educational institutions and providing other less-formal job-training programs.

In all, the contributions in this volume complement and add to our knowledge of labor market outcomes along the U.S.-Mexico border as they analyze a variety of overlapping themes related to such outcomes. Still, we realize that other important themes that potentially affect the border workforce are not explored here, including the role of unions, health, and safety, among many others. The intersections of such themes with those discussed in this volume should serve as fodder for future research. For example, while Anthony P. Mora mentions how women have figured prominently in grassroots activism and union involvement, an entire volume could be written on the theme of how gender relates to union activity on both sides of the border.[1] Another manuscript could address how changes in migration patterns (including those affected by restrictions in border-crossing abilities) relate to health outcomes among the border workforce.[2] And yet another could consider how safety issues, in both the workplace and community, affect the well-being of workers on both sides of the border.[3]

Over time, the list of labor-market themes along the U.S.-Mexico border will no doubt expand, and new permutations of these will grow. We should note that events such as the 2006 Lineae Terrarum conference and the many contributions of border scholars present forums to expand on these themes and their interactions. Throughout this book, the authors have made it clear that the border regions are of strategic economic and social importance to both Mexico and the United States. Indeed, if recent sociopolitical events such as the intensification of border-security policies are a precursor of things to come, this area of study will continue to grow in prominence among scholars, students, policymakers, and the public.

Appendix

Defining the Border and Data Appendix

Defining the Border

As observed throughout this manuscript, a variety of definitions exist when defining the U.S.-Mexico border region. These definitions usually depend on the level of geographic detail available in the different datasets.

MSA Approach

James T. Peach and Richard V. Adkisson (chapter 3); Pia M. Orrenius, Madeline Zavodny, and Leslie Lukens (chapter 8); and André Varella Mollick (chapter 11) primarily identify the U.S. border region using the metropolitan statistical area (MSA) approach. According to the Office of Management and Budget, to be classified as an MSA, areas must "have at least one urbanized area of 50,000 or more population, plus adjacent territory that has a high degree of social and economic integration with the core as measured by commuting ties." In this case, the border MSAs are Brownsville (including San Benito and Harlingen), El Paso, Laredo, and McAllen (including Edinburg, Mission, and Pharr) in Texas; Las Cruces in New Mexico; Tucson and Yuma in Arizona; and San Diego in California. Neither Tucson nor Las Cruces are located directly along the U.S.-Mexico border, but they are located in counties adjacent to Mexico. El Centro, California, is another MSA located along the U.S.-Mexico border, but it received its designation as an MSA in 2003, so that the chapters in this book (which use data from before 2003) exclude this MSA from their discussion.

The County and Municipio Approach

Chapters 2 (Fullerton, Holcomb, and Molina) and 3 (Peach and Adkisson) identify the U.S. border region in terms of the counties located near Mexico. There are twenty-three counties directly adjacent to Mexico [from west to east: San Diego and Imperial counties in California; Yuma, Pima, Santa Cruz, and Cochise counties in Arizona; Hidalgo, Luna, and Doña Ana counties in New Mexico; and El Paso, Hudspeth, Jeff Davis, Presidio, Brewster, Terrell, Val Verde, Kinney, Maverick, Webb, Zapata, Starr, Hidalgo, and Cameron counties in Texas]. Chapter 3 further includes both Culberson County and Dimmit County (in Texas) in the border definition because these counties, while not technically adjacent to Mexico, are located quite close to Mexico.

When using Mexican data, municipios (municipalities that are similar to U.S. counties) can be used to identify border regions, as in chapter 6 (Dávila, Mora, and Hales). Specifically, that chapter identifies the Mexican northern border region as the thirty-five municipios adjacent to the United States (Mexicali, Tecate, and Tijuana in Baja California; Acuña, Guerrero, Hidalgo, Jimenez, Ocampo, and Piedras Negras in Coahuila de Zaragoza; Ascension, Guadalupe, Janos, Juarez, Ojinaga, and Praxedis G. Guerrero in Chihuahua; Anahuac in Nuevo Leon; Agua Prieta, Altar, Caborca, Cananea, Naco, Nogales, Puerto Peñasco, San Luis Rio Colorado, Santa Cruz, and Saric in Sonora; and Camargo, Guerrero, Matamoros, Mier, Miguel Aleman, Nuevo Laredo, Reynosa, Rio Bravo, and Valle Hermoso in Tamaulipas).

The PUMA Approach

When using data from the Public Use Microdata Series (PUMS) and the Integrated Public Use Microdata Series (IPUMS-International), it is not possible to uniquely identify all the individual U.S. counties; the geographic coding combines less-populated counties into public-use microdata areas (PUMAs), which are constructed to contain at least one hundred thousand residents. Chapters 6 (Dávila, Mora, and Hales), 7 (Sáenz, Murga, and Morales), and 10 (Mora and Dávila) use PUMAs to identify the U.S. border region. Specifically, chapters 6 and 10 focus on the PUMAs that contain counties adjacent to Mexico. These chapters include in the U.S. border region the counties of Andrews, Brewster, Brooks, Cameron, Crane, Culberson, Dimmit, Edwards, El Paso, Gaines, Hidalgo, Hudspeth, Jeff Davis, Jim Hogg, Kenedy, Kinney, Kleberg, La Salle, Loving, Pecos, Presidio, Real, Reeves, Starr, Terrell, Upton, Uvalde, Val Verde, Ward, Webb, Willacy, Winkler, Zapata, and Zavala in Texas; Catron, Chaves, Doña Ana, Eddy, Grant, Hidalgo, Lea, Luna, Otero, Sierra, Socorro, and Torrance in New Mexico; Cochise,

Gila, Graham, Greenlee, Maricopa, Pima, Pinal, Santa Cruz, and Yuma in Arizona; and Imperial and San Diego in California. Chapter 7 also includes additional PUMAs—those that contain counties contiguous to those counties adjacent to Mexico (the counties used in chapters 6 and 10, plus Aransas, Bandera, Bee, Duval, Frio, Gillespie, Jim Wells, Kendall, Kerr, Live Oak, Maverick, McMullen, Medina, Nueces, Refugio, and San Patricio in Texas; Gila and Maricopa in Arizona; and Orange and Riverside in California). Note that some of the counties included in the PUMA-derived border definitions are technically not adjacent to Mexico. Nevertheless, given these counties' small population size, the authors are generally not concerned that their inclusion will distort our results.

State Approach

Yet other chapters, including the Hector J. Villarreal chapter (5) and the Catalina Amuedo-Dorantes and Cynthia Bansak chapter (9) broadly define the border to include the states along the U.S.-Mexico international boundary. Chapter 5 focuses on the six Mexican states (Baja California, Coahuila de Zaragoza, Chihuahua, Nuevo Leon, Sonora, and Tamaulipas), while chapter 9 uses the four U.S. states (Arizona, California, New Mexico, and Texas).

Data Appendix

This manuscript employs a variety of datasets, most of which are publicly available, to investigate labor market issues along the U.S.-Mexico border. It should be noted that the use of these secondary datasets does not mean that the research contained in this manuscript is not original, as the analysis and interpretation of the data provide key empirical evidence for the discussions in the different chapters. The chapter by John Sargent, Melissa Najera, and Linda Matthews (chapter 4) includes original qualitative data the authors obtained through the use of interviews. The remainder of this appendix describes the various quantitative datasets employed throughout the manuscript.

American Community Survey (ACS)

The American Community Survey (ACS) has been annually compiled by the U.S. Census Bureau since 2000. The 2005 version contains approximately 1 percent of the total U.S. population. Sampling weights, which were constructed by the Census Bureau, are included with the data to maintain the national representation of the samples. The ACS can be downloaded free of charge from the U.S. Census Bureau at www.census .gov or from the University of Minnesota Population Research Center at www.ipums.org.

Encuesta Nacional de Ingreso y Gasto de los Hogares

These data are based on an income-expenditure survey, representative at the national level, for Mexico. They are coordinated by El Instituto Nacional de Estadística, Geografía e Informática (INEGI) and can be obtained for a nominal fee at www.inegi.gob.mx.

Integrated Public Use Microdata Series (IPUMS)

These data are publicly available (and free of charge) from the University of Minnesota's Population Research Center at www.ipums.org. They are nationally representative samples of large-scale datasets collected by the U.S. Census Bureau. The full IPUMS contains samples drawn from the U.S. decennial censuses between 1850 and 2000, as well as from the ACS. Statistical weights are provided in the IPUMS to maintain the national representation of the samples; all chapters using these data employ the sampling weights in their analyses. The IPUMS data for 1980–2000 use the PUMS from the U.S. Census Bureau; for more information on the PUMS, see the description below. Annual data between 2000 and 2005 in the IPUMS are based on the ACS (see the ACS description above).

Integrated Public Use Microdata Series–International
(IPUMS-International)

These data can be downloaded free of charge from the University of Minnesota's Population Research Center at www.ipums.org. Before this book went into press, these data included large-scale nationally representative samples for twenty-six countries (including Mexico and the United States), collected by various countries' government census agencies (e.g., the U.S. Census Bureau). Statistical weights are provided in the International IPUMS to maintain the national representation of the samples. The IPUMS-International included a representative sample of 10.6 percent of the Mexican population in 2000 and 5 percent of the U.S. population.

Mexican Migration Project (MMP)

The MMP data are part of an ongoing collaborative research project, based at Princeton University and the University of Guadalajara, on Mexican migration to the United States. These data include information collected since 1982 in surveys administered every year in Mexico and the United States. The MMP114 version, which includes 114 communities, was released in June 2007; it represents the latest version of the dataset at the time this book went into press. Information on approximately 18,000 Mexican households, 900 U.S. households, and individual-level data on more than 125,000 persons are included in the MMP114 dataset; of these, detailed information is provided for more than 6,700 household heads with migration experience to the United States or Canada. The MMP114 files are available for public use and can be downloaded from the MMP Web site at mmp.opr.princeton.edu.

Public Use Microdata Samples (PUMS)

PUMS data are nationally representative samples based on the long-form version of the U.S. decennial census for 1980, 1990, and 2000. The long-form questionnaire was administered by the Census Bureau to one out of every six households; sampling weights, which were constructed by the Census Bureau, are included with the data to maintain the national representation of the samples. In addition to basic demographic information, the long-form version asked detailed questions about income, earnings, employment, education, and primary place of work, among other factors. The PUMS has two public versions: the 1 percent sample and the 5 percent sample, each containing approximately 1 and 5 percent of the U.S. population. The PUMS can be downloaded free of charge from the U.S. Census Bureau at www.census.gov or from the University of Minnesota Population Research Center at www.ipums.org.

Notes

Introduction

1. These figures are from the authors' estimates using 2000 census data in the Integrated Public Use Microdata Series (IPUMS-International); see the appendix for more details. The five million workers to which this chapter refers reside in the border region as defined using the county approach described in the appendix.

2. To illustrate, Keith Partridge, the executive director of the McAllen Economic Development Corporation, stated in June 2007, "The way we see our community of McAllen and Reynosa, Mexico, is that we're one city that happens to have a river running through it. Not that much different than any city in the world, except that we have to go through a Customs and Immigration every time we cross . . . Families are on both sides of the border. Business and commerce activities are going back and forth . . ." (Goodwyn 2007).

3. For example, using 2000 census data in the IPUMS–International, we estimate that in 2000, workers in the Mexican border region earned 1.5 times more on average per month than those in the Mexican interior ($577 versus $377), but only one-fifth of the average wages ($2,687) accrued by workers on the U.S. side of the border (defined using the county approach). On a related note, Joan B. Anderson (2003) finds that poverty rates on the Mexican side of the border are lower than those in the Mexican interior, but higher than the poverty rates on the U.S. side of the border (which themselves are higher than those in the U.S. interior).

4. For example, the University of Arizona Press recently published an entire manuscript focusing on women's issues in the U.S.-Mexico border region (*Women and Change at the U.S.-Mexico Border: Mobility, Labor, and Activism*, edited by Mattingly and Hansen, 2006).

Chapter 1

1. A note on nomenclature: Even terminology like "Mexican," "Hispanic," "Anglo," or "Chicano" is contested on the border. The term "Mexican," for instance, can obscure a great deal of diversity within that population. Though they often share certain cultural practices, like Catholicism or speaking Spanish, Mexicans could individually claim different racial and ethnic backgrounds. I do not intend to reduce the complexity of people's sense of racial, national, or ethnic identities. For simplicity, though, I use the term "Mexican" as it would have been understood at the border

during this time period. It will refer to individuals who claimed ancestry to the areas that had been part of the Mexican nation in 1821. I have also opted to use the more inclusive term "Euro American" over "Anglo" to describe non-Hispanic whites. Many of the Americans who lived along the nineteenth- and twentieth-century borders did not claim Anglo Saxon parentage. "Euro American" more aptly captures the variety of settlers who were either recent European immigrants or claimed ancestry in Europe. Not exclusively Anglo/Anglo Saxon, many of these settlers identified themselves as Irish, French, German, and so forth.

2. James Brooks' *Captives and Cousins* has meticulously documented how widespread slavery had been among both Native American and Mexican groups living at the northern frontier even after Mexico officially outlawed slavery in 1829 (Brooks 2002).

3. For a discussion of these differences, see Janet Lecompte (1981). While Lecompte traces the differences between Euro American and Mexican ideas about gender, work, and public activity, she sometimes overestimates the meaning of these differences for Mexican women. She frequently overstates the historical "independence" or "equality" of Mexican women, ignoring the ways in which institutionalized relationships of inequality divided power along gendered lines, configuring and enforcing male authority. See also Deena González (1999:44–50).

4. For more discussions about Mexicans' experiences in California, see Albert M. Camarillo (1979), Richard Griswold del Castillo (1979), Tomás Almaguer (1994), Genaro Padilla (1993), and Rosaura Sánchez (1995).

5. While most of their actions focused on pasture lands, the Gorras Blancas also occasionally interfered in trade. In some incidents, the vigilante group stopped contracted haulers and destroyed their cargo because they believed that the team leader had undercut prices for this service (Otero 1939:248–49).

6. For more discussion about the Texas Rangers' brutality, see Julian Samora, Joe Bernal, and Albert Peña (1979); Alfredo Mirande (1990), and Benjamin Johnson (2005).

7. For other discussions of Mexicans in twentieth-century Southern California, see Gilbert González (1994), Francisco Balderrama (1982), and Matt Garcia (2001).

8. At least fifteen thousand Mexicans worked in Michigan's beat fields by 1930 (Valdés 1988:3). Agricultural enterprises in Michigan, Illinois, and Indiana offered incentives for Mexican laborers to stay in the region during the winter. Factories throughout the Midwest benefited from these arrangements as those workers sought jobs during the off season. Cities like Chicago, Detroit, and Gary developed sizable Mexican enclaves. By 1930, the U.S. Census counted nearly twenty-one thousand Mexicans in Chicago, an increase of 1,700 percent from 1910 (Arredondo 1999:61).

9. In 1925, for instance, the director of California's Bureau of Tuberculosis published a report that claimed that Mexicans were a threat to public health. She argued that Mexicans, as a race, were less able-bodied and therefore more prone to disease than whites (Molina 2006:120–21). Similarly, Dr. Benjamin Goldberg, head of Chicago's tuberculosis sanatorium, declared that immigration from Mexico was a national health menace when public health officials met in Chicago in 1928. Goldberg out-

lined alleged racial differences between Euro Americans and Mexicans that he imagined made the latter more likely to carry a host of deadly aliments. Ending immigration across the border was necessary, Goldberg contended, because Mexicans were "a race sizzling with susceptibilities" (*Chicago Daily Tribune* 1928).

10. As translated by David G. Gutiérrez (1995:73).

11. The mid-2007 equivalent values are estimated using the Consumer Price Index.

12. For an extensive discussion on NAFTA's impact on Mexico, see Jorge Castañeda (1995).

Chapter 2

1. Financial support for this research was provided by El Paso Electric Company, Hunt Building Corporation, Hunt Communities, Wells Fargo Bank of El Paso, and a UTEP College of Business Administration Faculty Research Grant. Helpful comments were provided by an anonymous referee. Statistical research assistance was provided by George Novela.

2. The data discussed in this chapter are from the U.S. Census Bureau Decennial Census, the U.S. Census Bureau Quick Facts, the U.S. Census Bureau American Community Survey, and the U.S. Bureau of Economic Analysis. Contact the authors for details.

3. This issue goes beyond the scope of this chapter, but it warrants further research, particularly with respect to whether the patterns of economic growth in these younger counties differ from other counties. If so, how should policymakers respond to the differences?

4. Social pressures related to high-dependency ratios to some degree mitigate at the older ranges. However, low incomes on the U.S. side of the border offset many of these advantages and create other socioeconomic problems regarding public services that go beyond what the age profiles might otherwise imply (Zunker, Rutt, and Cummins 2004).

5. It should also be noted that infrastructure investment shortfalls also likely contribute to the income gaps observed along the border (García-Milà and McGuire 1992).

6. An interesting issue that arises from table 2.3 is whether trans-border shopping impacts the unemployment rates in these counties. Given that the factors that influence border region unemployment rates exhibit significantly more variation than what is observed in non-border labor markets (as will be discussed later in this volume by André Varella Mollick), a more detailed study is needed in order to fully examine such trends.

Chapter 3

1. This chapter is an expanded and updated version of our article "NAFTA and Economic Activity along the U.S.-Mexico Border," *Journal of Economic Issues* 34 (June 2000): 481–89.

2. Indeed, trade policy was controversial before the Declaration of Independence was signed—remember the Boston Tea Party. An intense debate over the nature of commerce among the states was resolved by granting Constitutional authority to Congress to regulate interstate commerce. Throughout the nineteenth century, import tariffs were the major source of U.S. federal government revenue. Also, given concerns over the impact of trade on U.S. jobs, Congress enacted the infamous Smoot-Hawley Act during the Great Depression, raising tariffs to levels high enough to significantly reduce U.S. international trade. The Bretton Woods Agreement at the end of World War II established a system of fixed exchange rates that was not lifted until the early 1970s, and it created the International Monetary Fund, the World Bank, and the GATT. Bretton Woods was a strong declaration among the Allied Powers that trade restrictions resulted in reduced economic activity and increased political instability. Although the GATT has now been replaced by the World Trade Organization (WTO), the Bretton Woods Agreement remains a powerful influence on trade and economic policy around the world. That trade policy remains controversial in the United States and elsewhere may be easily confirmed by the organized and unorganized protests at each WTO meeting.

3. John Sargent, Melissa Najera, and Linda Matthews look at such impacts on the Mexican side of the border in the following chapter.

4. This openness measure uses both imports and exports. Given the nature of some trade between Mexico and the United States—e.g., the maquiladora industry, in which raw materials and other inputs are exported from the United States to Mexico for assembly or manufacturing, and then the final products are exported from Mexico to the United States—there is some double counting.

5. The border region, of course, is the entry point for most Mexican migrants to the United States regardless of legal status or intended destination. (More on this migration issue will be discussed later in this volume by Villarreal [chapter 5] and by Orrenius, Zavodny, and Lukens [chapter 8].) The Pew Foundation (Haskins 2007) state-level estimates of illegal migrants indicate that Texas and California are also the states of residence for many illegal immigrants. The border region has traditionally experienced high rates of population growth and high in-migration rates despite its generally high unemployment rates and low per-capita incomes. Apparently, NAFTA has not substantially altered border region population growth patterns.

6. For example, border MSAs tend to have a relatively high share of employment in retail trade, in accommodations, and in food service, and—often—in warehousing and transportation, three traditionally low-wage industries. In the previous chapter, Thomas M. Fullerton Jr., James H. Holcomb, and Angel L. Molina Jr. see the trend somewhat differently. Their concern is that both nationally and along the border, many new jobs in the service sector require higher levels of education, leaving border residents at a disadvantage in the face of a changing industrial structure.

Chapter 5

1. Ricardo Cantu and Andrea Bereznak provided splendid research assistance for this project. The study also benefited from comments by an anonymous reviewer.

2. The result holds at least for what would be considered classical migration. There is a new demographic of migrants with professional education (e.g., engineers, grade school teachers, nurses, etc.) that may originate in the Mexican northern states (see some arguments in Alacron 1997). However, further research is needed on this topic.

3. Of course, there exist other pertinent reasons: a quality component within human capital (i.e., varying quality of schools), social networks, etc. However, given the availability of data, the two effects mentioned have received the most attention.

4. There is some dispute regarding the extent to which Nuevo Leon is a border state; strictly speaking, it does possess a border area (very small) but it does not have any city located on the border. Nonetheless, given its economic weight in the area and its commercial relations with several Texan cities, we will employ the strict definition and consider Nuevo Leon a border state.

5. In the United States, 28 percent of those people age twenty-five or older reported they had attained at least a bachelor's degree (http://www.census.gov/PressRelease/www/releases/archives/education/004214.html).

6. Alternative profiles might be tested. In the case of a different number of hours worked, the average salaries change linearly, as the simulations are based on salary per hour. In the case of other age profiles, patterns change non-linearly because the model is semi-logarithmic, and thus the wage differences between educational levels are larger for younger people and smaller for older people.

7. This study seems to contradict some previous results that skill-returns might have increased in Mexico, noticeably the findings of Cesar Bouillon, Arianna Legovini, and Nora Lustig (2003). However, their study analyzes a longer time period, and it also uses 1994 as the starting point; the economic returns to college were unusually high that year according to the available income-expenditure household surveys. Nevertheless, these results are corroborated by Gladys Lopez-Acevedo (2004) and Aashish Mehta and Hector J. Villarreal (2005).

8. A typical definition is the ratio to the mean of half the average over all pairs of the absolute deviations between people.

9. Standard "Mincerian equations" usually employ an additional quadratic term for experience to capture "obsolescence" of experience. In this chapter's initial analysis, the quadratic term was not always statistically significant, and its economic significance was small. The author therefore decided to drop the term to keep the number of parameters to a minimum.

Chapter 6

1. Additional evidence of the growing paid-employment opportunities can be observed in Lucinda Vargas (2001), who notes that the northern border cities in Mexico had some of the highest unemployment rates before the maquiladora program existed. However, with the growth in the maquiladora industry in the region, these cities now boast some of the lowest unemployment rates in Mexico. Similarly, during the 1990s, poverty rates declined more in Mexican border municipios along the major transportation routes for trade in goods than they did in other municipios (Anderson 2003).

2. It should be noted that in a related study (Mora and Dávila 2006), we provide evidence of the presence of self-employment push-factors in the U.S. border region for non-Hispanic white workers, but the presence of these factors is not dispropor-tionate to those in the rest of the United States. Moreover, when focusing exclusively on Mexican immigrants in the same study, our findings suggest that immigrants are *pulled* into self-employment along the border but pushed in the U.S. interior. The border region arguably provides Mexican immigrants with more lucrative entrepre-neurial possibilities than other workers because of their knowledge of the language, culture, and business practices prevalent in the region (see also Mora 2006).

3. Specifically, we estimate the earnings function for these two regions while con-trolling for factors related to self-employment propensities (including education, age, marital status, gender, and occupations) using the Heckman selection technique (Heckman 1976). The estimated selection variable λ was −3.08 (standard error = 0.005) for the Mexican interior, and 0.061 (0.015) for the Mexican border region. Details can be obtained from the authors.

4. Of interest, using the same methodology reported in note 1, we also find evi-dence of a positive selection into self-employment on the U.S. side of the border (with the estimated λ [standard error] = 0.070 [0.011]), but a negative self-employment selection in the U.S. interior (λ = −1.935 [0.013]). In a previous study, the first two authors of this chapter also detected positive self-employment selection among Mexi-can immigrants in the U.S. border region (Mora and Dávila 2006); we interpreted this finding in terms of immigrants purposely migrating to the U.S. border region with the intention of starting a business. The observation of positive self-employment selection on *both* sides of the U.S.-Mexico border suggests that *something* about the overall geo-graphic region foments business formation, and it could be attracting entrepreneurial migrants from other areas; this issue is worthy of future research.

Chapter 7

1. The procedure to identify Mexican immigrant jobs comes from previous research (Douglas and Sáenz 2008; Model 1993; Waldinger 1996). We calculate two sex-specific percentages: (1) the percentage of workers in a given occupation who are Mexican immigrants (p_o), and (2) the percentage of all workers—regardless of occupation—who are Mexican immigrants (p_t). Subsequently, we estimate the fol-lowing ratio for each sex across the four border states: Ratio = p_o/p_t. We then identify "Mexican immigrant jobs" as those in which this ratio is 1.5 or higher and there is a minimum number of workers in a given occupation (5,000 for females and 12,500 for males). This variable equals 1 for workers with such jobs; it equals zero otherwise.

2. Note that the multivariate analysis includes age, education, experience (age − years of education − 6), and experience squared. The simultaneous use of these four variables raises some concerns regarding multicollinearity. However, because the edu-cation variable is categorical, the regression equation can be identified. In addition, parallel analyses were conducted eliminating the experience and experience-squared variables. These results were consistent with those obtained when all four variables are included in the analysis (i.e., the results presented in this chapter).

3. The results indicate that immigrants' wages tend to be lower in New Mexico and Texas than in the other two border states, particularly among women. To illustrate, female Mexican immigrants earned 13.5 percent less and 11.3 percent less in New Mexico and Texas, respectively, than their otherwise similar counterparts in California and Arizona. Compared to their peers in California, Mexican-born men earned 6.6 percent less in New Mexico, 4.8 percent less in Texas, and 2.4 percent more in Arizona.

4. For example, Mexican women who do not hold a Mexican immigrant job along the border earn 10.5 percent less than their counterparts in the interior, while those who have a Mexican immigrant job along the border earn 5.6 percent less (= −10.5 + 4.9) than women in the interior.

Chapter 8

1. The views expressed here are those of the authors and do not necessarily reflect those of the Federal Reserve Bank of Dallas or Federal Reserve System.

2. Overviews of Mexican immigration to the United States include those of George Borjas (2007), Gordon H. Hanson (2006), and Douglas S. Massey et al. (1987).

3. We use the terms "immigrant," "migrant," and "foreign-born" interchangeably throughout this chapter.

4. Lower migration costs also have implications for the self-selection of migrants and, all other things equal, should make selection among border migrants less positive as compared with migrants to the U.S. interior (Chiquiar and Hanson 2005; Orrenius and Zavodny 2005). The issue of self-selection, however, is outside of the scope of this chapter.

5. Being able to cross the border legally does not mean that these migrants can work legally in the United States, although many of them work anyway. It is also common to overstay these visas, in which case the migrant loses legal status.

6. Alberto Dávila and Rogelio Sáenz (1990) find a negative short-run correlation between maquiladora employment growth and Border Patrol apprehensions. This is not inconsistent with a long-run relationship between growth in the maquiladora workforce and U.S. migration, but it suggests that the timing of the impact may depend on relative economic conditions. Elsewhere in this book, Sargent, Najera, and Matthews in chapter 4 discuss how the maquiladora industry has evolved in the post-NAFTA era. Despite the recent bust, maquiladoras in Mexican border states continue to employ almost one million workers.

7. It should be noted that wage inequality changed in Mexico over the sample period, rising in the late 1980s and early 1990s and falling in the post-NAFTA period (Chiquiar 2004; Robertson 2007). Recall from Villarreal in chapter 5 that this may have affected migration, although we do not investigate those potential effects here.

8. These data can be obtained from the Office of Population Research, Princeton University, at mmp.opr.princeton.edu. The appendix to this volume provides a basic description of this dataset. For a detailed discussion of the MMP surveys, see Jorge

Durand and Douglas S. Massey (2004). The MMP114 (also used in the next chapter by Catalina Amuedo-Dorantes and Cynthia Bansak) is one of the richest datasets available for studying Mexican migration to the United States.

9. This list excludes the Mexican states bordering the United States that are not in the MMP.

10. Specifically, we include San Diego, California; Yuma and Tucson in Arizona; Las Cruces, New Mexico; and El Paso, Laredo, McAllen, and Brownsville in Texas. Tucson and Las Cruces are not always considered U.S. border cities, since they are not located adjacent to Mexico. However, they are located in counties that are adjacent to the border and, given our small sample sizes, we chose to include them as border cities. The MMP does not include information on U.S. counties, so we cannot identify the non-MSA border region.

11. We define migrant networks at the community level so we can assign every migrant a network value (the MMP only asks household heads about their networks, not other household members). See this chapter's appendix for more details.

12. The MMP data reports these as "U.S. occupations," although these workers are, in all likelihood, employed in Mexico.

13. Alberto Dávila and Marie T. Mora (2008) also find that the earnings of Mexican immigrants along the border improved relative to those of Mexicans in the interior between 1990 and 2000, although they do not find that the difference goes to zero. Perhaps this seeming discrepancy reflects the datasets used; their analysis only includes Mexicans residing in the United States, whereas the MMP contains migrants who have returned to Mexico.

14. These regressions include less than half the original observations because of missing wage information. We also exclude the aggregate variables, such as economic conditions and immigration policy.

15. Probit regressions yield very similar results, so we chose the simpler specification for ease of interpretation.

Chapter 9

1. The MMP114 is one of the richest datasets available for studying Mexican migration to the United States. Recall that the MMP114 is also used in the previous chapter by Pia M. Orrenius, Madeline Zavodny, and Leslie Lukens. That chapter covers the same time period (1980s to the present) and discusses the differences between migration to the U.S. border and migration within the United States.

2. The survey is the result of a multidisciplinary study of Mexican migration to the United States, which contains detailed information from approximately 19,000 households in 114 representative communities in Mexico. More information about this dataset is presented in the appendix to this volume. See the Mexican Migration Web site (at www.mmp.opr.princeton.edu) for details on the geographic coverage of this survey. For each household, a complete life history is gathered for the household head, including detailed information on whether the head has migrated to the United States in the past. If so, he or she is extensively queried about that migration experi-

ence, and this information is what we use for this study. Additionally, we include information on migrants from the same communities in Mexico who have settled in the United States and no longer return home. While this is a snowball sample, its usage allows us to distinguish between shorter- and longer-term migrants by including both types of migrants and accounting for the length of migrants' last spells in the United States. The changing geographic scope of the survey over time may bias some of our results if, indeed, migrant selection changed over the time period being examined. To the extent to which it is achievable, we address this possibility by controlling for a variety of personal and job-related characteristics possibly affecting migrants' tax payments and public-service usage rates.

3. The MMP interviews were conducted in communities of various sizes, ethnic compositions, and stages of economic development that are typical source regions for U.S.-bound migrants. In addition, the sample expands over time to incorporate communities in newer sending states.

4. The median duration in the United States, however, is only ten months.

5. This study found that border counties spend $200 million per year to provide emergency medical services to undocumented immigrants. Given these findings, Congress included $1 billion over four years in the Medicare Modernization Act to reimburse health care providers for the cost of providing emergency medical care to undocumented immigrants.

6. A probit model is "a model for binary responses where the response probability is the standard normal cumulative distribution function evaluated at a linear function of the explanatory variables" (Wooldridge 2002).

7. These results are robust to the inclusion of occupational binary variables, as well as to the length of migrants' last U.S. trip—intended to, respectively, capture any changes over time in occupational distributions and capture differences in the usage of public services, depending on the temporary versus permanent nature of a migrant's trip.

8. Additional output, available from the authors upon request, shows that the increase was generalized to all migrants regardless of their legal status.

9. The usage in public health insurance coverage does not preclude the fact that some migrants may still incur co-payments and other health-related costs.

10. The most likely cause of the increase in the rate of public health insurance coverage following the passage of the PRWORA may be the significant twenty-three percentage-point reduction in the usage of such services with the enactment of the law (see table 9.4).

Chapter 10

1. Often, the discussion of maquiladora employment involves low-skill labor, but the capital infrastructure also implies that maquiladoras stimulate the demand for high-skilled workers, given the complementarity between skilled labor and capital. For more information on maquiladoras and recent changes in the industry, see Sargent, Najera, and Matthews (chapter 4) earlier in this volume.

2. Extant literature discusses how community experiences affect the employment and residential preferences of workers (Wegener 1991; Hanson and Pratt 1988, 1992). U.S. residents new to the border region and/or to the Mexican culture might view the scale of the community to include only U.S. cities. As such, these workers would probably prefer to work on the U.S. side of the border and would therefore accept employment in Mexico only if firms provided an economic incentive. This incentive should also be larger if individuals perceive working in Mexico as being less secure than working in the United States or if crossing the international border is stressful.

3. U.S. and Canadian business persons entering and staying in Mexico for fewer than thirty days at a time can alternatively obtain an Forma Migratoria de Negocios (FMN) visa, which is available at no cost at all ports-of-entry and can be renewed as many times as needed throughout the year. However, the FMN only applies to workers whose primary place of business is outside of Mexico. For more information on the FM3 and the FMN, see ciudadjuarez.usconsulate.gov/wwwhmvr.html.

4. Specifically, we use the Five Percent Public Use Microdata Sample (PUMS) for 2000 and the 1 Percent ACS for 2005, both made available by Ruggles et al. (2007) in the Integrated Public Microdata Series (IPUMS). These data are described in the appendix chapter of this volume. We employ the IPUMS-provided sampling weights in all of our analyses to maintain the national representation of the samples. To obtain a sample of workers with a relatively strong attachment to the labor force, we exclude individuals currently enrolled in school, as well as those who worked fewer than twenty hours per week or fewer than thirty-two weeks in the year prior to each census. One drawback with the 2005 data for this particular study is the relatively small sample size of cross-border workers, given that the 2005 ACS in the IPUMS is one-fifth the size of our 2000 sample. As such, the 2005 sample is not large enough to partition the cross-border sample into detailed demographic groups (such as U.S.-born Hispanics versus non-Hispanic whites, or self-employed versus salaried workers), as we have done in other studies using data from 2000 (Mora and Dávila 2007; Mora 2006). Nevertheless, the 2005 ACS represents one of the largest and most current datasets with which to study cross-border workers.

5. The annual income information technically pertains to the year prior to the survey, but for ease of discussion, we refer to the survey year as the year when the income was earned.

6. T-tests show that the mean earnings significantly differ (at the 1 percent level) between the cross-border and other workers in each year.

7. Some anecdotal evidence can be found in Ginger Thompson (2005a), who notes the case of Dr. Charles Rodgers, a Brownsville oncologist who ran a cancer clinic across the border in Matamoros. Dr. Rodgers was abducted at his clinic on December 9, 2004, and held hostage at gunpoint for several hours until his wife paid an $88,000 ransom. Nearly two months later, Dr. Rodgers had not been back to Mexico, stating he was "never going back." He began consulting through videoconferencing with the Mexican physicians with whom he left his clinic.

8. The possibility exists that the relatively small sample size of cross-border workers in 2005 (recall note 4) is responsible for the lack of statistical significance of the change in this earnings premium between 2000 and 2005. If so, these results would suggest that the cross-border premium increased in the early 2000s, so that the potential earnings-dampening effects of a reduction in commuting time and the slowdown in the maquiladora industry were more than offset by other factors, such as higher commuting costs (e.g., real gas prices), as well as by additional stress associated with increased scrutiny by immigration officials and growing concerns over safety.

9. The economic impact of Mexican nationals on the tourism, entertainment, and retail sectors in many U.S. border communities should not be ignored. For example, retail sales in Texas to Mexican shoppers were as high as $15 billion per year in the early 2000s (General Accounting Office 2003). Also recall also from Fullerton, Holcomb, and Molina in chapter 2 that many border communities have relatively high retail-to-income ratios because of the ability to sell goods and services to Mexican shoppers.

10. Hourly earnings are estimated by dividing the sum of wage and salary income plus self-employment income by the number of hours usually worked per week times the number of weeks worked. It should be noted that a small number of workers in our sample reported non-positive self-employment income; however, none of these individuals worked abroad. Following methods similar to those of George J. Borjas and Stephen G. Bronars (1989), as well as ourselves in past works (Mora 2006; Mora and Dávila 2006, 2007) and other authors, rather than deleting these individuals and upwardly skewing earnings, we set their income equal to the minimum positive income earned by workers in each census year.

11. Given the semi-logarithmic nature of equation (1), a more precise magnitude of the cross-border earnings premium than the β's can be estimated using the technique described by Peter Kennedy (1981). For ease of interpretation, however, we focus on the β's themselves.

Chapter 11

1. The unemployment rate and employment figures used in this chapter come from the U.S. Bureau of Labor Statistics (BLS); the BLS website (www.bls.gov) contains details on the sampling methodology.

2. See André Varella Mollick (2008a) for a detailed discussion and analysis of employment activities on the U.S. side of the border, as well as for a review of the literature on the relationship between national and local unemployment rates.

3. See Gordon H. Hanson (2001) for more on the cross-border effects of manufacturing production in Mexico and André Varella Mollick, Abigail Cortez-Rayas, and Rosa A. Olivas-Moncisvais (2006) for extensions to other sectors. Jesús Cañas, Roberto Coronado, and Robert Gilmer (2005) view the boom at the U.S.-Mexico border as a major factor compelling the Texas economy to outperform the U.S. economy in the 1990s.

4. For example, the industry with the largest employment concentration in Laredo was the trade, transportation, and utilities sector, in which 37.4 percent of total employment in the city was concentrated (specialized) in 1990; that is, Laredo's employment specialization index was 0.374. In contrast, the share of this sector for total U.S. employment was 20.7 percent that year. Dividing Laredo's trade specialization by the share of U.S. employment in the trade sector yields the RSI of 1.807 (= 0.374/0.207) in 1990.

5. Further evidence of relatively concentrated employment in the Texas-Mexico border MSAs is found through estimating Herfindahl indices (which equal the sum of the squared employment shares in each of the ten industries in an MSA). The smaller the value of the Herfindahl index is, the more diversified is employment in the MSA. These indices are higher for the Texas border MSAs than for the largest non-border Texas MSAs between 1990 and 2005 (ranging from 0.153 to 0.166 in Brownsville, 0.157 to 0.150 in El Paso, 0.214 to 0.197 in Laredo, 0.175 to 0.171 in McAllen, 0.136 to 0.126 in Dallas, and 0.131 to 0.127 in Houston). Therefore, employment is more concentrated in Texas-Mexico border MSAs than in Dallas and Houston. The three California MSAs studied here have similar Herfindahl indices (0.127 to 0.126 in San Diego; 0.132 to 0.124 in Los Angeles; and 0.130 to 0.126 in San Francisco).

Chapter 12

1. One recent example that discusses cross-border unions is a book by David Bacon (2005).

2. To illustrate, the issue of cross-border health care has been receiving increased attention by social scientists and policymakers, as rising costs and higher insurance premiums are causing more U.S. border residents to use healthcare facilities on the Mexican side of the border (e.g., Warner 2007; Bastida, Brown, and Pagán 2007).

3. We note in chapter 10 that the surge in violence in Mexican border cities between 2000 and 2005 may have deterred some U.S. residents from working in Mexico. Also, Sargent, Najera, and Matthews provide some ethnographic evidence on maquiladora workers' perception of safety at the workplace. However, we realize these discussions only scratch the surface of how perceptions of safety affect the well-being of the border workforce; future studies should provide more in-depth investigations.

Bibliography

Adkisson, Richard V., and Linda Zimmerman. 2004. "Retail Trade on the U.S.-Mexico Border during the NAFTA Implementation Era." *Growth & Change* 35:77–89.

Alacron, Rafael. 1997. "From Servants to Engineers: Mexican Immigration and Labor Markets in the San Francisco Bay Area." Center for Latino Policy Research Working Papers.

Alderman, Harold, Jere R. Behrman, David R. Ross, and Richard Sabot. 1996. "The Returns to Endogenous Human Capital in Pakistan's Rural Wage Labour Market." *Oxford Bulletin of Economics and Statistics* 58:29–55.

Aleman, E. 2006. "Is Robin Hood the Prince of Thieves or a Pathway to Equity?" *Educational Policy* 20:113–142.

Almada, Christa, Lorenzo Blanco-González, Patricia S. Eason, and Thomas M. Fullerton Jr. 2006. "Econometric Evidence Regarding Education and Border Income Performance." *Mountain Plains Journal of Business & Economics* 7:11–24.

Almaguer, Tomás. 1994. *Racial Fault Lines: The Origins of White Supremacy in California.* Berkeley: University of California Press.

Alonso, Ana María. 1995. *Thread of Blood: Colonialism, Revolution, and Gender on Mexico's Northern Frontier.* Tucson: University of Arizona Press.

Alvarado, Ignacio. 2008. "Mexicans Fleeing Drug War Help El Paso House Market." *San Diego Union-Tribune*, September 10.

Anderson, Joan B. 2003. "The U.S.-Mexico Border: A Half Century of Change." *Social Science Journal* 40:535–554.

Arredondo, Gabriela F. 1999. *"What! The Mexicans, Americans?" Race and Ethnicity, Mexicans in Chicago 1916–1939.* PhD thesis, University of Chicago.

Arredondo, Gabriela F., Aída Hurtado, Norma Klahn, Olga Nájera-Ramírez, and Patricia Zavella (eds.). 2003. *Chicana Feminisms: A Critical Reader.* Durham, NC: Duke University Press.

Ashenfelter, Orley C., and Cecilia E. Rouse. 1999. "Schooling, Intelligence, and Income in America: Crack in the Bell Curve." National Bureau of Economic Research (NBER) Working Paper Series, no. 6902.

Associated Press. 2005. "Kidnappings High along Mexico Border." *USA Today*, January 27.

Bacon, David. 2005. *The Children of NAFTA: Labor Wars on the U.S.-Mexico Border.* Los Angeles: University of California Press.

Bailey, John. 2004. "Security Imperatives of North American Integration: Back to a Future of Hub and Spokes." In Sidney Weintraub (ed.), *NAFTA's Impact on North America: The First Decade*. Washington, DC: Center for Strategic and International Studies, pp. 235–260.

Bailey, Thomas, and Roger Waldinger. 1991. "Primary, Secondary, and Enclave Labor Markets: A Training Systems Approach." *American Sociological Review* 56:432–445.

Baker, Susan González. 1997. "The 'Amnesty' Aftermath: Current Policy Issues Stemming from the Legalization Programs of the 1986 Immigration Reform and Control Act." *International Migration Review* 31(1): 5–27.

Balderrama, Francisco. 1982. *In Defense of La Raza: The Los Angeles Mexican Consulate and the Mexican Community, 1929–1936*. Tucson: University of Arizona Press.

Balderrama, Francisco, and Raymond Rodríguez. 1995. *Decade of Betrayal: Mexican Repatriation in the 1930s*. Albuquerque: University of New Mexico Press.

Baldwin, Percy M. 1938. "A Short History of the Mesilla Valley." *New Mexico Historical Review* 13(3): 314–324.

Banco de Mexico. http://www.banxico.org.mx.

Banks, James, Richard Blundell, and Arthur Lewbel. 1996. "Tax Reform and Welfare Measurement: Do We Need Demand System Estimation?" *Economic Journal* 106:1227–1241.

Bartel, Ann P. 1989. "Where Do the New U.S. Immigrants Live?" *Journal of Labor Economics* 7(4): 371–391.

Bastida, Elena, H. Shelton Brown, and José A. Pagán. 2007. "Health Insurance Coverage and Health Care Utilization along the U.S.-Mexico Border: Evidence from the Border Epidemiologic Study on Aging." In Jacqueline L. Angel and Keith E. Whitfield (eds.), *The Health of Aging Hispanics: The Mexican Origin Population*. New York: Springer, pp. 222–234.

Bean, Frank D., Barry Edmonston, and Jeffrey S. Passel, eds. 1990. *Undocumented Migration to the United States: IRCA and the Experience of the 1980s*. Lanham, MD: University Press of America.

Bedi, Arjun S., and Noel Gaston. 1997. "Returns to Endogenous Education: The Case of Honduras." *Applied Economics* 29:519–528.

Bergsten, C. Fred. 2005. "Preface." In Gary Clyde Hufbauer and Jeffrey J. Schott (eds.), *NAFTA Revisited: Achievements and Challenges*. Washington, DC: Institute for International Economics.

Betts, Dianne C., and Daniel J. Slottje. 1994. *Crisis on the Rio Grande: Poverty, Unemployment, and Economic Development on the Texas-Mexico Border*. Boulder, CO: Westview Press.

Blau, Francine D. 1984. "The Use of Transfer Payments by Immigrants." *Industrial and Labor Relations Review* 37:222–239.

Bonacich, Edna. 1976. "Advanced Capitalism and Black/White Race Relations in the United States: A Split Labor Market Interpretation." *American Sociological Review* 41:34–51.

————. 1987. "'Making It' in America: A Social Evaluation of the Ethics of Immigrant Entrepreneurship." *Sociological Perspectives* 30(4): 446–466.

Borjas, George J. 1987. "Self-Selection and the Earnings of Immigrants." *American Economic Review* 77:531–553.

————. 1999. "Immigration and Welfare Magnets." *Journal of Labor Economics* 17(4): 607–637.

————. 2001. "Welfare Reform and Immigration." In Rebecca Blank and Ron Haskins (eds.), *The New World of Welfare: An Agenda for Reauthorization and Beyond.* Washington, DC: Brooking Press, pp. 369–385.

————. 2003. "The Labor Demand Curve is Downward Sloping: Reexamining the Impact of Immigration on the Labor Market." *Quarterly Journal of Economics* 118:1335–1374.

————. 2007. *Mexican Immigration to the United States.* Chicago: University of Chicago Press.

Borjas, George J., and Stephen G. Bronars. 1989. "Consumer Discrimination and Self-Employment." *Journal of Political Economy* 97(5): 581–605.

Borjas, George J., and L. Hilton. 1996. "Immigration and the Welfare State: Immigrant Participation in Means-Tested Entitlement Programs." *Quarterly Journal of Economics* 111:575–604.

Borjas, George J., and Lawrence F. Katz. 2007. "Evolution of the Mexican-Born Workforce in the United States." In George J. Borjas (ed.), *Mexican Immigration to the United States.* Chicago: University of Chicago Press, pp. 13–55.

Bouillon, Cesar, Arianna Legovini, and Nora Lustig. 2003. "Rising Inequality in Mexico: Household Characteristics and Regional Effects." *Journal of Development Studies* 39:112–133.

Brinkley, Joel. 1986. "Meese Links Drugs and Illegal Aliens." *New York Times,* September 18.

Brooks, James. 2002. *Captives & Cousins: Slavery, Kinship, and Community in the Southwest Borderlands.* Chapel Hill: University of North Carolina Press.

Buckley, F. H. 1996. "The Political Economy of Immigration Policies." *International Review of Law and Economics* 16(1): 81–99.

Burfisher, Mary E., Sherman Robinson, and Karen Thierfelder. 2001. "The Impact of NAFTA on the United States." *Journal of Economic Perspectives* 15(1): 125–144.

Camarillo, Albert M. 1979. *Chicanos in a Changing Society: From Mexican Pueblos to American Barrios in Santa Barbara and Southern California, 1848–1930.* Cambridge: Harvard University Press.

Cañas, Jesús, Roberto Coronado, and Robert Gilmer. 2007. "Maquiladora Recovery: Lessons for the Future." *Southwest Economy* March/April: 3–7.

Cañas, Jesús, Roberto Coronado, and Robert Gilmer. 2004. "Maquiladora Downturn: Structural Change or Cyclical Factors." *Business Frontier* 2:1–8.

————. 2005. "Texas Border, Employment and Maquiladora Growth." *The Face of Texas: Jobs, People, Business and Change.* October, Federal Reserve Bank of Dallas. http://www.dallasfed.org/research/pubs/fotexas/fotexas_canas.pdf.

————. 2007. "Mexican Reform Clouds View of Key Industry." *Southwest Economy* May/June: 10.

Capps, Randolph, Michael Fix, Everett Henderson, and Jane Reardon-Anderson. 2005. "A Profile of Low-Income Working Immigrant Families." No. B-67 in Series, *New Federalism: National Survey of America's Families.* Washington, DC: Urban Institute.

Card, David. 2001. "Estimating the Return to Schooling: Progress on Some Persistent Econometric Problems." *Econometrica* 69:1127–1160.

Carrillo, Jorge, and Redi Gomis. 2003. "Los Retos de las Maquiladoras ante la Pérdida de Competitividad." *Comercio Exterior* 53(4): 318–327.

Carrillo, Jorge, and Arturo Lara. 2005. "Mexican Maquiladoras: New Capabilities of Coordination and the Emergence of a New Generation of Companies." *Innovation: Management, Policy, & Practices* 7:2–3.

Castañeda, Jorge. 1995. *The Mexican Shock: Its Meaning for the U.S.* New York: New Press.

Castillo, Melissa. 2003. *The Utilization of Perceived Needs Importance in Explaining and Predicting Responsiveness to Organizational Inducements.* Unpublished doctoral dissertation, University of Texas–Pan American.

Catanzarite, Lisa. 2000. "Brown-Collar Jobs: Occupational Segregation and Earnings of Recent Immigrant Latina/os." *Sociological Perspectives* 43:45–75.

———. 2002. "Dynamics of Segregation and Earnings in Brown-Collar Occupations." *Work and Occupations* 29:300–345.

Catanzarite, Lisa, and Michael Bernabé Aguilera. 2002. "Working with Co-Ethnics: Earnings Penalties for Latino Immigrants at Latino Jobsites." *Social Problems* 49(1): 101–127.

Cerrutti, Marcela, and Douglas S. Massey. 2001. "On the Auspices of Female Migration from Mexico to the United States." *Demography* 38(2): 187–200.

———. 2004. "Trends in Mexican Migration to the United States, 1965 to 1995." In Jorge Durand and Douglas S. Massey (eds.), *Crossing the Border: Research from the Mexican Migration Project.* New York: Russell Sage Foundation, pp. 17–44.

Chávez, Alicia Hernández. 2006. *Mexico: A Brief History.* Trans. Andy Klatt. Berkeley: University of California Press.

Chicago Daily Tribune. 1928. "Depicts Mexican Immigrants as Health Menace: Doctor Urges Bar to Halt Disease Invasion." October 19, 1928, p. 20.

Chiquiar, Daniel. 2004. "Globalization, Regional Wage Differentials, and the Stolper-Samuelson Theorem: Evidence from Mexico." Banco de México Working Paper No. 2004–06.

Chiquiar, Daniel, and Gordon H. Hanson. 2005. "International Migration, Self-Selection, and the Distribution of Wages: Evidence from Mexico and the United States." *Journal of Political Economy* 113:239–281.

Christman, John. 2005. *Mexico's Maquiladora Industry Outlook: 2005–2010.* Presentation made at the Maquiladora Industry Outlook Meeting, Laredo, TX, September 23, 2005.

Clark, Kenneth, and Stephen Drinkwater. 1998. "Ethnicity and Self-Employment in Britain." *Oxford Bulletin of Economics and Statistics* 60(3): 383–407.

Clark, Stephen D. 2007. "Estimating Local Car Ownership Models." *Journal of Transport Geography* 15:184–197.

Congressional Budget Office (CBO). 2003. *The Effects of NAFTA on U.S.-Mexican Trade and GDP.* http://www.cbo.gov/ftpdoc.cfm?index=4247&type=0 (accessed July 28, 2007).

Congressional Quarterly, Inc. 1994. *Congressional Quarterly Almanac 1993.* Washington, DC: CQ Press, 51-S, 140–141H.

Coronado, Roberto, Thomas Fullerton, and Don Clark. 2004. "Short-Run Maquiladora Employment Dynamics in Tijuana." *Annals of Regional Science* 38:751–763.

Cragg, Michael Ian, and Mario Epelbaum. 1996. "Why Has Wage Dispersion Grown in Mexico? Is It the Incidence of Reforms or the Growing Demand for Skills?" *Journal of Development Economics* 51:99–116.

Craig, Richard. 1971. *The Bracero Program: Interest Groups and Foreign Policy.* Austin: University of Texas Press.

Cummings, Judith. 1985. "Border Patrol is Troubled by Attacks on Agents." *New York Times*, May 19.

Dávila, Alberto, Alok K. Bohara, and Rogelio Sáenz. 1993. "Accent Penalties and the Earnings of Mexican Americans." *Social Science Quarterly* 74(4): 902–916.

Dávila, Alberto, and J. Peter Mattila. 1985. "Do Workers Earn Less along the U.S.-Mexico Border?" *Social Science Quarterly* 66(2): 310–318.

Dávila, Alberto, and Marie T. Mora. 2000. "English Skills, Earnings, and the Occupational Sorting of Mexican Americans along the U.S.-Mexico Border." *International Migration Review* 34(1): 133–157.

———. 2008. "Changes in the Relative Earnings Gap Between Natives and Immigrants along the U.S.-Mexico Border." *Journal of Regional Science* 48(3): 525–545.

Dávila, Alberto, José A. Pagán, and Montserrat Viladrich Grau. 1999. "Immigration Reform, the INS, and the Distribution of Interior and Border Enforcement Resources." *Public Choice* 99:327–345.

Dávila, Alberto, and Rogelio Sáenz. 1990. "The Effect of Maquiladora Employment on the Monthly Flow of Mexican Undocumented Immigration to the U.S., 1978–1982." *International Migration Review* 24:96–107.

Deaton, Angus. 1997. *The Analysis of Household Surveys: A Microeconometric Approach to Development.* Baltimore: Johns Hopkins University Press.

Department of Economic and Social Affairs. 2001. *World Population Ageing: 1950–2050.* New York: Population Division, United Nations.

Deutsch, Sarah. 1987. *No Separate Refuge: Culture, Class, and Gender on the Anglo-Hispanic Frontier in the American Southwest, 1880–1940.* New York: Oxford University Press.

Devlin, Robert, Antoni Estevadeordal, and Andres Rodríguez-Clare. 2006. *The Emergence of China: Opportunities and Challenges for Latin America and the Caribbean.* Boston: Harvard University Press.

Diaz, David A. 2007. "Border Leaders Finalizing Work for Legislative Assault on Border Wall." *Texas Insider*, June 6. http://www.texasinsider.org (accessed June 14, 2007).

Dill, Bonnie Thornton, Lynn Weber Cannon, and Reeve Vanneman. 1987. "Race and Gender in Occupational Segregation." In *Pay Equity: An Issue of Race, Ethnicity and Sex.* Washington, DC: National Committee on Pay Equity, pp. 11–70.

Dodson, M. E. III. 2001. "Welfare Generosity and Location Choices Among New United States Immigrants." *International Review of Law and Economics* 21(March): 47–67.

Donato, Katharine M. 1993. "Current Trends and Patterns in Female Migration: Evidence from Mexico." *International Migration Review* 27:748–771.

Donato, Katharine M., and Evelyn Patterson. 2004. "Women and Men on the Move: Undocumented Border Crossing." In Jorge Durand and Douglas S. Massey (eds.), *Crossing the Border: Research from the Mexican Migration Project.* New York: Russell Sage Foundation, pp. 111–130.

Donato, Katharine M., and Andrea Tyree. 1986. "Family Reunification, Health Professions, and the Sex Composition of Migrants to the United States." *Sociology and Social Research* 70:226–230.

Douglas, Karen Manges, and Rogelio Sáenz. 2008. "No Phone, No Vehicle, No English, and No Citizenship: The Vulnerability of Mexican Immigrants in the United States." In Angela Hattery, David Embrick, and Earl Smith (eds.), *Race, Human Rights and Inequality.* Lanham, MD: Rowman & Littlefield.

Driskell, Robyn, and Elizabeth Embry. 2007. "Mexican American Women's Labor Market Experience: The Effects of Regional and Ethnic Concentration." *Latino(a) Research Review* 6(1–2): 72–93.

Dunn, Timothy. 1996. *The Militarization of the U.S.-Mexico Border, 1978–1992: Low-Intensity Conflict Doctrine Comes Home.* Austin: University of Texas Center for Mexican American Studies.

Durand, Jorge, and Douglas S. Massey. 1992. "Mexican Migration to the U.S.: A Critical Review." *Latin American Research Review* 27(2): 3–42.

———. 2004. "What We Learned from the Mexican Migration Project." In Jorge Durand and Douglas S. Massey (eds.), *Crossing the Border: Research from the Mexican Migration Project.* New York: Russell Sage Foundation, pp. 1–14.

Durand, Jorge, Douglas S. Massey, and Rene M. Zenteno. 2001. "Mexican Immigration in the United States." *Latin American Research Review* 36:107–127.

Duranton, Gilles, and Diego Puga. 2000. "Diversity and Specialization in Cities: Why, Where and When Does It Matter?" *Urban Studies* 37(3): 533–555.

Dussel Peters, Enrique. 2005. *The Implications of China's Entry into the WTO for Mexico.* Global Issue Papers No. 24, Heinrich Böll Foundation.

Fernández-Kelly, María Patricia. 1983. *For We Are Sold, I and My People: Women and Industry in Mexico's Frontier.* Albany, NY: State University of New York Press.

Fernández-Kelly, Patricia, and Douglas S. Massey. 2007. "Borders for Whom? The Role of NAFTA in Mexico-U.S. Migration." *Annals of the American Academy of Political Science* 610:98–118.

Fix, M., and J. S. Passel. 1999. *Trends in Noncitizens' and Citizens' Use of Public Benefits Following Welfare Reform: 1994–97.* Washington, DC: Urban Institute.

Flota, Chrystell, and Marie T. Mora. 2001. "The Earnings of Self-Employed Mexican Americans along the U.S.-Mexico Border." *Annals of Regional Science* 35(3): 483–499.

Foley, Neil. 1997. *The White Scourge: Mexicans, Blacks and Poor Whites in Texas Cotton Culture.* Berkeley: University of California Press.

Fong, Lina Yuk-Shui. 1998. "Borderland Poverty: The Case of the Rio Grande Valley and the United States–Mexico Border." *Social Development Issues* 20(3): 107–115.

Freund, Caroline, and Caglar Ozden. 2006. "The Effect of China's Exports on Latin American Trade with the World." Working paper. Washington, DC: Office of the Chief Economist for Latin America and the Caribbean, World Bank. http://team .univ-paris1.fr/teamperso/sponcet/455/lecture%2024%20opportunites%20 and%20threat%20for%20LDC/Effect%20China%20exports%20on%20LA.pdf.

Fullerton, Thomas M., Jr. 2001. "Educational Attainment and Border Income Performance." *Federal Reserve Bank of Dallas Economic & Financial Review* (Third Quarter): 2–10.

———. 2003. "Recent Trends in Border Economics." *Social Science Journal* 40:583–592.

Fullerton, Thomas, and David Schauer. 2001. "Short-Run Maquiladora Employment Dynamics." *International Advances in Economics Research* 7(4): 471–478.

Gabriel, Stuart A., and Stuart S. Rosenthal. 1996. "Commutes, Neighborhood Effects, and Earnings: An Analysis of Racial Discrimination and Compensating Differentials." *Journal of Urban Economics* 40:61–83.

Gamboa, Erasmo. 1987. "Braceros in the Pacific Northwest: Laborers on the Domestic Front, 1942–1947." *Pacific Historical Review* 56(3): 378–398.

Garber, Paul Neff. 1923. *The Gadsden Treaty.* Philadelphia: University of Philadelphia Press.

García, Mario T. 1989. *Mexican Americans: Leadership, Ideology, and Identity, 1930–1960.* New Haven: Yale University Press.

Garcia, Matt. 2001. *A World of Its Own: Race, Labor, and Citrus in the Making of Greater Los Angeles, 1900–1970.* Chapel Hill: University of North Carolina Press.

García-Milà, T., and T. J. McGuire. 1992. "The Contribution of Publicly Provided Inputs to States' Economies." *Regional Science & Urban Economics* 22:229–241.

General Accounting Office. 2003. *International Trade: Mexico's Maquiladora Decline Affects U.S.-Mexico Border Communities and Trade; Recovery Depends in Part on Mexico's Actions* (GAO-03-891). Washington, DC: U.S. General Accounting Office, July.

Gilbreth, Chris, and Gerado Otero. 2001. "Democratization in Mexico: The Zapatista Uprising and Civil Society." *Latin American Perspectives* 28(4): 7–29.

Gilmer, Robert, Keith Phillips, Jesus Cañas, and Roberto Coronado. 2004. "Framing the Future: Tomorrow's Border Economy." *Business Frontier* 4:1–8.

Glaeser, Edward, Hedi Kallal, José Scheinkman, and Andrei Shleifer. 1992. "Growth in Cities." *Journal of Political Economy* 100(6): 1126–1152.

Gonzáles, Manuel. 1999. *Mexicans: A History of Mexicans in the United States.* Bloomington: Indiana University Press.

González, Deena. 1999. *Refusing the Favor: The Spanish-Mexican Women of Santa Fe, 1820–1880.* New York: Oxford University Press.

González, Gilbert. 1994. *Labor and Community: Mexican Citrus Worker Villages in a Southern California County, 1900–1950.* Urbana: University of Illinois Press.

González, Juan. 2000. *Harvest of Empire: A History of Latinos in America.* New York: Penguin Books.

Goodwyn, Wade. 2007. "Plans for 20-Foot Border Wall Rile Texas Residents." Transcript from *All Things Considered*, National Public Radio, June 15. http://www.npr.org (accessed June 22, 2007).

Graebner, Norman. 1978. "Lessons of the Mexican War." *Pacific Historical Review* 47(3): 325–342.

Greenlees, Clyde S. and Rogelio Sáenz. 1999. "Determinants of Employment of Recently Arrived Mexican Immigrant Wives." *International Migration Review* 33:354–377.

Grinspun, Ricardo, and Maxwell Cameron. 1995. "Mexico: The Wages of Trade." In Fred Rosen and Deidre McFadyen (eds.), *Free Trade and Economic Restructuring in Latin America.* New York: Monthly Review Press.

Griswold del Castillo, Richard. 1979. *The Los Angeles Barrio, 1850–1890: A Social History.* Berkeley: University of California Press.

———. 1990. *The Treaty of Guadalupe Hidalgo: A Legacy of Conflict.* Norman: University of Oklahoma Press.

Gruben, William C. 1990. "Do Maquiladoras Take American Jobs?" *Journal of Borderlands Studies* 5:31–46.

———. 2001. "Was NAFTA Behind Mexico's High Maquila Growth?" *Federal Reserve Bank of Dallas Economic & Financial Review* (Third Quarter): 11–21.

———. 2006. "NAFTA, Trade Diversion and Mexico's Textiles and Apparel Boom and Bust." *Southwest Economy* 5:11–13.

Gutiérrez, David G. 1995. *Walls and Mirrors: Mexican Americans, Mexican Immigrants, and the Politics of Ethnicity.* Berkeley: University of California Press.

———. 1999. "Migration, Emergent Ethnicity, and the 'Third Space': The Shifting Politics of Nationalism in Greater Mexico." *Journal of American History* 86(2): 481–517.

Gutiérrez, Ramón. 1991. *When Jesus Came, the Corn Mothers Went Away: Marriage, Sexuality, and Power in New Mexico, 1500–1846.* Stanford: Stanford University Press.

Haas, Lisabeth. 1995. *Conquests and Historical Identities in California, 1769–1936.* Berkeley: University of California Press.

Hadjimarcou, John, and John W. Barnes. 1998. "Retailing to Foreign Nationals in the Border Zone: The Impact of Currency Devaluation and Cross-Border Competition." *Journal of Global Marketing* 11:85–106.

Hansen, Niles. 1981. *The Border Economy: Regional Development in the Southwest*. Austin: University of Texas Press.

Hanson, Gordon H. 1996. "U.S.-Mexico Integration and Regional Economies: Evidence from Border-City Pairs." National Bureau of Economic Research (NBER) Working Paper Series, no. 5425. Cambridge, MA: National Bureau of Economic Research.

———. 2001. "U.S.-Mexico Integration and Regional Economies: Evidence from Border-City Pairs." *Journal of Urban Economics* 50:259–287.

———. 2005. "Emigration, Labor Supply, and Earnings in Mexico." National Bureau of Economic Research (NBER) Working Paper Series, no. 11412.

———. 2006. "Illegal Migration from Mexico to the United States." *Journal of Economic Literature* 44:869–924.

Hanson, Gordon H., and Raymond Robertson. 2006. "China and the Recent Evolution of Latin America's Manufactured Exports." In *Latin America and the Caribbean's Response to the Growth of China and India*. Washington, DC: Office of the Chief Economist for Latin America and the Caribbean, World Bank.

Hanson, Gordon H., and Antonio Spilimbergo. 1999. "Illegal Immigration, Border Enforcement, and Relative Wages: Evidence from Apprehensions at the U.S.-Mexico Border." *American Economic Review* 89:1337–1357.

Hanson, Susan, Tara Kominiak, and Scott Carlin. 1997. "Assessing the Impact of Location on Women's Labor Market Outcomes: A Methodological Exploration." *Geographical Analysis* 29(4): 281–297.

Hanson, Susan, and Geraldine Pratt. 1988. "Reconceptualizing the Links between Home and Work in Urban Geography." *Economic Geography* 64(4): 299–321.

———. 1992. "Dynamic Dependencies: A Geographic Investigation of Local Labor Markets." *Economic Geography* 68(4): 373–405.

Hardesty, Scarlett G., Malcolm D. Holmes, and James D. Williams. 1988. "Economic Segmentation and Worker Earnings in a U.S.-Mexico Border Enclave." *Sociological Perspectives* 31(4): 466–489.

Haskins, Ron. 2007. *Immigration: Wages, Education and Mobility*. Economic Mobility Project, An Initiative of Pew Memorial (July 2007 Trust). http://www.economicmobility.org/assets/pdfs/Pew_Economic_Mobility_Immigrants.pdf (accessed July 28, 2007).

Heckman, James. 1976. "The Common Structure of Statistical Models of Truncation, Sample Selection, and Limited Dependent Variables and a Simple Estimator for Such Models." *Annals of Economic and Social Measurement* 5:475–492.

Hernandez, Raymond. 2007. "Opinions, Far Apart, Underscore Immigration Bill's Obstacles." *New York Times*, June 5.

Hewitt de Alcantara, Cynthia. 1976. *Modernizing Mexican Agriculture: Socioeconomic Implications of Technological Change, 1940–1970*. Geneva: United Nations Research Institute for Social Development.

Hondagneu-Sotelo, Pierrette. 1994. *Gendered Transitions: Mexican Experiences of Immigration*. Los Angeles: University California Press.

———. 2001. *Domestica: Immigrant Workers Cleaning and Caring in the Shadows of Affluence.* Los Angeles: University of California Press.

Hondagneu-Sotelo, Pierrette, and Cynthia Cranford. 1999. "Gender and Migration." In Janet Saltzman Chafetz (ed.), *Handbook of the Sociology of Gender.* New York: Kluwer Academic/Plenum Publishers, pp. 105–126.

Hufbauer, Gary Clyde, and Jeffrey J. Schott. 2005. *NAFTA Revisited: Achievements and Challenges.* Washington, DC: Institute for International Economics.

Hungerford, T., and Gary Solon. 1987. "Sheepskin Effects in the Returns to Education." *Review of Economics and Statistics* 69:175–177.

Instituto Nacional de Estadística, Geografía e Informática. http://www.inegi.gob .mx/inegi.

International Labor Office (ILO). 2007. *ILO Database on Export Processing Zones (Revised).* http://www.ilo.org (accessed August 12, 2007).

Izraeli, Oded, and Kevin J. Murphy. 2003. "The Effect of Industrial Diversity on State Unemployment Rates and Per Capita Income." *Annals of Regional Science* 37:1–14.

Jasso, Guillermina, Mark R. Rosenzweig, and James P. Smith. 2000. "The Changing Skill of New Immigrants to the United States: Recent Trends and Their Determinants." In George Borjas (ed.), *Issues in the Economics of Immigration.* A National Bureau of Economic Research Conference Report. Chicago: University of Chicago Press.

Johnson, Benjamin. 2005. *Revolution in Texas: How a Forgotten Rebellion and Its Bloody Suppression Turned Mexicans into Americans.* New Haven: Yale University Press.

Johnson, Stefan H., and Michael S. Rendell. 2004. "The Fertility Contribution of Mexican Immigration to the United States." *Demography* 41:129–150.

Jones, Lonnie L., Teofilo Ozuna Jr., and Mickey Wright. 1991. "Economic Impacts." In Leslie Blair (ed.), *U.S.-Mexico Free Trade Agreement: Implications for Border Development: Proceedings of Symposium and Workshops Held in Las Cruces, NM 30 April–1 May 1991.* Las Cruces: New Mexico State University, pp. 83–93.

Juhn, Cjhinhui, Kevin M. Murphy, and Brooks Pierce. 1993. "Wage Inequality and the Rise in the Returns to Skill." *Journal of Political Economy* 101(3): 410–442.

Kaestner, Robert, and Neeraj Kaushal. 2005. "Immigrant and Native Responses to Welfare Reform." *Journal of Population Economics* 18(1): 69–92.

Kahane, Leo H. 1996. "Congressional Voting Patterns on NAFTA: An Empirical Analysis." *American Journal of Economics and Sociology* 55(4): 395–409.

Kanaiaupuni, Shawn Malia. 2000. "Reframing the Migration Question: An Analysis of Men, Women, and Gender in Mexico." *Social Forces* 78(4): 1311–1347.

Kaushal, N. 2005. "New Immigrants' Location Choices: Magnets without Welfare." *Journal of Labor Economics* 23(1): 59–80.

Kelley, Robin D. G. 1997. *Yo' Mama's Disfunkitional! Fighting the Culture Wars in Urban America.* Boston: Beacon Press.

Kennedy, Peter. 1981. "Estimations with Correctly Interpreted Dummy Variables in Semilogarithmic Equations." *American Economic Review* 71(4): 801.

Kessell, John. 2002. *Spain in the Southwest: A Narrative History of Colonial New Mexico, Arizona, Texas, and California*. Norman: University of Oklahoma Press.

Kmec, Julie A., 2003. "Minority Job Concentration and Wages." *Social Problems* 50:38–59.

Kogel, T. 2005. "Youth Dependency and Total Factor Productivity." *Journal of Development Economics* 76:147–173.

Kopinak, Kathryn. 2005. "The Relationship Between Employment in Maquiladora Industries in Mexico and Labor Migration to the United States." Working paper 120. San Diego: Center for Comparative Immigration Studies.

Krauze, Enrique. 1997. *Mexico, Biography of Power: A History of Modern Mexico 1810–1996*. New York: Harper Perennial.

Ladman, Jerry R. 1979. "Economic Interdependence of Contiguous Border Cities: Twin City Multiplier." *Annals of Regional Science* 13:23–28.

Lall, Sanjaya, and John Weiss. 2005. "China's Competitive Threat to Latin America: An Analysis for 1990–2002." *Oxford Development Studies* 33(2): 63–194.

Lecompte, Janet. 1981. "The Independent Women of Hispanic New Mexico, 1821–1846." *Western Historical Quarterly* 12(1): 17–35.

Lemoine, Francoise, and Deniz Ünal-Kesenci. 2004. "Assembly Trade and Technology Transfer: The Case of China." *World Development* 32(5): 829–850.

Light, Ivan, Georges Sabagh, Mehdi Bozorgmehr, and Claudia Der-Martirosian. 1994. "Beyond the Ethnic Enclave Economy." *Social Problems* 41:65–80.

López-Acevedo, Gladys. 2004. "Mexico: Evolution of Earnings Inequality and Rates of Returns to Education (1988–2002)." *Estudios Economicos*, pp. 211–284.

Lorey, David E. 1999. *The U.S.-Mexican American Border in the Twentieth Century: A History of Economic and Social Transformation*. Wilmington: Scholarly Resources, Inc.

Los Angeles Times. 1922. "Mexico Makes Protest: State Department Told Nationals are Murdered." November 16.

Lozano Ascencio, Fernando. 2002. "Interlacion Entre la Migracion Internacional y la Migracion Interna." *Papeles de Poblacion* 8(33): 81–100.

Lustig, Nora, Barry P. Bosworth, and Robert Z. Lawrence, eds. 1992. *North American Free Trade: Assessing the Impact*. Washington, DC: Brookings Institution.

Marcouiller, Douglas, Veronica Ruiz de Castilla, and Christopher Woodruff. 1997. "Formal Measures of the Informal-Sector Wage Gap in Mexico, El Salvador, and Peru." *Economic Development and Cultural Change* 45(2): 367–392.

Marquez, Raquel R., and Yolanda C. Padilla. 2004. "Immigration in the Life Histories of Women Living in the United States–Mexico Border Region." *Journal of Immigrant and Refugee Services* 2(1–2): 11–30.

Martinez, Guerillmo. 1948. "Los braceros: Experiencias que deben aprovecharse." *Revista Mexicana de Sociología* 10(2): 177–195.

Massey, Douglas S., Rafael Alarcón, Jorge Durand, and Humberto Gonzalez. 1987. *Return to Aztlan: The Social Process of International Migration from Western Mexico*. Berkeley: University of California Press.

Massey, Douglas S., Jorge Durand, and Nolan J. Malone. 2002. *Beyond Smoke and Mirrors: Mexican Immigration in an Era of Economic Integration*. Russell Sage Foundation: New York.

Massey, Douglas S., and Rene M. Zenteno. 2000. "A Validation of the Ethnosurveys: The Case of Mexico-U.S. Migration." *International Migration Review* 34(3): 766–793.

Mattingly, Doreen J., and Ellen R. Hansen. 2006. *Women and Change at the U.S.-Mexico Border: Mobility, Labor, and Activism*. Tucson: University of Arizona Press.

McQuaid, Ronald W., Malcolm Greig, and John Adams. 2001. "Unemployed Job Seeker Attitudes Toward Potential Travel-to-Work Times." *Growth and Change* 32: 355–368.

McWilliams, Carey. 1990. *North from Mexico: The Spanish-Speaking People of the United States*. Updated by Matt S. Meier. New York: Praeger.

Mehta, Aashish, and Hector J. Villarreal. 2005. "Inequality and Heterogeneous Returns to Education in Mexico (1992–2002)." Ibero America Institute for Economic Research (IAI), Discussion Papers 131.

Meyer, Michael C., and William L. Sherman. 1995. *The Course of Mexican History, Fifth Edition*. New York: Oxford University Press.

Meza, Liliana. 1999. "Cambios en la estructura salarial de Mexico en el periodo 1988–1993 y el aumento en el rendimiento de la educación superior." *El Trimestre Economico* 66:189–226.

Miller, Tom. 1981. "Bracero Program No. 3." *New York Times*, October 5.

Mincer, Jacob. 1974. *Schooling, Experience and Earnings*. New York: Columbia University Press.

Mirande, Alfredo, 1990. *Gringo Justice*. South Bend, IN: University of Notre Dame Press.

Mizuno, Keizo, Fumitoshi Mizutani, and Noriyoshi Nakayama. 2006. "Industrial Diversity and Metropolitan Unemployment Rates." *Annals of Regional Science* 40(1): 157–172.

Model, Suzanne. 1993. "The Ethnic Niche and the Structure of Opportunity: Immigrants and Minorities in New York City." In Michael Katz (ed.), *The Underclass Debate: Views from History*. Princeton, NJ: Princeton University Press, pp. 161–193.

Molina, Natalia. 2006. *Fit to Be Citizens? Public Health and Race in Los Angeles, 1879–1939*. Berkeley: University of California Press.

Mollick, André Varella. 2008a. "The Rise of the Skill Premium in Mexican Maquiladoras." *Journal of Development Studies* 44(9): 1382–1404.

———. 2008b. "What Explains Unemployment in U.S.-Mexican Border Cities?" *Annals of Regional Science* 42:169–182.

Mollick, André Varella, Abigail Cortez-Rayas, and Rosa A. Olivas-Moncisvais. 2006. "Local Labor Markets in U.S.-Mexican Border Cities and the Impact of Maquiladora Production." *Annals of Regional Science* 40:95–116.

Mollick, André Varella, and Karina Wvalle-Vázquez. 2006. "Chinese Competition and its Effects on Mexican Maquiladoras." *Journal of Comparative Economics* 34:130–145.

Montejano, David. 1987. *Anglos and Mexicans in the Making of Texas, 1836–1986.* Austin: University of Texas Press.

Montgomery, Claire A. 1996. "A Structural Model of the U.S. Housing Market: Improvement and New Construction." *Journal of Housing Economics* 5:166–192.

Montoya, María. 2002. *Translating Property: The Maxwell Land Grant and the Conflict over Land in the American West, 1840–1900.* Berkeley: University of California Press.

Mora, Anthony P. 2009 (currently under contract). *Local Borders: Race, Nation, and Space in Southern New Mexico, 1848–1912.* Durham: Duke University Press.

Mora, Marie T. 2005. "Changes in Occupational Earnings along the U.S.-Mexico Border between 1900 and 1920." *Journal of Economic Issues* 39:1043–1059.

———. 2006. "Self-Employed Mexican Immigrants Living along the U.S.-Mexico Border: The Earnings Effect of Working in the U.S. versus Mexico." *International Migration Review* 40(4): 885–898.

Mora, Marie T., and Alberto Dávila. 2006. "Mexican Immigrant Self-Employment along the U.S.-Mexico Border: An Analysis of 2000 Census Data. *Social Science Quarterly* 87:91–109.

———. 2007. "Cross-Border Earnings of U.S. Natives along the U.S.-Mexico Border." Unpublished manuscript, University of Texas–Pan American.

Moraga, Cherrie, and Gloria Anzaldúa. 1984. *This Bridge Called My Back: Writing by Radical Women of Color.* New York: Kitchen Table Women of Color Press.

Morales, Maria Cristina, and Cynthia Bejarano. 2008. "Border Sexual Conquest: A Framework for Gendered and Racial Sexual Violence." In Angela Hattery, David Embrick, and Earl Smith (eds.), *Race, Inequality and Human Rights.* Lanham, MD: Rowman & Littlefield, pp. 181–198.

Morelos, Jose B. 2005. "Tendencias y cambio structural de la participacion de la mujer en la actividad economica en 1970 y 2000." *Estudios Demograficos y Urbanos* 20(1): 125–150.

Morrison, Michael. 1992. "'New Territory versus No Territory:' The Whig Party and the Politics of Western Expansion, 1846–1848." *Western Historical Quarterly* 23(1): 25–51.

Mullins, Daniel R., and Sally Wallace. 1996. "Changing Demographics and State Fiscal Outlook: The Case of Sales Taxes." *Public Finance Quarterly* 24:237–262.

Munshi, Kaivan. 2003. "Networks in the Modern Economy: Mexican Migrants in the U.S. Labor Market." *Quarterly Journal of Economics* 118:549–597.

Nasatir, Abraham. 1965. "The Shifting Borderlands." *Pacific Historical Review* 31(1): 1–20.

New York Times. 1981. "We've Lost Control of Our Borders." August 2.

———. 1986. "Amnesty: Who is Eligible." November 3, p. A16.

———. 2003a. "Mexico's Jobless Rate Hits a 6-Year High." September 20.

———. 2003b. "A Fleeting Boom and Disillusionment." December 27.

North, David S., and Marion F. Houston. 1976. *The Characteristics and Role of Illegal Aliens in the U.S. Labor Market, An Exploratory Study.* Washington, DC: Linton.

Oaxaca, Ronald. 1973. "Male-Female Wage Differentials in Urban Labor Markets." *International Economic Review* 14:693–709.

Ordóñez, Sergio. 2006. "Crisis y Restructuración de la Industria Electronica Mundial y Reconversión en México." *Comercio Exterior* 56(7): 550–564.

Ornelas, Sergio. 2005. "Mexico's Aerospace Industry: Enormous Potential, Ideal Match." *Mexico Now* 17:13–26.

Orrenius, Pia M. 2001. "Illegal Immigration and Enforcement along the U.S.-Mexico Border: An Overview." *Federal Reserve Bank of Dallas Economic and Financial Review* 1:1–11.

Orrenius, Pia M., and Madeline Zavodny. 2005. "Self-selection among Undocumented Immigrants from Mexico." *Journal of Development Economics* 78:215–240.

Ortíz-González, Victor. 2004. *El Paso: Local Frontiers at a Global Crossroads.* Minneapolis: University of Minnesota Press.

Otero, Miguel A. 1939. *My Life on the Frontier, 1882–1897.* Albuquerque: University of New Mexico Press.

Padilla, Genaro. 1993. *My History, Not Yours: The Formation of Mexican American Autobiography.* Madison: University of Wisconsin Press.

Parrado, Emilio A., and Rene M. Zenteno. 2001. "Economic Restructuring, Financial Crises, and Women's Work in Mexico." *Social Problems* 48(4): 456–477.

Passel, Jeffrey S. 2004. *Mexican Immigration to the U.S.: The Latest Estimates.* Migration Policy Institute. http://www.migrationinformation.org/Feature/display.cfm?ID=208.

———. 2005. *Unauthorized Migrants: Numbers and Characteristics.* Washington, DC: Pew Hispanic Center.

———. 2006. *Estimates of the Size and Characteristics of the Undocumented Population.* Washington, DC: Pew Hispanic Center.

Patrick, J. Michael, and William Renforth. 1996. "The Effects of the Peso Devaluation on Cross-Border Retailing." *Journal of Borderlands Studies* 11:25–41.

Peach, James T. 1997. "Income Distribution along the United States Border with Mexico." *Journal of Borderlands Studies* 12(1–2): 1–15.

Peach, James T., and Richard V. Adkisson. 2000. "NAFTA and Economic Activity along the U.S.-Mexico Border." *Journal of Economic Issues* 34(2): 481–489.

Peach, James T., and James Williams. 2000. "Population and Economic Dynamics of the U.S.-Mexico Border Region." In Paul Ganster and David J. Pijawka (eds.), *The U.S.-Mexican Border Environment: A Road Map to a Sustainable 2020.* San Diego: San Diego State University Press.

Pear, Robert. 1982. "It's Time for Immigration Law Reform—Or Is It?" *New York Times,* January 3.

———. 1986. "President Signs Landmark Bill on Immigration," *New York Times,* November 7.

———. 2007. "Failure of Senate Immigration Bill Can be Lesson for Congress, Experts Say." *New York Times,* June 30.

Pear, Robert, and Carl Huilse. 2007. "Immigrant Bill Dies in Senate; Defeat for Bush." *New York Times*, June 29.

Pear, Robert, and Jeff Zeleny. 2007. "Senators Agree on Way to Revive Immigration Bill." *New York Times*, June 15.

Perot, H. Ross, and Pat Choate. 1993. *Save Your Job, Save Our Country: Why NAFTA Must be Stopped Now!* New York: Hyperion Books.

Pessar, Patricia R. 1999. "Engendering Migration Studies: The Case of New Immigrants in the United States." *American Behavioral Scientist* 42(4): 577–600.

Piore, Michael J. 1979. *Birds of Passage: Migrant Labor and Industrial Societies.* Cambridge, UK: Cambridge University Press.

Pisani, Michael J., and David W. Yoskowitz. 2002. "The Maid Trade: Cross-Border Work in South Texas." *Social Science Quarterly* 83(2): 568–579.

Poterba, James M. 1997. "Demographic Structure and the Political Economy of Public Education." *Journal of Policy Analysis and Management* 16:48–66.

Reid, Lori L. 1998. "Devaluing Women and Minorities: The Effects of Race/Ethnic and Sex Composition of Occupations on Wage Levels." *Work and Occupations* 25(4): 511–536.

Reinhold, Robert. 1986. "Illegal Aliens Hoping to Claim Their Dreams." *New York Times*, November 3.

Reisler, Mark. 1976. *By the Sweat of Their Brow: Mexican Immigrant Labor in the United States, 1900–1940.* Westport: Greenwood Press.

Reséndez, Andrés. 2002. "Getting Cured and Getting Drunk: State Versus Market in New Mexico and Texas, 1800–1850." *Journal of the Early Republic* 22(1): 77–103.

———. 2005. *Changing National Identities at the Frontier: Texas and New Mexico, 1800–1850.* New York: Cambridge University Press.

Reskin, Barbara F., and Patricia A. Roos. 1990. *Job Queues, Gender Queues: Explaining Women's Inroads into Male Occupations.* Philadelphia: Temple University Press.

Rivera-Batiz, Francisco L. 1986. "Can Border Industries be a Substitute for Immigration?" *American Economic Review* 76: 263–268.

Robertson, Raymond. 2007. "Globalization and Mexican Labor Markets." Lecture presented at the Trade, Migration, and International Development Conference. Dallas: Federal Reserve Bank of Dallas. http://www.dallasfed.org/research/pubs/migration/robertson.pdf.

Robles, Barbara J. 2002. "Latina Microenterprise and the U.S.-Mexico Border Economy." *Estey Centre Journal of International Law and Trade Policy* 3(2): 307–327.

Rocio Ruiz, María. 2005. *Visión Global de la Industria Manufacturera de Exportación.* Presentation made at the annual meeting of the National Maquiladora Association, Cancun, Mexico.

Rodriguez, Nestor. 2004. "Workers Wanted." *Work and Occupations* 31:453–473.

Roeckell, Lelia M. 1999. "Bonds Over Bondage: British Opposition to the Annexation of Texas." *Journal of the Early Republic* 19(2): 257–278.

Romalis, John. 2007. "NAFTA's and CUSFTA's Impact on International Trade." *Review of Economics and Statistics* 89(3): 416–435.

Rosen, Fred, and Deidre McFadyen, eds. 1995. *Free Trade and Economic Restructuring in Latin America.* New York: Monthly Review Press.

Rosen, Sherwin. 1974. "Hedonic Prices and Implicit Markets: Product Differentiation in Pure Competition." *Journal of Political Economy* 82:34–55.

Ruggles, Steven, Matthew Sobek, Trent Alexander, Catherine A. Fitch, Ronald Goeken, Patricia Kelly Hall, Miriam King, and Chad Ronnander. 2007. Integrated Public Use Microdata Series (machine-readable database). Minneapolis: Minnesota Population Center. http://www.ipums.org.

Ruiz, Vicki. 1987. *Cannery Women, Cannery Lives: Mexican Women, Unionization, and the California Food Processing Industry, 1930–1950.* Albuquerque: University of New Mexico Press.

———. 1998. *From Out of the Shadows: Mexican Women in Twentieth Century America.* New York: Oxford University Press.

Ruiz Durán, Clemente. 2006. "Value Chains and Software Clusters in Mexico." In Carlo Pietrobelli and Roberta Rabellotti (eds.), *Upgrading to Compete: Global Value Chains, Clusters, and SMEs in Latin America.* Washington, DC: Inter-American Development Bank.

Ruiz Durán, Clemente, Michael Piore, and Andrew Schrank. 2005. "Los Retos para el Desarrollo de la Industria del Software." *Comercio Exterior* 55(9): 744–753.

Sáenz, Rogelio, and Marie Ballejos. 1993. "Industrial Development and Persistent Poverty in the Lower Rio Grande Valley." In William W. Falk and Thomas A. Lyson (eds.), *Forgotten Places: Uneven Development in Rural America.* Lawrence: University Press of Kansas, pp. 102–124.

Sáenz, Rogelio, Maria Cristina Morales, and Maria Isabel Ayala. 2004. "United States: Immigration to the Melting Pots of the Americas." In M. I. Toro and M. Alicea (eds.), *Migration: A Global View.* Westport, CT: Greenwood Press, pp. 211–232.

Sakellariou, Chris. 2006. "Education Policy Reform, Local Average Treatment Effect and Returns to Schooling from Instrumental Variables in the Philippines." *Applied Economics* 38:473–481.

Samora, Julian. 1971. *Los Majados: The Wetback Story.* Notre Dame: Notre Dame University Press.

Samora, Julian, Joe Bernal, and Albert Peña. 1979. *Gunpowder Justice: A Reassessment of the Texas Rangers.* Notre Dame: Notre Dame University Press.

Samora, Julian, and Patricia Vandel Simon. 1993. *A History of the Mexican-American People.* Notre Dame: Notre Dame University Press.

Sánchez, George. 1993. *Becoming Mexican American: Ethnicity, Culture, and Identity in Chicano Los Angeles, 1900–1945.* New York: Oxford University Press.

Sánchez, Rosaura. 1995. *Telling Identities: The Californio "Testimonios."* Minneapolis: University of Minnesota Press.

Sanders, Jimy, and Victor Nee. 1996. "Immigrant Self Employment: The Family as Social Capital and the Value of Human Capital." *American Sociological Review* 61:231–249.

Sandos, James A., and Harry E. Cross. 1983. "National Development and International Labour Migration: Mexico 1940–1965." *Journal of Contemporary History* 18(1): 43–60.

Sargent, John. 1994. *Skills Acquisition in the Maquiladoras*. Unpublished doctoral dissertation, University of Washington.

Sargent, John, and Linda Matthews. 1999. "Exploitation or Choice? Exploring the Relative Attractiveness of Employment in the Maquiladoras." *Journal of Business Ethics* 18:213–227.

———. 2001. "Combining Export Processing Zones and Regional Free Trade Agreements: Lessons from the Mexican Experience." *World Development* 29(10): 1739–1752.

———. 2004. "What Happens When Relative Costs Increase in Export Processing Zones? Technology, Regional Production Networks, and Mexico's Maquiladoras." *World Development* 32(12): 2015–2030.

———. 2006. "Capital Intensity, Technology Intensity, and Skill Development in Post China/WTO Maquiladoras." Working paper. Edinburg: University of Texas–Pan American, Center for Border Economic Studies. http://ea.panam.edu/cbes/pdf/SargentMatthews.pdf (accessed August 14, 2007).

———. 2007. "China vs. Mexico in the Global EPZ Industry: Maquiladoras, FDI Quality, and Plant Mortality." Working paper. Edinburg: University of Texas–Pan American, Center for Border Economic Studies. http://ea.panam.edu/cbes/pdf/WorkingPaper1-06.pdf (accessed August 14, 2007).

Sayer, Liana C., Philip N. Cohen, and Lynne M. Casper. 2005. "Women, Men, and Work." In Reynolds Farley and John Haaga (eds.), *The American People Series: Census 2000*. New York: Russell Sage Foundation, pp. 76–106.

Schrover, Marlou, Joanne van der Leun, and Chris Quispel. 2007. "Niches, Labour Market Segregation, Ethnicity and Gender." *Journal of Ethnic and Migration Studies* 33(4): 529–540.

Scott, Robert E, Carlos Salas, and Bruce Campbell. 2006. "Revisiting NAFTA: Still Not Working for North America's Workers." Economic Policy Institute Working Paper #173. Washington, DC: Economic Policy Institute. http://www.epi.org.

Secretaría de Economía (Subsecretaría de Industria y Comercio). 2004. *Acciones Concretas para Incrementar la Competitividad*. http://www.economia.gob.mx (accessed October 15, 2006).

Segura, Denise A., and Beatriz M. Pesquera. 1999. "Chicana Political Consciousness: Renegotiating Culture, Class, and Gender with Oppositional Practices." *Aztlán* 24:7–32.

Senon, Philip, 1986. "'Startling' Surge is Reported in Illegal Aliens from Mexico." *New York Times*, February 21.

Sharp, John. 1998. *Bordering the Future: Challenge and Opportunity in the Texas Border Region*. Austin: Texas Comptroller of Public Accounts.

Simon, Curtis J. 1988. "Frictional Unemployment and the Role of Industrial Diversity." *Quarterly Journal of Economics* 103(4): 715–728.

Simon, Rita J., and Margo Deley. 1984. "The Work Experience of Undocumented Women Migrants in Los Angeles." *International Migration Review* 18(4): 1212–1229.

Simpson, Penny, and Jane LeMaster. 2006. *Winter Texan Survey: Winter 2006*. Edinburg: Valley Markets and Tourism Research Center, College of Business Administration, University of Texas–Pan American.

Singh, Vishal P., Karsten T. Hansen, and R. C. Blattberg. 2006. "Market Entry and Consumer Behavior: An Investigation of a Wal-Mart Supercenter." *Marketing Science* 25:457–476.

Sklair, Leslie. 1993. *Assembling for Development: The Maquiladora Industry in Mexico and the United States*. San Diego: Center for U.S.-Mexican Studies.

Smith, James P., and Barry Edmonston, eds. 1997. *The New Americans: Economics, Demographic, and Fiscal Effects of Immigration*. Washington, DC: National Academy Press.

Stanford Law Review. 1954. "Wetbacks: Can States Act to Curb Illegal Entry?" Volume 6(2): 287–322.

Stern, Alexandra Minna. 2004. "Nationalism on the Line: Masculinity, Race, and the Creation of the U.S. Border Patrol, 1910–1940." In Samuel Truett and Elliott Young (eds.), *Continental Crossroads: Remapping U.S.-Mexico Borderlands History*. Durham: Duke University Press, pp. 299–324.

Stoddard, Ellwyn R., ed. 1983. *Borderlands Sourcebook: A Guide to the Literature on Northern Mexico and the American Southwest*. Norman: University of Oklahoma Press.

———. 1991. "Frontiers, Borders and Border Segmentation: Toward a Conceptual Clarification." *Journal of Borderlands Studies* 6(1): 1–22.

Streeby, Shelley. 2002. *American Sensations: Class, Empire, and the Production of Popular Culture*. Berkeley: University of California Press.

Sutton, Paul D., and Frederick A. Day. 2004. "Types of Rapidly Growing Counties in the U.S., 1970–1990." *Social Science Journal* 41:251–265.

Tafoya, Audry, and Ralph Watkins. 2005. "Production Sharing Update: Developments in 2003." *Industry Trade and Technology Review* December/January: 9–34.

Tamborini, Christopher R. 2007. "Work, Wages and Gender in Export-Oriented Cities: Global Assembly versus International Tourism in Mexico." *Bulletin of Latin American Research* 26(1): 24–49.

Telles, Edward E., and Edward Murguia. 1990. "Phenotype Discrimination and Income Differences among Mexican Americans." *Social Science Quarterly* 71:682–696.

———. 1992. "The Continuing Significance of Phenotypic Discrimination among Mexican Americans." *Social Science Quarterly* 73:120–122.

Thompson, Ginger. 2005a. "Sleepy Mexican Border Towns Awake to Drug Violence." *New York Times*, January 23.

———. 2005b. "Mexico Rebukes U.S. for Drug Violence Alert." *New York Times*, January 28.

Thorbecke, Willem, and Christian Eigen-Zucchi. 2002. "Did NAFTA Cause a Giant Sucking Sound?" *Journal of Labor Research* 23:647–660.

Tiano, Susan. 1984. "Maquiladoras, Women's Work, and Unemployment in Northern Mexico." *Aztlan* 15:341–378.

———. 2006. "The Changing Composition of the Maquila Workforce along the U.S.-Mexico Border." In Mattingly, Doreen J., and Ellen R. Hansen (eds.), *Women and Change at the U.S.-Mexico Border: Mobility, Labor, and Activism.* Tucson: University of Arizona Press, pp. 73–90.

Tyree, Andrea, and Katharine M. Donato 1985. "The Sex Composition of Legal Immigrants to the United States." *Sociology and Social Research* 69:577–85.

U.S. Bureau of Economic Analysis. 1980–2004. *National Economic Accounts.* http://www.bea.gov.

U.S. Bureau of Economic Analysis. 1980–2004. *Regional Economic Accounts.* http://www.bea.gov.

U.S. Bureau of Labor Statistics. 1980–2004. *Current Employment Statistics.* http://www.bls.gov.

U.S. Customs and Border Protection (CBP). 2006. *Secure Electronic Network for Travelers Rapid Inspection (SENTRI).* November 1. http://www.cbp.gov/xp/cgov/travel/frequent_traveler/sentri/sentri.xml (accessed August 2, 2007).

U.S. Department of Commerce, Bureau of Economic Analysis. International Economic Accounts. Washington, DC. http://www.bea.gov/international/bp_web/simple.cfm?anon=71&table_id=10&area_id=22 (accessed July 6, 2007).

U.S. Department of Commerce, Bureau of Economic Analysis. Regional Economic Information System (REIS). Washington, DC. http://www.bea.gov/regional/reis/drill.cfm (accessed July 6, 2007).

U.S. Department of Homeland Security Office of Immigration Statistics. 2006. *Fact Sheet: Border Apprehensions 2005.* http://www.dhs.gov/immigrationstatistics.

U.S. Department of the State, Bureau of the Consular. http://travel.state.gov.

U.S. International Trade Commission (USITC). 2007. http://www.usitc.gov (accessed August 15, 2007).

U.S.-Mexico Border Counties Coalition (USMBCC). 2006. *At the Crossroads: U.S./Mexico Border Counties in Transition.* El Paso: Institute for Policy and Economic Development, University of Texas at El Paso.

Valdés, Dennis Nodín. "1988 Mexican Revolutionary Nationalism and Mexican Repatriation During the Great Depression." *Mexican Studies/Estudios Mexicanos* 4(1): 1–23.

Valdez, Zulema. 2006. "Beyond the Ethnic Enclave: The Effect of Ethnic Solidarity and Market Opportunity on White, Korean, Mexican and Black Enterprise." In Caroline Brettell (ed.), *Crossing Borders/Constructing Boundaries: Race, Ethnicity, and Identity in the Migrant Experience.* Lanham, MD: Lexington Books, pp. 341–385.

Vargas, Lucinda. 2001. "Maquiladoras: Impact on Texas Border Cities." *The Border Economy.* Dallas: Federal Reserve Bank of Dallas.

Vega Briones, German. 2003. "Migracion, Genero y Familia: Un Estudio de la Frontera Norte de Mexico." *Portularia: Revista de Trabajo Social* 3:11–333.

Vélez, William, and Rogelio Sáenz. 2001. "Toward a Comprehensive Model of the School Leaving Process among Latinos." *School Psychology Quarterly* 16:445–467.

Vila, Pablo. 2000. *Crossing Borders, Reinforcing Borders: Social Categories, Metaphors, and Narrative Identities on the U.S.-Mexico Frontier.* Austin: University of Texas Press.

———. 2003. "Gender and the Overlapping of Region, Nation, and Ethnicity on the U.S.-Mexico Border." In Pablo Vila (ed.), *Ethnography at the Border.* Minneapolis: University of Minnesota Press, pp. 73–104.

Villarreal, Hector J. 2006. "An Intertemporal Comparison of Income and Welfare for two Mexican Regions." Escuela de Graduados en Administracion Publica Campus Monterrey, Working Papers, 2006-2.

Waldinger, Roger. 1994. "The Making of an Immigrant Niche." *International Migration Review* 28(1): 3–30.

———. 1996. *Still the Promised City? African-Americans and New Immigrants in Postindustrial New York.* Cambridge, MA: Harvard University Press.

Warner David C. 2007. "Cross Border Health Insurance and Aging Mexicans and Mexican Americans." In Jacqueline L. Angel and Keith E. Whitfield (eds.), *The Health of Aging Hispanics: The Mexican Origin Population.* New York: Springer, pp. 202–210.

Weber, David. 1982. *The Mexican Frontier 1821–1846: The American Southwest Under Mexico.* Albuquerque: University of New Mexico Press.

———. 1994. *The Spanish Frontier in North America.* New Haven: Yale University Press.

———. [1973] 2003. *Foreigners in Their Native Land: Historical Roots of the Mexican Americans.* Albuquerque: University of New Mexico Press.

Weber, Devra. 1994. *Dark Sweat, White Gold: California Farm Workers, Cotton, and the New Deal.* Berkeley: University of California Press.

Wegener, Bernd. 1991. "Job Mobility and Social Ties: Social Resources, Prior Job, and Status Attainment." *American Sociological Review* 56:60–71.

Weintraub, Sidney. 1993. "The North American Free Trade Agreement as Negotiated: A U.S. Perspective." In Steven Globerman and Michael Walker (eds.), *Assessing NAFTA: A Trinational Analysis.* Vancouver: Fraser Institute, pp. 1–31.

———. 1997. *NAFTA at Three: A Progress Report.* Washington DC: The Center for Strategic and International Studies.

Welch, Finis. 2000. "Growth in Women's Relative Wages and in Inequality among Men: One Phenomenon or Two?" *American Economic Review* 90(2): 444–449.

Wooldridge, Jeffrey M. 2002. *Econometric Analysis of Cross Section and Panel Data.* Cambridge, MA: MIT Press.

World Bank. 2007. *World Development Indicators.*

Yamada, G. 1996. "Urban Informal Employment and Self-Employment in Developing Countries: Theory and Evidence." *Economic Development and Cultural Change* 44(2): 289–314.

Zavodny, Madeline. 1997. "Welfare and the Location Choices of New Immigrants." *Economic Review (Federal Reserve Bank of Dallas)*, Second Quarter, pp. 2–10.

———. 1998. "Determinants of Recent Immigrants' Location Choices." *International Migration Review* 33:1014–1030.

Zax, Jeffrey S. 1991. "Compensation and Commutes in Labor and Housing Markets." *Journal of Urban Economics* 30:192–207.

ZFacts.com. 2007. Current Gas Prices and Price History. http://zfacts.com/p/35.html (accessed September 6, 2007).

Zunker, C., C. Rutt, and J. Cummins. 2004. "Older Women on the U.S.-Mexico Border." *Journal of Women & Aging* 16:105–117.

About the Editors

Marie T. Mora is currently a full professor of economics at the University of Texas–Pan American (UTPA). Prior to joining UTPA in 2002, Mora was a tenured faculty member at New Mexico State University. She obtained her PhD in economics from Texas A&M University in 1996, after completing her BA and MA degrees (also in economics) from the University of New Mexico in her hometown of Albuquerque. Mora's research interests include the economics of the U.S.-Mexico border, Hispanic labor markets, and the economics of language. Her work has been published in such refereed journals as the *Journal of Regional Science, Social Science Quarterly, Economic Development and Cultural Change, Industrial Relations*, the *Journal of Population Economics, Annals of Regional Science, Economics of Education Review, International Migration Review, Economic Inquiry*, and the *Journal of Economic Issues*. Mora is currently serving in her second term as the president of the American Society of Hispanic Economists, and her other professional activities include serving on: the editorial board of the Social Science Quarterly, the American Economic Association's Committee on the Status of Minority Groups in the Economics Profession, and the national advisory board of the Robert Wood Johnson Foundation Center for Health Policy Program at the University of New Mexico.

Alberto Dávila is currently a full professor of economics and V. F. "Doc" and Gertrude M. Neuhaus Chair for Entrepreneurship at the University of Texas–Pan American (UTPA). He is also serving as department chair for the Department of Economics and Finance, a position he has held since January 1997. Before joining the faculty at UTPA in 1996, Dávila was a tenured faculty member at the University of New Mexico. He earned his PhD degree in economics from Iowa State University in 1982, with his doctoral dissertation focusing on U.S.-Mexico border wage differentials. Dávila also has an MS degree in economics from Iowa State and a BA degree in economics from UTPA. Dávila's research interests include the economics of the U.S.-Mexico border, the economics of immigration, and Hispanic labor markets. Dávila has published on border-related topics since 1982, first appearing in the Federal Reserve Bank of Dallas' *Economic Review*. Dávila's more recent work has been published in such refereed journals as the *Journal of Regional Science, Economic Development and Cultural Change*, the *American Journal of Agricultural Economics, Industrial Relations*, the *Journal of Population Economics, Economic Inquiry, Public Choice, Review of Development Economics, Social Science Quarterly, Economics of Education Review*, and

International Migration Review. Moreover, he has received such professional honors as the Small Business Administration District Research Advocate Award for the Lower Rio Grande Valley (2003) and the Distinguished Alumnus award from the College of Business Administration at UTPA's seventy-fifth anniversary (fall 2002).

About the Contributors

Richard V. Adkisson is the Wells Fargo professor of economics and international business at New Mexico State University, where he has been on the faculty since 1994. Adkisson serves as immediate past president of the Western Social Science Association and as editor of the *Journal of Economic Issues*, and he has recently completed a term as president of the Association for Institutional Thought. His research interests include institutional economics, public policy, and U.S.-Mexico border issues. Published papers can be found in the *Journal of Economic Issues*, the *International Trade Journal*, *Growth and Change*, the *Journal of Borderlands Studies*, *Social Science Journal*, and *Policy Studies Review*. Recent articles include "Living Large: Evolving Consumer Credit Institutions and Privately Induced Transfer Payments" (with Randy McFerrin), "Ceremonialism, Intellectual Property Rights, and Innovative Activity," and "Retail Trade on the U.S.-Mexico Border during the NAFTA Implementation Era" (with Linda Zimmerman).

Catalina Amuedo-Dorantes is a full professor of economics at San Diego State University and was Western Michigan University's first recipient of a PhD in applied economics in 1998. She earned a JD degree from Universidad Nacional de Educación (UNED) in Spain in 1996 and a BA in economics from Universidad de Sevilla in Spain in 1992. Amuedo-Dorantes worked at the Center for Human Resource Research at Ohio State University prior to joining the San Diego State University in 1999. She is also a research fellow for the IZA Institute of Labor in Germany, and has been a visiting scholar at the Institute for Research and Poverty at the University of Wisconsin and at the Public Policy Institute of California. Amuedo-Dorantes has received awards from the National Institutes for Health, the Joint Center for Poverty Research, the Robert Wood Johnson Foundation, the William & Flora Hewlett Foundation, and the W. E. Upjohn Institute for Employment Research. Her primary research area is labor economics, with a focus on contingent work, immigration, and remittances.

Cynthia Bansak is an assistant professor of economics at St. Lawrence University. Prior to this position, she was an assistant professor at San Diego State University and an economist at the Board of Governors of the Federal Reserve System. Bansak received a PhD in economics from the University of California at San Diego and a BA in economics from Yale University. Her research and teaching interests fall broadly within the field of labor economics. Bansak has published research on immigration regarding the effect of employer sanctions on wages and examining the relationship between banking and remittances. In addition, her current work explores aspects of poverty alleviation programs in the United States such as the Personal Responsibility and Work Opportunity Reconciliation Act (PRWORA) and the State Children's Health Insurance Program (SCHIP).

Thomas M. Fullerton Jr. is the Wells Fargo professor of economics and finance in the College of Business Administration at the University of Texas at El Paso (UTEP). In addition to conducting research on borderplex business conditions, Fullerton teaches graduate and undergraduate economics and econometrics courses. He obtained his PhD in economics from the University of Florida. Fullerton also holds an MS in economics from Iowa State University and an MA in business economics from the Wharton School of Finance at the University of Pennsylvania. As a UTEP undergraduate, Fullerton majored in economics and finance. Fullerton's research has been published in academic journals on six continents and has been cited by articles in the *Wall Street Journal*, the *New York Times, Barron's, USA Today, Investor's Business Daily*, and *U.S. News & World Report*. He has also appeared on national newscasts aired by ABC, CNN, and *The News Hour with Jim Lehrer* on PBS.

Alma D. Hales is a PhD student at the University of Texas–Pan American (UTPA) pursuing a doctoral degree in business administration with emphasis on international business. She received her BA degree in economics, with a minor in English, from UTPA in December 2003. In addition, Hales participated in the American Economic Association's Summer Minority Program in Economics at the University of Colorado at Denver in 2003 and at Duke University in 2004. Her research interests include Hispanic labor markets and the economics of language and education.

James H. Holcomb is an associate professor of economics at the University of Texas at El Paso (UTEP). Holcomb earned a PhD in economics from Texas A&M University in 1985. He also has an MA in economics from Texas Tech University and a BBA in economics and finance from UTEP. Holcomb's research areas are behavioral economics and finance and experimental methods, and he has published in such journals as the *Journal of Economic Behavior and Organization, Rationality and Society*, and the *Journal of Socio-Economics*. He previously served at UTEP as an associate vice provost for research and sponsored projects and as the associate dean of the College of Business Administration.

Leslie Lukens interned in the Research Department of the Federal Reserve Bank of Dallas during the Summer of 2007 assisting in immigration research. Lukens holds a master's degree from the LBJ School of Public Affairs at the University of Texas at Austin and BS degrees in economics and business administration from the University of Kansas.

Linda Matthews is currently an associate professor of management at the University of Texas–Pan American. She received her PhD from the University of Washington in organizational behavior and human resource management. Matthews' research interests currently include human capital development in, and sustainability of, the

Mexican maquiladora industry, transfer of training, and motivation. Her work has been published in such journals as *World Development*, the *Journal of World Business*, *Business Horizons*, and the *Journal of Business Ethics*.

Angel L. Molina Jr. is an associate economist at the University of Texas at El Paso (UTEP) with the Border Region Modeling Project. Molina earned his MS degree in economics from UTEP in May 2007. He also obtained a BBA in finance from UTEP in December 2003. Molina's research areas include applied econometrics and border economics. His thesis study on "Economic Growth in the El Paso-Ciudad Juarez Borderplex: Which Causes Which?" received a faculty research award from the International Academy of Business and Public Administration Disciplines. A member of the American Society of Hispanic Economists and the Rio Grande Economics Association, Molina has published research on cross-border regional growth patterns.

André Varella Mollick has been working as an associate professor of economics at the University of Texas–Pan American since the fall of 2004. He has held previous positions at Mexico's Instituto Tecnológico y de Estudios Superiores de Monterrey (ITESM) in Monterrey and in the U.S. private sector. Mollick's PhD in economics is from the University of Tsukuba, Japan, in 1996, and his research interests are in development economics, international economics, macroeconomics, and regional economics. Mollick's most recent publications have appeared in such peer-reviewed journals as the *Global Economy Journal*, the *Cambridge Journal of Economics*, the *Annals of Regional Science*, the *Global Finance Journal*, the *Journal of Development Studies*, and the *Journal of Comparative Economics*.

Anthony P. Mora is currently an assistant professor of American culture, Latino/a studies, and history at the University of Michigan. He received his BA degree in history from the University of New Mexico and his PhD in history from the University of Notre Dame in 2002. Mora's principal research interests focus on the historical construction of race, gender, and sexuality. His first book, *Local Borders: The Changing Meanings of Race, Nation, and Space in Southern New Mexico, 1848–1912* (under contract with Duke University Press), explores the ways in which racial and national ideologies influenced the meaning of Mexican identity along the nineteenth-century border. Mora has also started another major research project on the relationship between African Americans and Mexican Americans in the early twentieth-century Midwest. Before joining the University of Michigan, he was a member of the history faculty at Texas A&M University and a visiting scholar at the American Academy of Arts and Sciences.

Maria Cristina Morales received a PhD from Texas A&M University and is currently an assistant professor of sociology at the University of Texas at El Paso. Her research areas of interest include social inequality (race/ethnic, gender, and immigration/citizenship), labor, and structural violence. Morales has published in the areas of immigration, race and ethnic demography, spatial inequality, education, Latina/o labor, and globalization and violence.

Lorena Murga is a PhD candidate in the Department of Sociology at Texas A&M University. Her areas of interests are racial/ethnic relations, Latina/o sociology, and immigration/migration studies. Murga is currently conducting research on immigration policies and the racialization of labor.

Melissa Najera is an assistant professor of management at the University of Houston–Clear Lake. She received her BBA, MBA, and PhD in international business from the University of Texas–Pan American. She has recently published in the *International Journal of Commerce and Management* and the *Journal of International Business and Entrepreneurship Development*. Her research interests include the retention of workers, maquiladora employment, and international management.

Pia M. Orrenius is a senior research economist and advisor at the Federal Reserve Bank of Dallas. She received her PhD in economics from the University of California at Los Angeles and BA degrees in economics and Spanish from the University of Illinois at Urbana-Champaign. Her recent publications include "Does Immigration Affect Wages? A Look at Occupation-Level Evidence" in *Labour Economics* and "Self-Selection among Undocumented Immigrants from Mexico" in the *Journal of Development Economics* (both co-authored with Madeline Zavodny), "On the Determinants of Optimal Border Enforcement" in *Economic Theory* (with Mark Guzman and Joseph Haslag), and "Crime on the U.S.-Mexico Border: The Effect of Undocumented Immigration and Border Enforcement" in *Migraciones Internacionales* (with Roberto Coronado). In addition to her Fed duties, Orrenius is a senior fellow at the Tower Center for Political Studies at Southern Methodist University and a research fellow at the IZA Institute of Labor in Bonn, Germany.

James T. Peach is currently Regents professor of economics and international business at New Mexico State University (NMSU); he previously held the Robert O. Anderson Professorship. Peach obtained his PhD from the University of Texas at Austin. Before joining NMSU in 1980, Peach served as a consultant to the U.S. Agency for International Development in Bangladesh and taught at Southwest Texas State University. Peach is a former editor of the *Journal of Borderlands Studies* (1986–1995). He has served as president of the Rocky Mountain Council on Latin American Studies (1989), the Association of Borderlands Studies (2000), the Association for Evolutionary Economics (2003), and the Western Social Science Association (2005). His research interests include income distribution, economic development, and demography, with a particular focus on U.S.-Mexico economic relations and development of the U.S.-Mexico border region. Peach's recent publications appear in the *Journal of Economic Issues, Social Science Journal, Economics of Education*, and the *Journal of Borderlands Studies*.

Rogelio Sáenz is a full professor in the Department of Sociology at Texas A&M University. He received his PhD in sociology from Iowa State University in 1986. Sáenz is the author of numerous publications on various topics, including the demography of Latinos, immigration, social inequality, and race and ethnicity. He is the author of the census report titled *Latinos and the Changing Face of America* and a co-editor of the book titled *Latinas/os in the United States: Changing the Face of América* (Springer 2007). Sáenz has co-edited three special issues on "Latinos in the South" (*Southern Rural Sociology*), "The Latino Experience in the United States" (*Sociological Focus*), and "Spatial Inequality and Diversity" (*Rural Sociology*). He received the American Association of Higher Education Hispanic Caucus Outstanding Latino/a Faculty Award in Research and Teaching in Higher Education in 2003, and the American Sociological Association Latino/a Sociology Section Distinguished Contribution to Research and Scholarship Award in 2005.

John Sargent is an associate professor of international business at the University of Texas–Pan American. Sargent received his PhD in Organizational Behavior and International Business from the University of Washington. His research focuses on the evolution of the maquiladora industry, the impact of China's export success on the Mexican economy, and Latin American business groups. Sargent's research has appeared in outlets such as *World Development*, the *Journal of World Business*, *Latin American Business Review*, and the *Journal of Borderlands Study*.

Hector J. Villarreal is currently the director general of Centro de Estudios de las Finanzas Públicas (since February 2008), the budgeting office and public finance research center of the Mexican Congress. He is founding faculty (currently on leave) of the Public Policy School of Tec de Monterrey (La Escuela de Graduados en Administración Pública y Política Pública, Instituto Tecnológico y de Estudios Superiores de Monterrey) and a member of the National Researchers' System in Mexico. Villarreal received his PhD from the University of Wisconsin at Madison, majoring in applied microeconomics, while also serving as a research assistant and associate researcher for the Food System Research Group at that university. His research areas include welfare measurements, the economics of education, and household decisions. At present, he is working on the microfoundations of welfare and the impact of social programs on poverty alleviation.

Madeline Zavodny is an associate professor of economics at Agnes Scott College in Decatur, Georgia, and a research fellow at the IZA Institute of Labor in Bonn, Germany. She was formerly an associate professor of economics at Occidental College and a research economist and associate policy advisor at the Federal Reserve Bank of Atlanta. Zavodny received her PhD in economics from the Massachusetts Institute of Technology and her BA in economics from Claremont McKenna College. Her recent publications related to immigration include "Does Immigration Affect Wages? A Look at Occupation-Level Evidence" in *Labour Economics* and "Self-Selection among Undocumented Immigrants from Mexico" in the *Journal of Development Economics* (both co-authored with Pia M. Orrenius), as well as "Immigrants, English Ability and the Digital Divide" in *Social Forces* (co-authored with Hiroshi Ono). Zavodny also conducts research on fertility behavior and the effects of marriage on wages.

Index